The Vietnam Experience

War in the Shadows

by the editors of Boston Publishing Company

Boston Publishing Company / Boston, MA

Boston Publishing Company

President and Publisher: Robert J. George
Editor-in-Chief: Robert Manning
Managing Editor: Paul Dreyfus
Marketing Director: Jeanne Gibson

Series Editor: Samuel Lipsman
Senior Editor: Gordon Hardy
Design Director: Lisa Bogle
Senior Writer: Denis Kennedy

Picture Editor: Wendy Johnson
Picture Department Coordinator/Researcher:
Jennifer Atkins

Assistant Designer: Sherry Fatla

Text Researcher: Michael Hathaway

Business Staff: Amy Pelletier, Amy Wilson

Special contributors to this volume:
Picture Researcher: Lynne Weygint
Editorial Production: Emily Betsch, Dalia Lipkin, Theresa S. Manning, Patricia Leal Welch

About the editors

Editor-in-Chief: *Robert Manning* is a long-time journalist and has previously been editor-in-chief of the *Atlantic Monthly* magazine and its press. He served as assistant secretary of state for public affairs under Presidents John F. Kennedy and Lyndon B. Johnson. He has also been a fellow at the Institute of Politics at the John F. Kennedy School of Government at Harvard University.

Editor for this volume: *Samuel Lipsman* is series editor for *The Vietnam Experience*. A former Fulbright Scholar, he received his M.A. and M.Phil. in history at Yale. He has written and edited other volumes of *The Vietnam Experience*.

Authors: *Douglas Pike* (Chapter 1) is a former foreign service officer who spent fifteen years in Vietnam. He is the author of numerous books and articles, including *Viet Cong* and *War, Peace, and the Vietcong*. He is currently director of the Indochina Studies Program at the University of California at Berkeley. *John Prados* (Chapter 2) received his Ph.D. in international relations from Columbia and writes on national security policy. His Vietnam publications include several articles and the book, *The Sky Would Fall: Operation Vulture, The U.S. Bombing Mission in Indochina, 1954*. *James William Gibson* (Chapter 3) received his Ph.D. in sociology from Yale and is currently professor of sociology at Southern Methodist University. He is the author of *The Perfect War: Technowar in Vietnam*. *Shelby Stanton* (Chapter 4) is a Vietnam veteran and former captain in the U.S. Army Special Forces. His books include *Vietnam Order of Battle, The Rise and Fall of an American Army*, and *Green*

Berets at War. Colonel Rod Paschall (Chapter 5) served for six years as a U.S. Special Forces adviser and infantryman in Indochina. He is the author of many articles on military affairs and is currently director of the U.S. Military History Institute at Carlisle Barracks, PA. *John Morrocco* (Chapter 6) has researched and written extensively on the air war in Vietnam and wrote *Thunder from Above* and *Rain of Fire*, two other volumes in *The Vietnam Experience*. He received his M.A. from the London School of Economics and Political Science. *Benjamin F. Schemmer* (Chapters 7 & 8), a former Army officer and senior Pentagon official, has been editor of *Armed Forces Journal International* since 1968. He is the author of the most complete account of the Son Tay rescue attempt, *The Raid*.

Cover Photo:

While a comrade stands guard, Pathet Lao troops meet in a cave on the Plain of Jars in eastern Laos.

Library of Congress Catalog Card Number: 87-73527

ISBN: 0-939526-38-7
10 9 8 7 6
5 4 3 2 1

Contents

The Vietcong Secret War

The Vietnam War differed vastly from any conflict the U.S. has ever experienced. Only its nineteenth-century encounters with the American Indian and its turn-of-the-century experiment with colonialism in the Philippines foreshadowed the unique combat environment it found in Indochina. As a perceptive journalist observed at the time, Vietnam was a war for people with double vision, fought against a two-faced enemy using two kinds of combat, one open and orthodox and the other clandestine with few rules.

At work in Vietnam, making such a war probable, even inevitable, were a peculiar set of sociopolitical influences that collectively can be termed the cultural context of the war. Central in this was the unique strategy Hanoi and its Vietcong confederates practiced on the South Vietnamese and their American and other allies. The result was a condition of permanent ambiguity. The war was difficult to explain and tough to assess. There was no reliable way to distinguish friend from foe, no sure way of

measuring the war's course, no certain means of determining who was winning. The Americans and the South Vietnamese never had more than an approximate idea of the size of their foe and his weapons inventory. The intelligence community in Saigon was charged with providing the two standard military intelligence estimates—enemy capability and enemy intentions—but the nature of the war made impossible anything like a precise, scientifically determined, statistically rooted estimate either of enemy prowess or battle plans. The best the community could offer was educated, often shrewd, guesses from experienced analysts hardened in the fires of repeated failure. As was sardonically observed by working-level intelligence officers throughout the war: Anyone who is not thoroughly confused just does not know what is going on.

The clandestine tradition

Indochina—which is to say Vietnam, Cambodia, and Laos—has a thousand-year history of violence, conspiracy, and exotic bloody-handed warfare. Accounts from their ancient kingdoms are filled with tales of warfare mixed with grandeur and duplicity in equal measure, of conspiratorial politics and secret organizations, and of plots and counterplots and spasms of bloody political struggle. Violence and duplicity are themes running through the record of the peninsula back to the dawn of its civilization.

Vietnam's historical experiences both contributed to and resulted from clandestinism. The major contributor probably was China's millenia-long effort to establish hegemony, during which for long periods it controlled day-to-day activities. Clandestine politics became the only effective mechanism by which Vietnamese could deal with the local ruling Chinese mandarin and his minions. When the Chinese hand was weak or absent, politics in Vietnam reverted to the traditional court-village system—the politics of the royal entourage at the court in Hue on one hand and coterie politics in the Vietnamese village on the other, but still essentially clandestine.

French colonialism raised clandestine politics to the level of high art and turned Indochina into a labyrinth of political intrigue probably unequaled in the world. French colonialists contributed by precipitating local political rivalries, fostering factionalism in the court at Hue, and exacerbating the hostility of geographic regionalism. They created a climate in which all loyalties were uncertain, betrayal commonplace, and only secret understandings and hidden political arrangements had much chance of succeeding.

Thus, there was fertile soil for the politically radical

organizers who began to appear on the scene in the late 1920s: the Communists (three separate brands including a strong Trotskyite movement) and the Nationalists (non-Communist revolutionaries, most important of whom were the Dai Viets and the Vietnam Quoc Dan Dang). The distorted Vietnamese political environment they found provided Vietnamese revolutionaries of all stripes with ideal conditions to advance whatever cause they espoused.

Clandestinism had its own operational code, its own value system, and its own definition of proper behavior by leader and led. The organization itself was always bifurcated, with an overt element known to the world and a covert organization known only to insiders, not two parts of a whole but separate identities often with different functions. For example, the Cao Dai and Hoa Hao were both overt, genuine religious movements and covert, authentic Nationalist organizations.

The leader of a clandestine Vietnamese organization needed to be skilled at stage-managing politics and to be a master of the techniques of intrigue; a political magician whose success, as with any magician, derives from his ability to deceive by diverting attention. The publicly acknowledged leader of such an organization, for example, almost never was the true leader. If one was clever and penetrated the system, he found the person behind the official leader, only to discover later that a second figure was put there for him to discover and that the true power behind him was a third figure, or perhaps a fourth or fifth. The most impressive clandestine leader in Vietnam, a very model, was, of course, Ho Chi Minh.

For five decades the man now known to the world as Ho Chi Minh played a phantasmagoric role behind perhaps a dozen aliases. Most Vietnamese believe his real or original name was Nguyen Tat Thanh, with Nguyen being the family name. He chose his two most commonly employed appellations, Nguyen Ai Quoc and Ho Chi Minh, for their significance in Chinese ideographs, the former meaning Nguyen, the Patriot, and the latter, Ho, the Enlightened One. His choice of aliases during the 1920s in Canton apparently was made lightheartedly. He was known then as Ly Thuy, Lee Suei, and Vuong Son Nhi, all ideographic word plays on each other. Nearly an entire decade of his life, the 1930s, remains unaccounted for, leading to speculation that there has been more than one Ho Chi Minh. Some maintain that he died in a Hong Kong prison in 1933 under the name of Nguyen Ai Quoc or in a Soviet prison, in either case replaced by an unknown who went on to become the ruler of North Vietnam. No other world leader in modern times was as enigmatic as Ho Chi Minh. And, in the tradition of the best clandestine organization leaders, he did nothing to clear up the mystery. Far from it, he gave journalists and others over the years a series of contradictory explanations, behaving in Vietnamese eyes exactly as a good leader should.

Preceding page. *Vietcong agent Nguyen Van Troi, the mastermind behind several terrorist bombings in Saigon, is prepared for his execution in October 1964.*

The result of all this—the centuries of Chinese occupation, the psychological scars of French colonialism, the lingering tradition of political intrigue, ubiquitous secret sociopolitical movements—was to thrust the Vietnamese people into the modern world singularly ill-prepared to deal with it. The immutable lesson they had learned from the past was to expect betrayal. As one of the wisest of present-day Vietnamese, Dean Thuc, formerly of the Saigon University, expressed it: The history of Vietnam can be written in terms of the double-cross. This heavy burden of political clandestinism carried into the twentieth century made predictable, even inevitable, subsequent Vietnamese history. At root it is a semiparanoiac heritage, the world seen as a place of cheaters where duplicity is the norm and betrayal inevitable, with the concomitant general inability to trust. In short, clandestinism was a great force of negation that warped the society and made Vietnam a natural habitat for secret war.

The strategy of deception

Deception is the heart of warfare as it has been practiced throughout history, particularly in the East. The legendary early Chinese general, Sun Tzu, author of *The Art of War*, the earliest known writing on the subject, wrote around 600 B.C.:

All warfare is based on deception. Hence, when able to attack, we must seem unable; when using our forces, we must seem inactive; when we are near, we must make the enemy believe that we are away; when far away, we must make him believe we are near. Hold our baits to entice the enemy. Feign disorder, and crush him. If your opponent is of choleric temper, seek to irritate him. Pretend to be weak, that he may grow arrogant. If he is taking his ease, give him no rest. If his forces are united, separate them. Attack him where he is unprepared, appear where you are not expected. These military devices, leading to victory, must not be divulged beforehand.

Sun Tzu's precepts, and others by later Chinese strategists including Mao Tse-tung, were drilled into every Vietcong recruit. Also cited was Vietnam's own military history, rampant with examples of deception. For example, instructors told recruits that the three components of an eleventh-century Vietnamese army were the "real army" (*Chinh Binh*), the military force; the "hidden army" (*Ky Binh*), a covert, invisible, guerrilla-like force; and the "phantom army" (*Nghi Binh*), which did not exist at all but which a good Vietnamese general could make his enemy believe existed so as to dishearten and intimidate him.

The Vietnam War was very much a war of wits in which the Vietcong sought to make up with deception, cunning, and surprise what they lacked in prowess. The essence of this was covert organization work. Villages under Vietcong control provided the necessary organizational base for the secret war. Well-organized and disciplined Vietcong armed-propaganda teams challenged the government of

Ho Chi Minh, the enigmatic leader of North Vietnam whose early career was a mystery even to his countrymen, dines aboard a yacht during a 1957 visit to Communist Poland.

South Vietnam (GVN) in the villages it controlled. Highly organized Vietcong penetration agents effectively infiltrated Vietnamese and American installations. While spirit, strategy, and leadership contributed much to Vietcong victory, it was its superb organization that enabled it to mobilize the villagers, sabotage the urban areas, and destabilize the South Vietnamese society so as to deliver final victory.

The grand strategy concept used by Hanoi and the Vietcong in pursuit of this goal was called *dau tranh*, which in English literally means *struggle* but in the original Vietnamese has a far more powerful, emotive connotation.

The essence of *dau tranh* and that which chiefly differentiates it from other strategies, is the sense of totality. Today's warfare and today's politics are a single seamless web, it is held, and no meaningful distinction can be drawn between combatant and noncombatant. By definition, all people without exception have a place and a role in the conduct of war. There is no such thing as a disinterested bystander; not even children are excluded—particularly not even children, one might say. This is people's war and the people are the weapons—to be forged and hurled into battle.

Vietcong recruits (and Vietnamese Army [PAVN] recruits still today) were taught that the concept of *dau tranh* should be visualized as a pincer with two prongs, like ice tongs, closing on the enemy. One prong is political *dau tranh*, the other armed *dau tranh*. Another metaphor used was hammer and anvil. The one immutable principle of this concept is that the two arms must work in close coordination, never one alone against the enemy.

Dau tranh is a strategy that combines Marxist-Leninist, Maoist, and indigenous Vietnamese military doctrines. It is chiefly distinguished by its breadth of definition and involves programs and activities not normally associated with armed forces and war making. Tactics are socio-psychological in nature: use of the united front organization to establish a mass base of support and heavy use of various communication devices to foment social strife. Great stress is placed on the class struggle. The ultimate objective is seizure of power. The strategy employs force, defined as "revolutionary" to distinguish it from the enemy's use of force, and is of two types: military and political. Diplomatic force may be regarded as a third type or as part of the political force. The two types *always* operate simultaneously and in coordinated fashion. The strategy is seen as political in the sense that any revolution is political, and while violence is regarded as necessary, it is not seen as the essence. Military force manifests itself as combat, either guerrilla war or "big unit" war, but also as kidnapings and assassinations. Political force is thought of as the people (particularly the villagers) "struggling" in "uprisings" and other forms of organized protest, dissidence, and rioting. The people are organized, and once organized, mobilized; then motivated. The resultant trinity—organization, mobilization, motivation—becomes a murky no man's land wedged in between orthodox politics and orthodox warfare.

The struggle is deliberately prolonged, drawn out in time so as to enervate and dishearten the enemy. It is called protracted conflict. Throughout, the objective is to change attitudes and perceptions, which then alters the balance of forces and eventually the tide of battle. Victory can come away from the battlefield, in which case major credit goes to the political struggle, or through increased tempo and magnitude of armed struggle that eventually seeks, fights, and wins the final battle.

South Vietnamese villagers in Dinh Luong Province mill about the bodies of canal workers murdered by the Vietcong on December 12, 1965.

A Vietcong assassin, captured in October 1966 and now turned informant, directs U.S. soldiers to the tunnel hideaway of his former terrorist ring.

Such was the nature of the Vietnam War, especially in the early years. Gradually its character changed. By mid-1968 it had broadened and became a more orthodox, limited, small-scale war employing what General Vo Nguyen Giap called his "regular force" strategy. Even in the later years, however, the tactics of deception continued to be employed.

Techniques of secret war

Many and varied were the devices employed by the Vietcong in pursuit of victory. Their cadres in the field, particularly in the halcyon early years of true revolutionary guerrilla warfare, demonstrated considerable skill, ingenuity, and technological sophistication.

The front line for this secret war was the villages of South Vietnam—2,560 of them—where about 80 percent of all the people lived at the time. The village was, and still is, the heart and soul of Vietnam.

To the villages came first the Armed-Propaganda Team,

a conceptual military unit invented during World War II in the caves of Cao Bang in the mountains of the North by Gen. Giap and Ho Chi Minh. It was well named—armed, but only for defensive purposes, and there to make propaganda, as that word is defined by Lenin: communication for the purposes of organization, motivation, and mobilization. In villages where they were not betrayed the teams molded the villagers into tight-knit, self-controlled, self-contained, sociopolitical organizations called "liberation associations." In the GVN areas, of course, these were deeply covert, a hierarchical shadow standing alongside the GVN governmental structure. During the Vietminh war the French called this "the parallel inventory." Others later termed it the organizational weapon.

For the villager this struggle was not secret so much as it was inconspicuous. To outsiders it was not so much inconspicuous as ambiguous. Vietcong activity—particularly the assassinations and kidnapings—obviously was well known. The difficulty outsiders had in grasping the idea of the secret war was that the incidents, while often tragic, seemed relatively minor: a hamlet chief executed; a bus held up and Vietcong "war bonds" sold to the passengers; a dozen villagers taken off to serve as porters on the Ho Chi Minh Trail. Single acts in the calculus of this kind of war can grow weighty only when multiplied by the total number of villages involved and that figure multiplied by the days of the years of protracted conflict. Further, Vietcong strategy sought to divert attention from the silent, deadly struggle in the village and focus it on the visible tip of the revolutionary iceberg: authoritarian GVN behavior, the Paris talks, antiwar activity, prominent foreigners touring North Vietnamese bomb damage, accidental civilian war casualties. These became the visual images that dominated American television and shaped world perception. Television could not photograph the invisible war of the Vietnamese village.

Tactics employed by the Vietcong in their secret war consisted of three major *action* (or *van*) programs or mechanisms. The first was called *dich van*, or *action among the enemy*, meaning the general South Vietnamese population. It consisted of organizational work, propaganda, disinformation, espionage, bombings, sabotage, sapper attacks, assassinations, and kidnapings. The second was *binh van*, or *action among the military* (originally *binh van-chinh van*—the latter meaning *civil servant*—or B and C program). These were nonmilitary activities directed against enemy soldiers and civil servants, chiefly proselytizing efforts that ideally would induce desertion or defection, or, at the least, reduce effectiveness and commitment. The third was the *dan van*, or *action among the people* program, meaning people in villages controlled by the Vietcong and chiefly involving administration of the "liberated" area.

Battle was primarily joined in the GVN-controlled villages, whose number over the years ranged from 50 percent to 90 percent of the total villages, depending on the fortunes of war. The *dich van* activity here was less organizational and more operational—systematic harassment to coerce or intimidate the villagers with or without the taking of life; sabotage and destruction of state property; and specific acts of terror against individuals such as assassination, execution, or kidnaping.

For the citizen in a government-controlled village this had a great impact. The common characteristic of this violent activity against individuals is that it was directed at the village leader, usually the natural leader—that individual who, because of age, sagacity, or strength of character, was the one to whom people turned for advice or leadership. Many were religious figures, schoolteachers, or simply people of integrity and honor. Since they were superior individuals, these persons were more likely to stand up to the insurgents when they came to the village and thus were most likely to be the first victims. Potential opposition leadership was the NLF's most feared enemy. Steadily, quietly, and with a systematic ruthlessness, the NLF in six years wiped out virtually an entire class of Vietnamese villagers. The assassination rate declined steadily from 1960 to 1965 for the simple reason that there was only a finite number of persons to be assassinated. Many villages by 1966 were virtually depopulated of their natural leaders.

Assassination efforts were directed against the best and worst enemy officials—the highly popular, effective civil servant and the most corrupt and oppressive local official—which stimulated mediocrity in the GVN. The major assassination targets were GVN officials representing the most direct threat to the Vietcong, that is, the National Police Field Force, the Revolutionary Self-Defense Force, the Revolutionary Development Teams, and other "pacification" workers. The Vietcong employed a bounty system for assassinating key figures. For instance, in May 1969, leaflets surreptitiously distributed in Saigon offered a "reward" of $500 to anyone who assassinated the Saigon police chief. Payments for other killings ran as high as $1,000.

Assassination of other "enemies of the people" as authorized in official instructions included: "Capitalists, businessmen and wealthy farmers; servicemen of the Puppet Army of South Vietnam [ARVN]; personnel of the Puppet Administration [GVN]; personnel of enemy intelligence, police, psychological warfare and pacification agencies; members of enemy political organizations; members of religious organizations; defectors [*hoi chanh*] or individuals arrested and then released by the enemy; deserters and draft dodgers [from Communist forces]; moral degenerates and other undesireables; enemy POWs; dependents of detainees of the Revolution [i.e., prisoners] who are antirevolutionary." The pattern in urban assassinations appeared to be to kill those who represented the greatest threat to the cause. Most of these people were little known

This death notice, which Vietcong agents left on the body of assassinated hamlet chief Danh Hanh, accuses him of having been a lackey for the American-Diem clique. Hanh was judged to have "carried out treacherous activities against our country and incurred the deep hatred of the people of the hamlet." He was, therefore, "made to pay for his crimes."

even in Vietnam and their deaths went largely unnoted, although at the Indochina Archive of the University of California there is a thick book listing biographical information on the countless victims of assassinations.

Typical of the more prominent assassinations was Le Thanh Cac, one of Vietnam's best and most popular athletes, a bicycle champion regarded as Olympic material. He was executed while training on Plantation Road at the edge of Saigon in 1962. A defector later said the execution was ordered, even though Cac was highly popular among Vietnamese youth, because he was forming an athlete organization that it was feared would be anti-Vietcong.

Other notable examples included Nguyen Van Bong, who was director of the National Institute of Administration, which trained Vietnamese bureaucrats. A first assassination attempt in 1959 failed. A plastique bomb placed in his car in November 1971 proved fatal. Ta Chung, editor of *Chinh Luan*, Saigon's third-largest newspaper, was killed in 1967 after the Vietcong publicly warned him to desist editorial criticism, which he ignored. Subsequently, he was shot down at the front entrance of his home. The paper continued its editorial attack, and a year later, police apprehended a Vietcong squad breaking into the editorial office to plant a bomb. The GVN minister of education, Le Minh Tri, was killed in Saigon on January 6, 1969, when a motorcycle pulled up alongside his car. The rider opened the door and tossed in a hand grenade.

In addition to individual killings and kidnapings the most common form of violence in the secret war was harassment: use of explosives (mines, booby traps, secretly planted bombs) or small-arms fire. The latter was particularly common in rural areas. A half-dozen rounds of sniper fire would be directed into a village, usually in the evening. The village defenders, alerted, could not be sure whether a full-scale attack was under way. They would radio word to the nearby ARVN post. The ARVN commander had to decide whether this was only harassing fire, a full-scale attack, an attack to draw his relief force into ambush, or a diversion to draw him away from the scene of a real attack elsewhere. His correct decision, from a military standpoint, was to do nothing for the moment and await developments. That, of course, undermined villager confidence in ARVN, which was the Vietcong intent in the first place. Harassing fire into a village might continue sporadically for weeks, usually accompanied by nocturnal megaphone taunts, threats, and appeals. Sometimes, after a few weeks of softening up, a full-scale attack would be launched. Harassing fire was cheap and could be assigned to inexperienced guerrillas. It created a great sense of anxiety within the village, keeping villagers awake at night, thus impairing their farming and other normal daytime activities.

Such violence had a high cast of rationality about it. The chief purpose of course was to eliminate opposition in the Vietnamese countryside. Assassinations in the early years were so extensive as to amount to genocide—the elimination of an entire class of rural Vietnamese, the official and natural leadership class. This contributed to a second purpose, to disorient and isolate the individual villager psychologically. It also destroyed the structure of authority, previously a source of security. Violence also isolates; a villager can no longer draw strength from customary social supports. And it served other purposes: to advertise the Vietcong cause, to provoke GVN retaliation, and to sustain or raise Vietcong morale.

A major dimension of the secret war in the Vietcong-controlled village was internal security measures to protect the organization. The enemy here was the GVN penetration agent, himself a product of the Vietnamese heritage of clandestinism. He often worked in his native region and could in many instances match the Vietcong in penetration skills. More numerous as a threat were the free-lancers who supplied the GVN with information. Some did so to avenge a Vietcong wrong; others were *attentistes*, or fence sitters, serving both sides; still others were "target of opportunity spies," those who happened on information they knew could be sold to local GVN officials.

The urban front

The Vietcong's secret war in the cities differed markedly from that of the rural areas. Urban centers were always under close GVN control even during the government's most tenuous moments. Hence Vietcong activities had to be deeply covert. Activity also differed in kind. There was more emphasis on espionage and less on violence. There was less direct organizational work and more indirect motivational efforts (what the Communists call "legal actions") directed at the South Vietnamese society, particularly its social organizations and mass media. The operational principle practiced throughout was that urban *dich*

van agents were to be assisted knowingly or otherwise by vast numbers of ordinary South Vietnamese. Spying, for instance, was not regarded as reserved for the professional *dich van* agent. Rather, it was the domain of all Vietnamese patriots under the label of the "people's espionage system." Such mass-support involvement, cadres were told, could be arranged when the people were properly motivated. Hence, the *dich van* agents devoted most of their time and energy to this end.

The Vietcong penetration agent was instructed to give highest priority to protecting himself and his *apparat*; he or she was cautioned to live conventionally and do nothing to draw the attention of neighbors or the police. Agents received a carefully constructed fictitious identity, or "legend." Random behavior was to be practiced to avoid observable patterns of activity. Safe houses, codes, ciphers, recognition signals, and courier routes were to be changed frequently and immediately if a security breach was suspected. Above all a discernible modus operandi was to be avoided.

Vietcong spies did score intelligence coups during the war. That much is certain, since hard evidence proves a few of them. A copy of the top-secret 1961 Staley-Thuc Plan, by which President Kennedy first committed the U.S. to the war in Vietnam, was found in 1963 in a Vietcong headquarters in Tay Ninh Province when overrun by ARVN troops. The 1970 ARVN-Joint General Staff Combined Plan for Military Region (MR) III, master pacification plan for the entire region, was found under similar circumstances. An ARVN major later confessed to selling it to a Vietcong agent for $2,000. In 1971 a Vietcong defector shocked his interrogators by rattling off almost verbatim an outline of the GVN negotiating strategy at the Paris talks. On the body of a *dich van* agent killed in Hue in 1968 was found a notebook containing the names of virtually every top South Vietnamese official along with extensive (and factually correct) information on each: home address, automobile license plate number, working habits, and other information considered useful ("the general carries a pistol in the glove compartment of his car").

How significant, in the final resolve, this urban penetration and espionage effort was is a matter that historians are still debating. Since the activity was deeply covert, the successful operation never became public. Only the failed missions, those uncovered by counterespionage efforts or accidentally "blown," are known. However, while the extent of success can be debated, the fact of it cannot.

Equally difficult for historians to determine are the numbers involved in the urban *dich van* program. It was commonly asserted throughout the war that the GVN was "flooded with spies," the minimal figure being put at 5,000 to 6,000. The most determined effort to fix a precise number came in 1972 in a White House–ordered Central Intelligence Agency (CIA) study, part of a broader effort to estimate the GVN's viability after U.S. troop withdrawal.

The CIA estimated that there were 30,000 infiltrators in the GVN and ARVN. Of these about 20,000 were held to be trained professionals (i.e., *dich van* agents). The remainder were of lesser status, such as couriers, safe house operators, or free-lance informers and others willing to perform tasks on commission. The study said the enemy's goal, to be achieved in 1975, was 50,000 agents, or one spy for every twenty persons in the GVN-ARVN. Some in the intelligence community challenged the study, maintaining that the true figure could not possibly be higher than 10,000. One veteran intelligence officer in Saigon stated, "You simply cannot 'run' 30,000 agents and even with 10,000 they would be tripping over each other." Further complicating the effort to tabulate the total number was the fact that many of the Vietcong agents were known to be "sleepers," that is, individuals who had infiltrated enemy installations with orders to work themselves into key positions but do nothing, not even report, pending some final, ultimate moment when they would be called to action. For years defectors told of hearing that Saigon Port had been infiltrated with several thousand such "sleepers" who were

Rescue workers sift through the wreckage of the Thai Thanh restaurant in Bac Lieu, South Vietnam, following the explosion of a Vietcong plastic bomb on June 22, 1965.

to come out of the woodwork at the right moment and paralyze port activities. That crucial moment never came, hence even to this day we do not know how much truth there was in the reports, nor, of course, the numbers involved. Unfortunately for historians, these matters were not resolved after the war. A few covert agents did surface in victorious Saigon in 1975 but not more than 100 at the most, hence the size of the Communist spy network remains unknown.

The most accomplished spy, among those few about whom anything is known, probably was Huynh Van Trong. He admitted to his loyalties in 1971 after being uncovered while serving as President Nguyen Van Thieu's special assistant, a post he obtained through the recommendation of a Catholic bishop. Trong's job was to prepare position papers for the president on political and diplomatic matters. This involved reading and evaluating a

South Vietnamese soldiers await the command to execute Vietcong saboteur Nguyen Van Troi. He was shot despite pleas from Communist nations around the world that he be spared.

My Friend An

by Douglas Pike

Pham Xuan An (second from right), who may have been an agent of Hanoi, lunches with three women including the author's wife, Myrna Pike, at a restaurant outside Saigon in 1963.

vast number of official reports sent to the president's office. Trong was in a position to know most of what Thieu knew. Obviously he was also in a position to influence presidential thinking.

The most skillful Vietcong saboteur known is Nguyen Van Sam, who operated for years in Saigon before his betrayal in the late 1960s. He told interrogators that he had been in charge of three of the most important bombings of the past decade: the Brinks Billet (and U.S. Army Officer Club) explosion on Christmas Eve, 1964; the bombing of the original American embassy in Saigon; and the destruction of the My Canh Floating Restaurant, a favorite haunt of Americans. His captors were impressed by his technical knowledge of explosives and timing devices.

Perhaps the best-known Vietcong agent was Nguyen Van Troi. He masterminded several bombings in Saigon. He was apprehended while mining a bridge near Tan Son Nhut Airport over which U.S. Secretary of Defense Robert McNamara's car was to pass while visiting Vietnam. Troi subsequently was tried, convicted, and shot, despite an

international propaganda campaign mounted by Hanoi to save him. His death is still observed each year as an official anniversary. Many socialist countries have issued postage stamps bearing his image. The Hanoi histories say Jane Fonda named her son Troy after him.

An enigmatic spy figure was Pham Ngoc (Albert) Thao; exactly who he was remains in some doubt. Thao was an early mover and shaker on the Saigon political scene, highly influential in GVN circles, and a central actor in several of the coups d'état of the mid-1960s when he came close to becoming the GVN ruler. It was his penchant for political intrigue that brought him down, assassinated by political rivals. Although he was never uncovered as a Vietcong spy, postwar reports from Hanoi indicated that he had been promoted posthumously to the rank of colonel in PAVN and was buried in Go Vap Hero Cemetery outside of Saigon. Some Vietnamese believe that Hanoi adopted Thao as its own after the war for political effect. Others maintain he was not committed to either side but was simply an opportunist determined to advance his career.

During the Vietnam War, Pham Xuan An was a professional associate of a number of prominent American journalists and American embassy officials in Saigon, and a confidant and friend of a few, including myself. It now appears An was also a long-time professional Hanoi *dich van* agent.

One of An's first jobs was to work for Dr. Tran Kim Tuyen, a lapsed student for the Jesuit priesthood, who ran what euphemistically was called the Presidential Social Research Service, a fledgling CIA and action agency for Ngo Dinh Diem's Can Lao Party, run by Diem's brother Ngo Dinh Nhu. An's job was to evaluate intelligence reports for Dr. Tuyen. Later An became an important employee of the Reuters News Bureau in Saigon, then moved on to *Time* magazine as a staffer whose name appeared on the masthead for several years.

After the war An surfaced as a self-proclaimed Hanoi agent. Rumors about him abound. He has talked to at least one former *Time* colleague in a Saigon park, although what he said was guarded, offering few details and no explanation about his past. In 1985 there was a reliable report that he had been seen outside the U.N. building in New York by a Vietnamese who had known him well. This witness later learned that he was work-ing for the DRV U.N. Mission under the name Hoang Mong Bich. However, efforts to trace him further came to naught.

There are at least three explanations for An's behavior. First, he might have been an agent of Hanoi from at least the early 1960s, because of either ideological commitment or opportunism. Second, he might have been an "April 30 cadre," one of those South Vietnamese able to switch sides after the Communist victory and accepted by Hanoi for their usefulness. Third, he could have been a double agent who worked for the Americans then and still does, now in the most deadly arena possible. Each of these hypotheses can call on some supporting evidence and internal logic.

In thinking back on my own association with An, two things stand out that did not at the time. First, almost never did I see An alone. He was always in the company of his friend Nguyen Hung Vuong, my closest Vietnamese friend. When I invited them to my home An would come either with Vuong or not at all. Second, An never tried to press any propaganda line or policy ideas on me. Quite the opposite. He seemed to avoid political discussion, offering the most mundane, conventional answers to my questions— unlike Vuong, whose replies were rich and varied. At the time I assumed that An simply was not a political animal. Later I was puzzled to hear *Time* praise his acumen and sophistication in interpreting Vietnamese politics.

An was deeply Confucian—of this I am sure, and it may be an important clue in understanding him. He was a moral person, so regarded himself, and consistently acted on the basis of Confucian values. One of these values concerns rules of friendship. It stresses loyalty and precludes any exploitation of a friend. If An were a Communist agent *and* a Confucianist, he would be willing to peddle disinformation to *Time*, but he would not do so with me, a friend. The best way for him to avoid this conflict would be to bore me with banal answers to questions on politics.

Because reasonable doubt remains, I am not yet prepared to condemn An. Perhaps I am only avoiding the bruised ego that would come if I acknowledged that I was fooled for fifteen years. In any case, I remain unsure.

What I am sure of is that An's career is a metaphor for the Vietnam War. His life personifies those times, with all of their ambiguities, claims and counterclaims, and varied interpretations, a world in which nothing was ever quite what it seemed to be, one about which the whole truth will probably never be known.

Whether he was a true *dich van* agent or a political plotter playing both sides probably never will be known.

Vu Ngoc Nha, whose network of forty-three agents was uncovered by GVN police in 1969, is another important Vietcong agent about whom much is known. At his trial Nha, a Catholic, said he had joined the Communist party in Hanoi in 1948 at the age of twenty-nine and had been sent south as a *dich van* agent in 1956. A puzzling aspect of his career, indicative of the murky world of Saigon politics, was his arrest, trial, and sentence to three years in jail in 1958 as a Communist agent. After that he returned without apparent difficulty to his spy work in Saigon. By 1969 he had moved into the upper levels of the GVN and was working in President Thieu's office. Nha was sentenced to life imprisonment and was presumably released by the Communists in 1975.

Tran Ngoc Hien, a *dich van* agent born in Hue and a veteran of the Vietminh war, was among the most intriguing figures because of his prominent brother. In 1954 Hien opted to remain in Hanoi while his brother, Tran Ngoc Chau, went south where he attained success and fame and eventually became a cause célèbre. Hien moved south to Saigon in 1965 and began his rise up the South Vietnam political ladder. When apprehended in April 1969 he told his interrogators that he had been chief of what was termed the Saigon B–22 Strategic Intelligence Unit. His work was "legal," that is, chiefly organizational and motivational rather than intelligence or sabotage. Hien was also under orders to "turn" his brother Chau but was unsuccessful, he said.

Tran Ba Thanh, police official and assistant director of the National Police after 1963, was revealed in 1975 to have been a long-time Vietcong agent. And then there is the interesting case of Nguyen Thanh Trung. He told Western journalists after the war that he had become a Vietcong agent after his father (an early party member) was killed by GVN troops in the Mekong Delta in 1963. He said he changed his name, joined the party, and became a *dich van* agent. He was "run" by a Comrade K., under whose guidance Trung joined the VNAF, was sent to the U.S. for two years of fighter pilot training, then returned to Vietnam and eventually rose to the rank of lieutenant colonel. In the closing days of the war Trung bombed the presidential palace in Saigon from his F–5E fighter plane, on orders from Hanoi, he said.

A separate category consists of what might be called the highly dubious or alleged Vietcong agent, about whom hard evidence is absent or questionable. One is Nguyen Lau, London School of Economics graduate and publisher of the largest English-language newspaper in Saigon, sentenced to five years in prison for espionage in July 1969 after admitting he had met and talked with members of the Saigon B–22 Strategic Intelligence Unit. Another is Nguyen Xuan Oanh, Harvard-educated economist, later GVN deputy prime minister and still later, governor of the National Bank of Vietnam, known to his many American friends by his Western name, Jack Owen. Oanh stayed in Vietnam after 1975, and his fortune under the Communists fluctuated. In 1987 his career was again on the rise with his election to the new Vietnamese National Assembly. It seems doubtful that Oanh was a Vietcong agent during the war. Many Vietnamese believe that his wife was a true *dich van* cadre. Other possible "sleepers" who revealed themselves after the war are Nguyen Van Hao, former GVN deputy minister of economy; Nguyen Anh Tuan, ex-GVN planning minister; and Pham Bieu Tam, dean of the Saigon Medical School.

VC spies: an assessment

What little can be learned about the effectiveness of Vietcong espionage, indeed about the entire *dich van* program, has come from four main sources: GVN penetration agent reports, captured Vietcong documents, Vietcong defector testimony, and the trial transcripts of exposed agents. As far as can be determined, GVN agents penetrating the Vietcong camp never collected much crucial information about the operation of the *dich van* program, or if they did it remains secret today. Captured documents and interrogation of prisoners and defectors yielded much rumor but minimal verifiable information. Most of these individuals had little access to sensitive information when working in the Vietcong ranks. The most reliable source was the Saigon trials of captured spies. For instance, a great deal was learned in the summer of 1969 when the GVN smashed three separate *dich van* networks in Saigon and arrested a total of eighty-two persons. Trial testimony offered insight into Vietcong penetration operations. First priority always went to "defensive" intelligence: penetrating enemy police, security, and counterintelligence agencies to learn details of the GVN "pacification" program in the countryside and to reduce breaches of security in its own headquarters. Second priority went to forthcoming enemy military operations and third priority to data on general enemy thinking and activity in the political and diplomatic fields. It was clear from the evidence presented at these trials that the Vietcong had succeeded in planting agents widely within the GVN, including the inner office of President Thieu and the GVN delegation at the Paris talks. There was also evidence of spying on the U.S. Mission in Vietnam but nothing that indicated penetration of the higher decision-making levels of either the U.S. military or civilian commands.

Information uncovered in these trials, plus that gleaned from other sources, allows some conclusions to be drawn about Vietcong espionage. First, it is clear that the Vietcong fielded a large number of spies. While the exact number has not been determined, it was, in any event, equal if not excessive to need. Second, these spies managed to reach into virtually every key GVN and U.S. installation, and while they may not have gotten into the most inner sanctums, the fact remains that Vietcong eyes and ears were virtually everywhere. Undoubtedly this means that the Vietcong headquarters in the jungle was inundated with "raw" intelligence, that is, narrow reports from individual agents about specific subjects mostly obtained at a low level—from drivers and clerks—and almost always unverified. The task then was to evaluate each report and get independent corroboration, if possible. Was the report true? Had the agent erred? Was the report an enemy "plant?" Firm evaluation was often difficult, sometimes impossible—a problem both sides shared throughout the war.

Even if it is assumed that Vietcong spies were everywhere and able to report up to 90 percent of all available intelligence, the question remains: How did this affect the final outcome of the war? We cannot rely upon Hanoi's historians for the answer. Since the end of the war they have been lavish in detailing many aspects of the struggle but have offered virtually nothing on the *dich van* program in general or Vietcong espionage in particular. There are several plausible explanations for this: the secrecy naturally and forever inherent in spying, a desire to protect successful spy methods that may again be called into use, and a reluctance to shift credit for victory away from PAVN. Or perhaps the historians, after examining the program, considered it to be of no particular success. In any event we can learn little from Hanoi. Nor have we received much postwar documentation from the American counterintelligence community about Vietcong spy successes—perhaps because, in fact, there were only a few or because of a reluctance to acknowledge that the Americans had been outfoxed. The only method remaining is to consider individual case histories and apply basic principles of historical logic.

A widely reported case concerns the U.S. Air Force (USAF) B–52 bomber raids. From the start of the bombings in 1965, rumors persisted in the U.S. Mission, largely based on reports by Vietcong defectors, that the enemy had penetrated the Air Force bomb-targeting system and knew in advance when and where the bombs would fall. There were a few clear instances, based on verifiable eyewitness accounts, of Vietcong installations receiving early warning and being able to scatter personnel moments before a raid began. Additional accounts have been given by postwar Vietcong officials. None of these, however, has ever satisfactorily explained how the information was obtained. One explanation, the simplest, was that the Vietcong had an effective air-raid warning system. They did indeed have watchers in the trees or at other elevated positions who would bang an alarm gong when they spotted approaching enemy planes. The difficulty with this explanation is that the B–52s flew at altitudes that made spotting difficult and usually impossible, even on cloudless days. Possibly the spotters may have had primitive listening devices. Another explanation was that American traitors were at work—in Guam, Okinawa, or Washington—who supplied targeting information, presumably to Soviet agents who quickly relayed it to South Vietnam. The FBI and USAF counterintelligence agents repeatedly investigated these reports, commonly administering polygraph tests and shadowing suspects, but to no avail. Or perhaps the advance knowledge came via electronic intelligence. According to this theory Soviet "fishing boats" heavily laden with electronic surveillance equipment were anchored off the end of the Guam runway and monitored the B–52s as they took off on their raids. Other Soviet surveillance vessels then tracked the planes en route to Vietnam. This would allow them to warn the Vietcong as to approximately when a raid was to come but not exactly where. Still another explanation was poor communication discipline by the B–52 crew members, that is, "loose pilot chatter," as the planes approached Vietnam. The pilots may have believed that the enemy did not have the sophisticated monitoring equipment necessary to listen in on conversations, when in fact they did have such a capability. One puzzling aspect of this case is that the security leaks, if that is what they were, extended only to U.S. Air Force strikes. As far as is known, U.S. Navy planes, taking off from carriers, were not similarly compromised.

The second case history of Vietcong espionage involves statistical analysis of data that suggests the enemy had advance information on most military operations mounted

A Vietcong weapons cache, containing mostly American-made armaments, stands abandoned by the enemy during the May 1970 incursion into eastern Cambodia by U.S. troops.

against it. The common belief was that "Charlie always knew," that is, neither American, allied, nor ARVN operations could be planned, staged, and launched in secrecy. The result was the "empty hootch" syndrome—arriving forces finding only a recently abandoned enemy camp. The Lam Son 719 operation—the 1971 South Vietnamese invasion into Laos—usually is cited as the most embarrassing example.

The statistical evidence relies on the fact that about 75 percent of all military engagements fought during the Vietnam War were at the choosing of the Vietcong, with respect to time, place, and duration. The logic of this statistic is that the Vietcong knew of impending enemy operations and could decide in advance whether to close in battle. However, it can also be argued that such a statistic is simply indicative of the kind of war being fought. Indeed, a central characteristic of the war was infrequency of engagement. For instance, throughout most of the war the number of allied small-unit operations averaged about 1 million per year. Of the 1 million, less than 1 percent resulted in enemy contact of any sort; and if ARVN small-unit operations are factored in, the percentage drops to .1 percent. The Vietcong chose to engage the enemy in only 7 of every 1,000 operations mounted against it (or 7 of every 10,000 operations if ARVN is taken into consideration). An equally strong conclusion here is that the statistics are more a commentary on the nature of the war than on Vietcong espionage abilities.

The balance sheet

It is still premature to render a final judgment on the efficacy of the Vietcong's secret war. Given its shadowy nature, the absence of crucial data, and the many fictions that already have grown around it, a clear and certain historical judgment may never be possible.

However, it seems unarguable that the strategy and operations of the Vietcong represent one of the major reasons why Hanoi won. Other reasons, of equal or greater importance, include the singular, implacable determination of Hanoi leadership; American loss of will in the final resolve; the faulty GVN/ARVN institutional and political structure; and the enormous change in the sociopolitical climate of America during the 1960s, the so-called world cultural revolution. All of these factors contributed to the final outcome. Had any one of them been absent the outcome might have been different. One can therefore conclude that the Vietcong's secret war strategy, in general application, was one critical element in the Communist victory.

The chief difficulty encountered by historians, in Hanoi and elsewhere, in assessing the overall meaning of the secret war is an inability to determine objectively how to divide credit for victory between armed *dau tranh* and political *dau tranh*. Efforts to distinguish meaningfully

between the two are traceable to a great debate over military doctrine that divided the Hanoi Politburo throughout the war. This debate pitted the doctrines of General Vo Nguyen Giap and PAVN against those of Truong Chinh and party agitprop and organizational cadres. While the two sides agreed that both forms of struggle were necessary, there was enormous room for argument over specific implementation, especially in allocation of resources such as manpower. General Giap argued that "the only way to win is militarily, on the ground, in the South." Truong Chinh (a party name meaning Long March, a gesture to Mao Tse-tung's revolutionary guerrilla war doctrine) argued that with political struggle as the hammer smashing the enemy on the anvil of armed struggle, victory could be achieved off the battlefield, in the villages of South Vietnam and in Washington. The war ended so ambiguously, as far as this doctrinal dispute is concerned, that the argument was not settled but simply continued in Hanoi during the postwar years. Its new manifestation is a debate over which deserves primary credit for victory, armed or political *dau tranh*.

In the year following the end of the war, Gen. Giap and others tended to give extensive credit to political *dau tranh*, which, of course, meant crediting the entire range of Vietcong secret war activities. Later Giap reversed himself and assigned primary credit to armed *dau tranh*, and that is now official historical dogma in Hanoi.

However, the matter is far from settled. Subsequent Vietnamese military failures and disappointments, in Cambodia and in meeting the threat posed by China, badly undercut the reputation of armed *dau tranh*'s prowess and caused a re-evaluation and upgrading of political *dau tranh*'s potency. Further, of course, are the vested interests in Hanoi that cloud objective judgment. Factional political infighting at the Politburo level is at stake, since the armed struggle position is essentially that of the PAVN generals while political struggle belongs to the upper-level Communist party cadres.

The three *van*, or action, programs representing the totality of secret war activity are a useful yardstick to measure its effectiveness. The *binh van* program (action among the GVN bureaucrats and nonmilitary action among ARVN) clearly deserves much credit for Communist victory. The estimated 35,000 *binh van* cadres working ceaselessly through the war were able to influence South Vietnamese thinking and soften GVN/ARVN institutions to such an extent that the final dénouement was simple collapse. The end of the Vietnam War resembled nothing so much as the fall of France in 1940 rather than the end of World War II in Europe. While not all credit for the final disorganization and destabilization goes to the *binh van* cadres, major credit must be assigned to them.

The *dan van* (action among the people) program chiefly involved the "liberated" and "contested" villages of South Vietnam and essentially concerned mobilizational work.

In a "liberated" South Vietnamese village, a young Communist militiaman poses with his AK47 rifle beneath two yellow-starred Vietcong flags.

The program established the necessary base. Its cadres organized, communicated to, and motivated the villagers to support the cause. In doing this, they provided the Vietcong with vitally needed supplies, intelligence, and manpower and, equally important, denied them to the GVN. The kind of war fought would not have been possible without the contribution of these *dan van* cadres.

The *dich van* program (action among the enemy), involving the narrower range of Vietcong activities such as espionage, urban sabotage, and terrorism, by its nature is more difficult to evaluate. Vietcong spying was ubiquitous and the fruit of it must have been significantly valuable, a conclusion that seems justified even though the exact extent of such espionage is still unknown. Probably the infiltration agents did not seriously influence GVN and U.S. policymaking or strategic thinking. That is the judgment of most counterintelligence professionals, who argue that an enemy agent penetrating the decision-making level cannot advocate measures or take other actions that will in effect help his enemy lose the war without immedi-

ately becoming suspect. Such an agent, they contend, is far too valuable as a source of information to risk exposure trying to sabotage strategic planning or policymaking. That seems a reasonable conclusion.

The most important meaning of the Vietcong secret war, on final balance, appears to be that the Vietcong introduced to the world a superb politico-military strategy. It outflanks modern weaponry, is in tune with the temper of the times, and successfully harnesses social forces already loosened by others elsewhere. Because of it, militant "struggle" has become to the last half of the twentieth century what Marxism was to the nineteenth century and Jeffersonian democracy to the eighteenth century. More troubling, it is a strategy for which no counterstrategy was ever successfully devised in Vietnam—or after.

The Golden Triangle

By the early 1970s, Southeast Asia had become the hub of a thriving clandestine drug trade. The region produced an estimated 1,000 tons of opium annually—perhaps 70 percent of the global supply—surely enough to meet the needs of opium, morphine, and heroin addicts in the major cities of Asia and beyond.

Southeast Asia's drug trail began in the remote tri-border region of Laos, Thailand, and Burma known as the "Golden Triangle." There, nomadic hill tribes such as the Hmoung, Yao, Lisu, Akha, Lahu, and Karens tended thousands of acres of opium poppies. They had cultivated the poppy for centuries, using it in tribal rites and as a cash crop in local trade.

From the mountains of the Golden Triangle, the opium entered a vast trafficking network that generally followed two corridors to market. The first led through Thailand. After processing and packaging, most of the opium grown in Burma and Thailand came under the control of armed bands, most notably the remnants of the Nationalist Chinese armies that fled China in 1949.

The second route passed through Laos. Primarily controlled by prominent military officers in Laos and South Vietnam, this transport network saw most of northern Laos's opium converted into heroin at laboratories in the Golden Triangle. It then traveled by air to Saigon, where smugglers could ship it to points in Europe and the United States.

The U.S. Central Intelligence Agency played a complicitous—if unwitting—role in this drug trade. In Burma, the CIA backed the Nationalist Chinese forces de-

A field of poppies—soon to be harvested by Lisu tribeswomen—blankets a hill in northern Thailand in the Golden Triangle.

spite the fact that they were better opium traders than guerrilla warriors. By the 1960s, they reportedly controlled one third of the world's illicit opium supply.

In Laos, the CIA recruited Hmoung and Yao hill tribesmen in the fight against communism, but along with the tribesmen's support came their cash crop—opium. The CIA did little to stop the tribes' use and production of the drug. The agency reported intelligence on opium movement and made a few attempts to encourage the tribes to raise potatoes in place of poppies, but overall it viewed the problem with benign neglect.

The CIA airline, Air America, played a more direct role in the tribes' opium trade. According to persistent reports, Air America helicopters helped transport Hmoung opium to the Laotian cities of Long Cheng and Vientiane. Although airline policy forbade the carrying of narcotics on company aircraft, enforcement depended largely on the pilots themselves. Some undoubtedly took advantage of the chance to make lucrative profits in drug running. Many more probably hauled opium-filled boxes without inquiring as to their contents.

While the CIA treated the drug trade with ambivalence, the U.S. Embassies in Indochina ignored or glossed over accusations that prominent figures in Laos, Thailand, and South Vietnam were trafficking in heroin. Yet increasing amounts of evidence pointed toward high-ranking officers and officials. General Ouane Rattikone, for example, former commander-in-chief of the Royal Laotian Army, openly admitted his role in Laos's pervasive drug trade; he allegedly controlled the largest heroin refinery in Southeast Asia. And the prevalence of the drug—and its enormous profits—in South Vietnam make it virtually certain that some high-ranking military or government officials were protecting the trade. Rumors surrounded numerous such officials, but attempts by the U.S. to gain solid evidence failed.

U.S. tolerance of the Southeast Asian drug trade came to an end in June 1971. Sparked by the heroin crisis among GIs in South Vietnam and the growing epidemic at home, President Nixon declared a "war on drugs" and pressured Southeast Asian allies for stronger antidrug measures. Such belated efforts, however, could only begin to affect the region's monstrous drug web.

A poppy plant still retaining its petals (top) *signifies that it is not yet ready for harvesting. On ripe poppy bulbs* (above), *opium sap congeals along incisions cut by Hmoung women with specially designed three-pronged knives. They later collect the opium* (right) *with shovel-like tools and store it in containers about their necks.*

A Chinese Nationalist guerrilla (left) guards the entrance to one of the many clandestine heroin refineries in the Golden Triangle, while an opium trader (above) examines bags of raw opium before they are shipped south by caravan. Colorful labels identify packets of high-quality opium (right) and Double U-O Globe heroin (below).

Left. *As Lisu villagers look on, an Air America airplane parks near a poppy field along the Thai-Burmese border in 1973. According to some, Air America's assistance to anti-Communist tribes in the Golden Triangle included transporting their opium from outlying villages to collection centers. Above. Tribesmen from the Shan states in Burma lead a small mule caravan carrying 1,000 kilos of opium. Larger caravans traveling out of Burma, usually guided by Nationalist Chinese guerrillas, sometimes involved hundreds of pack horses and armed guards and could extend for a mile along the Golden Triangle's narrow mountain trails.*

A Hmoung tribesman smokes opium at a village near Laos's royal capital of Luang Prabang. The hill tribes of the Golden Triangle smoke or eat much of the opium they produce but rarely use its more expensive derivative, heroin.

Confiscated packets of heroin are burned on a Saigon street in 1973. Such public events were part of a U.S.-sponsored crackdown by Southeast Asian governments on the production, use, and trafficking of Golden Triangle opium and heroin.

jammed with three battalions of tough paratroopers from the Vietnamese airborne brigade, the army trucks packed into Saigon under cover of darkness on November 11, 1960. By 3:00 A.M. they had surrounded Ngo Dinh Diem's presidential palace and before dawn were exchanging fire with the presidential guard. Saigon's citizens ran for cover. One man caught in the crossfire was William E. Colby, the chief of station for the U.S. Central Intelligence Agency. Colby barricaded his family into a top-floor hallway of his home and hours later made his way to his post at the United States Embassy.

The CIA station was operating at peak efficiency. Colby found officers in touch with the paratroopers, their political supporters, and President Diem in the palace. Diem's brother and counselor, Ngo Dinh Nhu, persuaded Colby to mediate talks with the coup plotters to gain time for the arrival of troops loyal to the president.

Diem was the major victor that day. The coup leader fled to Cambodia and many of his political

supporters went to jail. One politician, in touch with the CIA, convinced his contact to hide him and arrange his escape aboard an embassy courier flight. Diem was furious when he learned of the CIA's action; afterward, Nhu had angry words for William Colby. This action went beyond the stated U.S. position of neutrality in the coup attempt.

The CIA was also a victor that day. Colby had taken appropriate actions; the crisis passed with U.S. interests secure. William Colby was not new to such emergencies. His first Vietnam crisis occurred on the very day of his arrival in 1959, when CIA agents and equipment were exposed during the breakup of a cabal against Prince Norodom Sihanouk in Cambodia. Colby, then a subordinate at the CIA station, plunged into that crisis even before reaching his office from Tan Son Nhut Airport. In both 1959 and 1960 Colby's response was to order a low profile for CIA officers and bases involved, while backing up his agency men.

The CIA station had been coping with Saigon crises since the advent of Ngo Dinh Diem's rule in 1954. As the first CIA station chief in Vietnam, Edward G. Lansdale played a critical role in assisting Diem's rise to power. In fact, American intelligence officers had been talking with Vietnamese politicians since 1945, when men from the wartime Office of Strategic Services (OSS) were in contact with Ho Chi Minh.

With the United States government heavily involved in the "war in the shadows" in Vietnam, by 1960 the CIA stood at the forefront of that effort. Long before American combat troops arrived in Southeast Asia, the CIA was conducting covert operations and programs to bolster the South Vietnamese government. Once secret, many of those activities have since become well known to the American public. For others, the veil of secrecy is only now beginning to lift. Some may never be known. What follows is an overview of CIA efforts in the early days of the Vietnam conflict, when the seeds were sown for what happened later in the war.

The CIA's task during those first years of the war was exceedingly complex. With its primary mission of gathering intelligence, the CIA had to be everywhere, while, in its role of supporting the Vietnamese government, it had to stand with the occupant of the presidential palace. These roles often conflicted in Vietnam, leaving the CIA in a crossfire between the U.S. Embassy or military and its Vietnamese ally.

The CIA began the Kennedy administration with a spectacular failure that haunted its activities in Vietnam. That failure came in Cuba. Within three months of the inauguration of John Fitzgerald Kennedy, and after first assuring the new president of success, the agency mounted an open invasion of Cuba. The exile force recruited, trained, and armed by the CIA found itself defeated in three days of furious fighting.

President Kennedy publicly accepted full responsibility for the CIA failure. Privately he was outraged. Expecting his Cuban policy to symbolize the dynamism of the administration, Kennedy instead was saddled with failure. JFK told friends he wished he could shatter the agency into a thousand fragments (see sidebar, page 37).

The Central Intelligence Agency helped restore its standing by embracing the vital interest John Kennedy had in counterinsurgency. He believed the U.S. lacked the necessary capability to respond with flexibility to any level of conflict. Kennedy especially worried about limited, or "brush fire," wars. In February 1961, after less than two weeks in office, President Kennedy ordered a government-wide effort on "counterguerrilla warfare." He followed up with periodic exhortations thereafter.

Officers of the CIA were both lecturers and frequent participants in the counterinsurgency seminars JFK soon ordered for Washington officials. An agency officer headed the government inventory of paramilitary resources Kennedy ordered in June 1961. Vietnam had an insurgency problem; it seemed an ideal laboratory to test the new techniques. With broad access in Vietnamese society, and its ability to conduct unconventional missions, the CIA appeared well suited to counterinsurgency operations. President Kennedy even considered making Edward Lansdale the U.S. ambassador to South Vietnam.

A report from Lansdale awaited Kennedy on inauguration day. The paper advised sending a new team of Americans, including a senior chief for psychological operations; making greater efforts at contacting the South Vietnamese political opposition; and continued support for President Ngo Dinh Diem. Kennedy understood Lansdale's report as a warning of grave problems in the Republic of Vietnam, and he instructed an interagency task force to assemble a list of options. Lansdale served as adviser to the chairman of this committee, Deputy Secretary of Defense Roswell Gilpatric. At an April 29 meeting of the National Security Council (NSC), the president's top policy board for defense and foreign affairs, Kennedy approved many of the paper's proposed options.

President Kennedy set his policy in the National Security Action Memorandum (NSAM) he signed on May 11. The directive, NSAM-52, had several elements affecting intelligence in Vietnam. It approved an expansion of U.S. psychological warfare actions, the use of American air crews plus other nationalities as necessary, and covert

Preceding page. *MACV commander General Paul Harkins, CIA Director John McCone, and Defense Secretary Robert McNamara (left to right) meet in 1963 on the balcony of the old MACV headquarters in Saigon.*

Right. *In July 1965, before huge numbers of U.S. troops arrived in Vietnam, U.S. military police stand guard outside the American embassy in Saigon. The embassy also housed station headquarters for the Central Intelligence Agency in South Vietnam.*

flights over North Vietnam. The CIA and military were to cooperate in sponsoring forays by parties of Vietnamese into southeastern Laos and emplacing spy networks in North Vietnam, to create "covert bases and teams for sabotage and light harassment." The U.S. Military Assistance Advisory Group (MAAG) in Vietnam received instructions to build a capability for raids on the North within the South Vietnamese Ranger force.

In the fall of 1961 Kennedy sent his military representative, General Maxwell Taylor, along with NSC deputy Walt Rostow, to Vietnam to evaluate progress there. Edward Lansdale joined them for the trip. His recommendations in the Taylor-Rostow report included support for a Vietnamese central intelligence service and providing two helicopters and two light aircraft for a clandestine action unit in the Vietnamese service. Lansdale also wanted the

---

Ngo Dinh Nhu, who, as brother of President Diem and his deputy for intelligence affairs, was in frequent contact with CIA station chiefs, holds a press conference in September 1963.

U.S. to get Diem's approval for the use of third-country nationals as instructors and air crews in the covert operations. Lansdale proposed that the CIA have jurisdiction over the third-country personnel in Vietnam.

The Taylor-Rostow recommendations, indeed all Vietnam programs, were among the first responsibilities Kennedy assigned to an NSC unit he formed in January 1962, the Special Group Counterinsurgency (CI). The interagency committee focused on the implementation of NSC Vietnam decisions. Those Special Group (CI) programs carrying the code name Gold bore the highest priority within the U.S. government. The NSAM–52 initiatives were all Gold programs. The intelligence war was clearly heating up.

CIA's several Vietnam wars

The CIA faced formidable obstacles in performing its missions in Vietnam. The agency's function of supplying the U.S. government with information on the South Vietnamese government and society placed it in competition with the State Department, which also had a responsibility for reliable reporting. The CIA and MAAG had overlapping roles in paramilitary operations, while the U.S. military saw an obvious role for itself assisting the South Vietnamese in collecting intelligence on the enemy. The agency's Saigon station worked diligently to overcome divisiveness within the embassy and achieve more efficient prosecution of the war.

Bureaucratic rivalries within the U.S. Mission paled in comparison with the challenge posed by Diem. Diem resented as an intrusion into his country's internal affairs any CIA "spying" activities on his government or relations with his opposition. The CIA's interest in an efficient, consolidated Vietnamese intelligence service also flew in the face of Diem's divide-and-conquer domestic political strategy.

Still, the agency was not without resources of its own. When it came to political contacts in Saigon, the CIA was ahead of everyone else in the U.S. Embassy. Saigon station had a head start because Lansdale, choosing the Vietnamese over the French in 1954, began forging relationships that served the agency throughout the conflict. His successors, Nicolas Natsios and William Colby, continued many of these relationships and established new ones. Agency contacts ranged from top politicians like Dr. Phan Quang Dan to generals like Tran Van Don and Duong Van Minh. At the highest level of the Vietnamese government, Ngo Dinh Nhu had constant contact with the CIA station chief.

A significant dispute emerged between Saigon station and CIA headquarters over counterintelligence. James Angleton, CIA's legendary counterintelligence chief, wanted to mount operations that penetrated the South Vietnamese government to uncover secret Vietcong sym-

Cuba, Vietnam, and the CIA

by John Prados

Members of the South Vietnamese Civilian Irregular Defense Group patrol the Mekong Delta with their U.S. Special Forces advisers in 1963.

A week after the last stand of the Cuban-exile invaders at the Bay of Pigs, President John Kennedy ordered an investigation of the Cuban failure. Kennedy resuscitated the President's Foreign Intelligence Advisory Board, a civilian watchdog group he had recently abolished. The board considered proposals for reorganizing the intelligence community as its first order of business. The president also gave extra responsibilities in the intelligence area to his brother Robert F. Kennedy, the attorney general. The recommendations and decisions that followed these initial actions helped shape the Central Intelligence Agency's role in the Vietnam War.

General Maxwell Taylor, the president's special military representative, chaired the Cuba study panel. Serving with him were Director of Central Intelligence (DCI) Allen Dulles, Admiral Arleigh Burke, and the attorney general. Robert Kennedy accurately reflected his brother's views: a mixture of general admiration for the agency, annoyance with the CIA for its failure in Cuba, and a perception that the U.S. would need the CIA's expertise in paramilitary operations and political action, especially in Vietnam. Thus, the CIA suffered less than might be expected in the Taylor board report. But the shaky chain of command revealed by the Cuban fiasco had to be corrected. The

Taylor board recommended that the military be given primary responsibility for large paramilitary operations and that the president establish an NSC committee for "Cold War operations."

President Kennedy assigned "Cold War" functions to the existing special group at the NSC that monitored covert action. In several national security action memoranda of June 1961, Kennedy made the Joint Chiefs of Staff his primary advisers on paramilitary operations and directed that the military take charge of large-scale paramilitary actions. It was under these arrangements that the CIA acted in 1962 to shift the CIDG program to military control.

Kennedy also initiated the first of a series of changes in intelligence community leadership. Near the end of 1961 the president appointed John A. McCone as his new DCI. McCone was a California businessman who had made a fortune in defense production during World War II, a former chairman of the Atomic Energy Commission, and a staunch Republican, touchy but sharp as nails. He believed in enhancing the role of the CIA. Vietnam seemed the place to do it and counterinsurgency the instrument. McCone represented the CIA on the NSC Special Group (CI). He projected a "can do" attitude and gave field officers wide latitude, in return expecting their total loyalty.

McCone seemed quite satisfied with the CIA's performance in Vietnam. Though he replaced many division heads and station chiefs in his first year as DCI, McCone retained William Colby as Saigon station chief and Colby's superior, Desmond FitzGerald, as chief of the Far East Division of the clandestine service. When FitzGerald later moved over to work on Cuba, McCone promoted Colby to replace him.

The Saigon station grew as the American involvement in Vietnam deepened, from about 40 in 1959 to perhaps 200 CIA personnel in 1962. Over the next two years it doubled in size, to become the largest station in the Far East Division. At the height of the war the CIA had 700 officers working on Vietnam matters, and 600 of them were assigned to the Saigon station. The CIA contingent included a substantial number of political officers, military intelligence specialists, paramilitary experts, some officers for psychological warfare, and support personnel. A signals intelligence component arrived in 1961, and the station was soon assigned its own intelligence analysts. With the changes after Cuba, the advent of John McCone, and the growth of CIA resources in the Saigon station, the agency was ready for its Vietnam War.

pathizers working for it. Station chief Colby, fearing that any such step would sow mistrust in Saigon, preferred to unite behind the South Vietnamese and get on with the war. Desmond FitzGerald, chief of the Far East Division of CIA's clandestine service, sided with Colby. Later, when Colby himself became division chief, he continued to resist a primary counterintelligence mission for the Saigon station. The CIA did penetrate the Saigon government, but its primary purpose was to gather information and influence events.

Angleton revived his proposals for counterintelligence operations several times during the war but repeatedly lost the bureaucratic battle in the CIA clandestine directorate. It may have been a grave mistake. Vietcong infiltration of South Vietnamese institutions bedeviled the U.S. throughout the war. Though never adequately measured, the extent of Vietcong penetration was significant and produced a constant leak of intelligence about U.S. and South Vietnamese activities.

The other major mission of the Saigon station, improving South Vietnamese intelligence capabilities, often seemed an impossible task. CIA officers wanted the Vietnamese to have a unified intelligence service. Diem, mindful of the possibility that a powerful service might be used against him, instead established several units each directly responsible to the president.

The ensuing Vietnamese efforts to create services and collect intelligence in the North were plainly ineffective. The CIA established networks in North Vietnam under Lansdale, but the North Vietnamese rooted them out in about two years. President Diem formed a clandestine activity unit under his own control in February 1956 but it accomplished little. American MAAG commanders repeatedly complained of the inadequacy of intelligence and tried to add an Army field team of their own. This led to an early dispute between the military and the CIA.

The Army invited two senior Vietnamese intelligence officials to Japan in 1959 for a ten-day orientation to convince them to work with the military. Though Nicolas Natsios, then CIA's station chief, knew of the plans all along, he waited until the Vietnamese were in Japan to object that delicate CIA negotiations were being impeded. For months Natsios worked with the Vietnamese on an agreement to support an upgraded clandestine unit in return for joint CIA-Vietnamese control over its operations. The Army initiative evaporated. In August 1958 the CIA informed MAAG that it had made satisfactory arrangements with the Vietnamese.

The Vietnamese unit became the 1st Observation Group, which stood outside the normal South Vietnamese chain of command. Its operations were separately approved by Diem in much the same fashion as U.S. covert actions are by an American president. CIA assigned nine paramilitary officers to the group, but agency support did not make much difference to Vietnamese performance. The MAAG remained dissatisfied with the quality of the intelligence it received. In September 1959, when the Vietnamese chief of staff asked for U.S. Army training in intelligence collection on enemy territory, the request rekindled the military-CIA dispute. The CIA finally accepted the inclusion of Army intelligence teams in the advisory group in October 1960.

With NSAM–52 in May 1961 the 1st Observation Group received a big boost. The directive, which also added forty more officers to the Saigon CIA station and $1.5 million to its budget, sanctioned expansion of the clandestine unit. Based at Nha Trang, it had sixteen 14-man teams in July 1961. Authorized total strength of 305 increased by 500, with the goal of maintaining twenty 15-man teams backed by two 160-man Airborne Ranger companies. The 1st Observation Group quickly grew to 340 and selected 400 more recruits for special training.

Lansdale, for one, worried that the "overall command" of Vietnamese intelligence would be "inadequate to ensure proper emphasis and allocation of personnel to the tasks at hand." In his contribution to the Taylor-Rostow report, Lansdale recommended creation of a new Vietnamese clandestine action service of 3,000 men, divided between intelligence collection and paramilitary action. Formation of the unit could be accelerated, he observed, "by the assignment of additional American trainers and of already trained Vietnamese Army personnel."

Ngo Dinh Diem in fact established a Central Intelligence Organization (CIO) in May 1961, but it never became the kind of unified agency the Americans favored. Diem resisted giving CIO a charter enabling it to levy requirements on other Vietnamese services. The CIO grew to 1,400 officers in divisions responsible for foreign intelligence, counterespionage, support, training, and an interrogation center. The foreign intelligence division had stations in France, Hong Kong, Bangkok, Phnom Penh, and two cities in Laos. Plans for stations in the United States and Singapore never materialized. However, its commissioner lacked clout with Diem, while its personnel structure was top-heavy, with 60 percent supergrade officers and only 20 percent young vigorous men.

Far from consolidating Vietnamese intelligence, Diem fragmented it. The CIO became one of his personal organizations, along with the euphemistically named Social and Political Research Department. A third Diem service was the Presidential Survey Office, consisting of the officers of the 1st Observation Group with its commander as director. In turn, the Vietnamese national police increasingly became an intelligence service of the prime minister. Crosscutting loyalties further reduced the effectiveness of South Vietnamese intelligence, to the chagrin of CIA's Saigon station.

As the Vietnamese clandestine services grew, the U.S. military assumed a greater intelligence role alongside CIA. In July 1961 MAAG had twenty-nine intelligence

specialists, including a headquarters staff of ten; six in psychological warfare; and three teams of four each for intelligence/counterintelligence, photographic interpretation, and clandestine collection. There was only one man assigned to the Vietnamese 1st Observation Group, plus a dozen Special Forces men on temporary duty training Vietnamese Rangers.

Rapid growth in military intelligence personnel followed the approval of NSAM–52. By December 1961 the 1,209 people working on classified projects exceeded MAAG's official strength of 1,062. Classified projects personnel included the first of 400 Special Forces approved by Kennedy, 78 communications intelligence specialists, 230 serving with Vietnamese intelligence units, and about 350 in the recently arrived, secret air-support unit code named Farmgate, otherwise known as Detachment 2 of the 4400th Combat Crew Training Squadron, or "Jungle Jim." While the CIA also increased the strength of its Saigon station, the military easily matched and overmatched the agency's additions. The MAAG was a jealous custodian of its military prerogatives, and conflicts between the military and the Central Intelligence Agency continued as a feature of life at the U.S. Mission.

General Paul D. Harkins, commander of MAAG, was not wholly comfortable with the tactics of unconventional warfare. Harkins was Old Army: a staff officer under George Patton in World War II, a cavalryman turned to

South Vietnamese air force personnel and American air commandos watch in December 1961 as ground crews load rockets onto T–28 aircraft at Bien Hoa Air Base.

armor, a polo player, proper and polite. In Harkins's advisory group the operations section managed intelligence and could rewrite its reports, which became much more optimistic than CIA reporting. It was the beginning of a dispute over intelligence estimates between CIA analysts and military staffs that persisted throughout the Vietnam War.

Even Harkins had to make concessions to President Kennedy's enthusiasm for CI doctrine. With a burgeoning war and the popularity of counterinsurgency there were also opportunities for the CIA and military to put aside their rivalry and work together. An important one came in the fall of 1961, with a proposal for a paramilitary program in South Vietnam's central highlands. The plan allowed the CIA to work with the military in unprecedented fashion and ushered in the most active phase of agency operations in Vietnam.

The Montagnards and pacification

Diem had not been fully candid with the Taylor-Rostow mission when it visited Saigon in late October 1961. A few weeks later a senior Vietnamese intelligence official told

Rice sacks are parachuted into an outpost along the Laotian border in the early 1960s. Such airdrops were essential to maintaining the CIDG program's remote montagnard camps.

Americans that the Vietnamese president specifically warned his men to say nothing of the precarious situation of Republic of Vietnam troops in the central highlands who, according to the official, "could not withstand concentrated VC effort."

William Colby's CIA station detected the weakness in the highlands and wanted to arm villagers to defend themselves. The chief of Colby's Combined Studies Group, with authority over both paramilitary action and assistance to the Vietnamese Special Forces, worked with proponents to assemble a project called the Village Defense Program. Colby added an economic component and political framework and secured Vietnamese government approval in December 1961. The program began with a model project at the village of Buon Enao, near Ban Me Thuot. The CIA went to the Army to request Special Forces soldiers to train and lead the village defense forces.

The highlands were populated by mountain tribes (collectively known as montagnards, from the French). The tribe at Buon Enao, ethnic Rhade from a group of about 120,000, were only one of the many major and minor tribes and religious sects inhabiting Vietnam. Overall the montagnards numbered 600,000 to 800,000, some nomadic, others sedentary, of different cultures and even races. Among the better-known tribes were the Hre, Sedang, Stieng, Bahnar, Bru, Jarai, Jeh, Ma, M'nong, and Muong. There were also the Nung, mostly refugees from the North. Many tribes held animosities toward each other but all feared the lowland Vietnamese. Americans found work with the montagnards immensely challenging, but the CIA and Special Forces men with the tribes had to walk a delicate line between tribal loyalty and Vietnamese government authority.

The Village Defense Program began with one CIA officer and a Special Forces medic at Buon Enao, a village of 400. They spent a few weeks building rapport with the villagers, while the Rhade built a fence surrounding the village, both for defense and as a symbol of their participation. Inside the fence a dispensary and a training center were erected and shelters built. In mid-December 1961 the Rhade held a ceremony at which, with their spears and crossbows, they pledged that no Vietcong would enter their village or receive any help. A fifty-man Vietnamese security detachment came to defend Buon Enao while U.S. advisers armed and trained the Rhade. The village units soon came to be called Civilian Irregular Defense Groups (CIDGs), and that became the name of the program.

Supplies for the CIDGs and operational command came from the CIA at Saigon. The need for American advisers swiftly outstripped Colonel Gilbert Layton's contingent of CIA paramilitary experts, who turned to U.S. Army Special Forces for additional resources. Because this was a Gold program, the Army response was highly classified. In early February 1962, Captain Ron Shackleton, commander of Detachment A–113 on Okinawa, was alerted to prepare half his team, six men, for duty in Vietnam. The men left Kadena Air Force Base on February 13, 1962, in civilian clothes aboard an unmarked aircraft.

In Saigon, CIA officers took the Green Berets to a villa for a detailed briefing. Everything remained top-secret. Only two days before, a Farmgate SC–47 psychological warfare plane had crashed near Da Lat, killing eight Americans and a Vietnamese. Worried by the high American toll (the largest single loss thus far in the Vietnam War), President Kennedy put restrictions on U.S. air operations. Colby appreciated the secrecy. He had overruled, on grounds of inadequate cover and deniability, proposals of the CIA proprietary Air America to take over the covert air mission in Vietnam. For operational security, Colby had the Green Berets flown to Ban Me Thuot on an unmarked C–46 with a Nationalist Chinese crew. The CIA briefers told Capt. Shackleton's team they need not obey the orders of any local Vietnamese or U.S. authority; their orders would come directly from the agency at Saigon.

Buon Enao turned into a notable success. Within a week of the arrival of the Green Berets, Rhade were beginning to line up for admission to training. It became the secure base for expansion of the CIDG program, first to enclose 40 villages within a fifteen-kilometer radius, then 200, later throughout South Vietnam. Colby took Ngo Dinh Nhu, whom Diem had made intelligence chief, to see for himself. Nhu approved the countrywide expansion. Buon Enao became the first village considered secure enough to revert to full administration by the Vietnamese government.

Expansion meant even greater demands for American manpower. For the 200-village CIDG complex, which included four new base areas, Special Forces sent eight more of its A–detachments, basic teams of two officers and ten specialist sergeants. The CIA asked the Army for another sixteen teams of Special Forces before the end of June 1962.

In view of the anticipated large increase in Green Beret strength, the CIA reassessed its participation in the CIDG program. President Kennedy clearly intended that the military control large paramilitary actions, while the CIDG effort outgrew CIA support capabilities. At CIA headquarters Desmond FitzGerald approved a recommendation that the military be asked to assume full control of the CIDGs. William Colby, who soon succeeded FitzGerald as chief of Far East operations, supported the changeover, which became known as Operation Switchback.

The U.S. Army also reconsidered its CIDG participation. Two generals, William P. Yarborough, the head of Special Forces and the Special Warfare Center, and William B. Rosson, visited Vietnam in April 1962 to survey field activity. Their report was complimentary about the CIDG effort, but Rosson criticized the program on May 28 in conversation with Gen. Taylor. Deployment of additional Special Forces, Rosson felt, should be for offensive missions into Laos and North Vietnam, not for the CIDGs. The Army, however, ultimately rejected Rosson's view.

One partial step was a June agreement between the CIA Saigon station, the U.S. Mission, and the new U.S. military headquarters, Military Assistance Command, Vietnam (MACV), for joint coordination of the CIDGs. The CIA proposal for Switchback became the subject of a conference held in Hawaii that July. Initially Gen. Harkins objected since he feared MACV would not be able to duplicate CIA's unique logistical system, but Colonel George C. Morton, MACV special warfare chief, won him over. The Army set up a reimbursable account dedicated to Special Forces through which CIA handled actual procurement. Within a month Secretary of Defense Robert S. McNamara approved a phased takeover of the CIDGs to be completed by July 1, 1963.

The CIA side of Switchback, particularly its logistics aspects, was handled by the deputy chief of the Combined

Services Group, Gilbert Strickler, a reserve Army colonel on detached service at the agency. For the Special Forces, Col. Morton handled Switchback as commander of an ad hoc group, Special Forces Vietnam (Provisional), established in September 1962. Initially headquartered at Saigon, by January 21, 1963, the Green Berets had 62 officers and 258 enlisted specialists, 4 percent of total MACV manpower. In February Morton moved his group to Nha Trang, a major air transport base on the coast nearer the central highlands. When Morton turned over his command to Colonel Theodore Leonard in late 1963, the Special Forces numbered 674 with a headquarters staff of 98, for 6 percent of MACV strength. As a proportion of MACV manpower, Special Forces peaked at 7 percent in late 1964, about the time the 5th Special Forces Group (Airborne) became the official Green Beret unit. An additional number of Special Forces were detached to the MACV Studies and Observation Group (SOG) (see Chapter 4).

Rhade tribesmen, recruited by the CIA in late 1961 to provide local defense, await target practice at a U.S. firing range.

As the Special Forces contingent grew the CIDG program expanded. The 200-village complex, completed in October 1962, protected 60,000 montagnards with 10,600 hamlet militia and 1,500 men, called "strikers," in mobile strike force units. At the completion of Switchback in July 1963, 52,636 militia; 10,904 strikers; 3,803 mountain scouts; 946 trail watchers; and 515 medical workers protected 879 villages. Militia strength fell to 43,376 in December 1963 but strike forces increased to 18,000.

To a large degree, airlift made the CIDG program possible. Each new Special Forces detachment required 60 tons of supplies in its first month and 17 tons a month thereafter. Mostly accessible only by air, often only by parachute drop, the CIDG camps were dependent upon Army C–7 Caribous, Air Force C–47s and C–123s (from Farmgate), and, until May 1963, CIA aircraft. For the first half of that year the monthly tonnage moved by air averaged 1,776. Total monthly deliveries increased to 2,536 tons in July 1964, 85 percent of which was brought by aircraft. Airfields were improved or built to accommodate the airlift, many by Navy Seabees, a useful side benefit of the CIDG program.

The Vietnamese Special Forces, trained by Green Berets, played a major role in the program. In November 1961 the 1st Observation Group, redesignated the 77th Group, received its first increment of twenty-eight American trainers. Vietnamese were with the CIDG from the beginning at Buon Enao, where an eleven-man detachment worked with the Green Berets. Redesignated again as Airborne Special Forces (*Luc Luong Dac Biet*) in March 1963, the Vietnamese continued to put counterpart teams in each CIDG camp. Indeed, the Vietnamese team leader was also the camp commander, though in the heat of battle the Green Beret advisers often assumed leadership roles.

Troubles in the mountains

Though very successful in organizing the montagnards, the CIDG program could not seal off South Vietnam's borders. The camps denied sources of food to the Vietcong and blocked some infiltration routes but functioned best as listening posts rather than strongpoints. The strikers specialized in patrol actions rather than pitched battles. At first the Vietcong limited their response to probes, but they gradually stepped up operations against Special Forces and the CIDGs. On November 23, 1963, Hiep Hoa in the Mekong Delta was the first camp that the enemy momentarily penetrated. And on July 6, 1964, Special Forces Captain Roger H. Donlon, commander of Detachment A–726, won the first Medal of Honor awarded in the Vietnam War for his defense of the Nam Dong CIDG camp.

Only two days before the battle at Nam Dong, the Green Berets lost a CIDG camp for the first time, at Polei Krong in the highlands. Defended by Captain William Johnson's A–122 detachment, a Vietnamese team, and less than 100

strikers, Polei Krong lay up against a riverbank and had poorly cleared fields of fire. On the eve of the attack the Vietnamese camp commander had neglected to put out warning posts, manned only half his guard posts, and had two of his striker companies on overnight leave after returning from a patrol. The first mortar shell hit the Green Beret team house. Some Vietcong were inside the camp, near the kitchen, even as the battle began, while others quickly breached the south wall. Green Berets and Nung strikers did their best but lost access to the ammunition depot. Survivors scrambled to the riverbank. At the southwest corner of the camp a montagnard machine-gun unit held out for forty minutes. They were the last defenders of Polei Krong.

Hiep Hoa, Polei Krong, and Nam Dong were high points in a Vietcong campaign that amounted only to sporadic harassment of the camps. Ironically it was the lowland Vietnamese who posed a more serious problem for the CIDG program in those early years. They continued to treat the montagnards with contempt. Buon Enao and 31 other villages reverted to full Vietnamese control in September 1962; 107 more villages reverted in March 1963. The Vietnamese province chief took CIDG status away from the Rhade, mixed the units, dispersed them to remote garrisons, and left them unpaid for months on end.

In the summer of 1964 the Vietnamese began to convert the CIDGs into Civil Guards and draft the strikers for their Ranger force. That fall friction reached a boiling point. The montagnards had enjoyed autonomy under the French and wanted the same from South Vietnam. The Vietnamese actions instead demonstrated a will to dominate. Strikers at five Rhade camps rebelled.

Three parachute flares fired from a mountain on the night of September 19–20 proved to be the signal for the revolt. About 3,000 strikers participated, and 1,000 of them marched on the town of Ban Me Thuot where they almost captured the radio station and other key objectives. Captain Vernon Gillespie, by forceful but diplomatic appeals, averted a revolt at Buon Brieng. In some camps Green Berets and Vietnamese Special Forces were held hostage; in a few the Vietnamese were killed. Americans like Gillespie and Colonel John F. Freund stalled the rebels while the Vietnamese army brought up its 47th Regiment and faced down the rebels after nine tense days. The Vietnamese lost twenty-nine Special Forces and fifteen militiamen in the rebellion.

As the arrival of the rainy season soon precluded active operations, the montagnards presented political demands, including representation in the Saigon government, direct U.S. aid, command of their own armed forces, return of tribal land, permission to travel abroad, and the appoint-

Special Forces Captain Vernon Gillespie and his team of Rhade tribesmen contact a helicopter flying overhead while on patrol near the Buon Brieng CIDG camp in late 1964.

ment of montagnard province and district chiefs. In late December 1964, U.S. intelligence warned of a possible renewed rebellion, but the Vietnamese made cosmetic reforms and tension subsided. Within a year the government closed all five rebellious CIDG camps. The Vietnamese did adopt special laws for the highlands in 1967 and installed a montagnard commissioner in Saigon, but they proceeded with the Civil Guard conversions. The Americans took over the mobile strike force from CIDG, creating the renowned "Mike Forces." Disaffected montagnard leaders fled to Cambodia and formed a group to fight both the Vietnamese and Vietcong.

Although the Central Intelligence Agency had abandoned its role in the CIDGs, it remained active in pacification. In 1964 the CIA started another paramilitary program that gained increasing prominence. It began with a suggestion from a Vietnamese instructor at the CIA school at Vung Tau, whose friends living in Quang Ngai felt they had grievances against the Vietcong and asked for weapons to police their villages. The CIA officer at Vung Tau saw an opportunity to field local defense groups. The station funded a pilot program at Quang Ngai and coined the name People's Action Teams (PATs) for the units. By the winter of 1964 twenty platoon-size PATs were active, and the CIA had a new training camp to support the effort. Located near Vung Tau, the camp had a capacity for 5,000 trainees.

MACV marveled at the success of the PAT program. MACV engineers envied the speed with which the CIA built its training camp. But for a long time the military resisted massive expansion of the PATs for fear the CIA's recruiting would impede growth of the Vietnamese army. The PAT concept nevertheless contributed to the later innovation of "revolutionary development" teams and Provincial Reconnaissance Units (PRUs).

While these programs proceeded in the countryside, American and Vietnamese attention increasingly focused on Saigon, where the drama of Vietnamese politics frequently overshadowed the war. It was in Saigon that the CIA—with its panoply of contacts within South Vietnamese society—truly demonstrated its greatest capability.

Diem and after

At the highest level of the Saigon station, the station chief maintained contacts with important Vietnamese, including Diem's deputy for intelligence matters, Ngo Dinh Nhu. Many Vietnamese actively hated Nhu for his highhanded methods and reputed corruption. But William Colby's successor as station chief, John H. ("Jocko") Richardson, remained one of Nhu's biggest supporters. In 1963 Richardson's support put the CIA at odds with the ambassador and divided the station itself.

Jocko Richardson was big, bald, and articulate. In Italy during World War II, Richardson made his reputation in counterintelligence and as an expert at emplacing Allied military governments in Italian villages. He worked for the CIA and its predecessors in Austria, Trieste, and later as division chief in charge of covert action in Albania. Richardson had been with Lansdale in the Philippines. He came to the Saigon station in the summer of 1962, a senior officer, symbolic of the post's new importance within the CIA.

The four or five languages that Richardson mastered included French and this he used to effect in his dealings with Nhu. That language is well suited to nuance, and the Kennedy administration was trying desperately to make plain to Diem and Nhu that continued U.S. support depended upon real reforms. Nhu was one of the main channels to Diem. Richardson faithfully conveyed Washington's messages, but within the U.S. Embassy he tried to put Diem's and Nhu's actions in the best possible light.

To inhibit the growth of Buddhist political power, in 1963 Diem restricted rights of assembly and speech. Already thought to favor Catholics, Diem now openly challenged the majority religion of Vietnam. The confrontation built through the summer into a political crisis. In May the government prevented the Buddhists from flying their flag at the celebration of the Buddha's 2,527th birthday. On June 11 a Buddhist monk publicly immolated himself in downtown Saigon, a haunting picture that is one of the enduring images of Vietnam. On August 21, trusting no one else, Diem sent Vietnamese Special Forces to raid a number of Buddhist pagodas.

Kennedy suspended aid to Diem. Immediately after the pagoda raids, American officials considered informing Vietnamese generals that the U.S. would stand aside in any coup against Diem. Having reached a consensus on this, Washington sent a cable to inform Ambassador Henry Cabot Lodge, who had arrived in Saigon only three days earlier. Richardson opposed the initiative strenuously. When Lodge overruled him, the CIA station chief sent back-channel cables to headquarters. He persuaded division chief Colby to convince the CIA's director (DCI), John McCone, to demand reconsideration of the policy. McCone and McNamara took the issue to JFK. Lodge's instructions were modified within the week, earning Richardson the lasting enmity of the ambassador.

Meanwhile, Richardson worked at cross-purposes with some of his own CIA people, many of whom had concluded that Diem would never implement true reforms. In addition to informal contact through counterparts in the Vietnamese chain of command, two CIA officers had special contacts among the Vietnamese generals. Lieutenant Colonel Lucien Conein and Alphonso G. Spera were long-standing friends of many generals. Spera was even the brother-in-law of one. Conein had been in Vietnam with the original Lansdale mission in 1954. With the approval of Lodge and reluctant acquiescence of Richardson, Conein and Spera passed U.S. policy statements to the generals and kept themselves informed on subsequent plotting. The generals also had independent contact with Lodge and MACV commander Harkins, who opposed the coup and tried to dissuade the Vietnamese.

There were at least eighteen contacts between Conein or Spera and the generals in the period from August to late October. Nhu and Diem became aware at some point that coup plotting was under way. The generals soon learned of Diem's knowledge; they could not determine whether Richardson had told Nhu or Harkins had tipped off Diem. Senior General Tran Van Don, who most often met Conein at his dentist's office, grilled the CIA man on how Harkins knew of the coup. On October 26 the generals allowed the scheduled date for their coup to pass without incident.

President Kennedy followed developments but remained indecisive. By fall Kennedy favored the coup but again wavered in the last days of October, and instructed national security adviser McGeorge Bundy to tell Lodge to call off the generals. Lodge was to order Conein to tell the generals that their plans did not offer sufficient prospects for quick results. Instead, Lodge cabled Washington to protest the change and delayed giving instructions to Conein. In the meanwhile the Vietnamese generals decided to proceed, and the coup occurred on November 1, 1963.

Quickly isolated in the presidential palace, Diem and Nhu later managed to escape through an underground passageway. They took refuge at a French Catholic church in the Chinese Cholon section of Saigon. After telephone negotiations with the generals they surrendered, expecting to go into exile. Instead the brothers were murdered inside the M113 armored personnel carrier sent to pick them up. In the aftermath the generals ordered the execution of Colonel Le Quang Tung, Diem's Special Forces commander. The CIA sent officer Peer de Silva to replace Richardson, who was too closely identified with Diem.

The Americans had been mistaken to believe Diem's overthrow would end Saigon political difficulties. The coup in fact began an interregnum of twenty months of musical-chairs governments and more coups. The extent of CIA's political penetration proved more important than ever. For example, several coups were mounted or parried by General Nguyen Khanh, the strongman between January 1964 and February 1965. The CIA knew in advance of all these moves. In a September 1964 coup that failed, CIA knew the plotters, the politicians supporting them, and identities of rebel military units and their movements, as well as the details of Khanh's countermeasures, including loyal units and their estimated times of arrival at key points. All the data went to Washington as quickly as it became known at Saigon. On January 27, 1965, following another such coup experience, McGeorge Bundy wrote McCone to commend CIA's excellent reporting, which had "made a very tricky and fast-moving situation comprehen-

sible, and has permitted us to anticipate the developments as they have emerged."

But Washington still grappled with questions of policy. An ironic coincidence with the Diem coup was the assassination of John F. Kennedy in Dallas only three weeks later. Lyndon Baines Johnson, who followed JFK's footsteps into Vietnam, succeeded him as president. LBJ preserved consensus but gave the military most of what it wanted each time it came to ask. With military power predominant in Vietnam, the United States came ever closer to open intervention.

President Johnson sanctioned reprisal bombing after the Gulf of Tonkin incident in August 1964, accepted plans for "tit for tat" bombing late that year, and implemented them in early 1965, after the Vietcong shelling of a U.S. base at Pleiku. The Vietcong responded with a car bombing of the Saigon embassy on March 30. CIA station chief Peer de Silva only with difficulty regained sight in one of his eyes,

U.S. Ambassador Henry Cabot Lodge after his first meeting with South Vietnamese President Ngo Dinh Diem on August 26, 1963, during that summer's tense Buddhist crisis.

after being grievously wounded by glass shards from shattered embassy windows. One of his secretaries was killed.

Burdened by Vietnam, President Johnson demanded fresh policy initiatives and approved an initial commitment of U.S. combat troops. The first two Marine battalions landed on March 8, 1965. Maxwell Taylor, then ambassador in Saigon, advocated a whole series of options including increased use of the CIA's People's Action Teams. After an NSC meeting on March 26, John McCone added twelve proposals from the CIA, including organizing and supplying "development communities" and local partisan groups, expansion of harassment teams working in VC areas, use of irregular troops to infiltrate and capture VC communications centers, and deployment of political action teams to disputed areas. LBJ ordered "urgent exploration" of the CIA proposals.

John McCone was unhappy with Johnson's policy of partial responses. He favored more dramatic action, such as bombing the North. Ground operations, he warned Johnson in an April 1 letter, might be less effective than expected and should be accompanied by bombing. McCone believed limited action "offers great danger of simply encouraging Chinese Communists and Soviet support." Dissatisfied with the degree of his access to LBJ, and unable to shift Johnson from his moderate policy, McCone resigned and left the CIA on April 28. Johnson appointed retired Admiral William F. Raborn to replace him.

Present at the escalation

At one of his very first NSC meetings John Kennedy asked about the possibility of mounting guerrilla operations inside North Vietnam. The CIA director told him the agency had trained four teams of eight agents but that funds were limited and the CIA contingency fund low. JFK pursued the matter on March 9, 1961, requesting reports on "guerrilla operations on Viet Minh territory." The CIA responded on March 25 and a few days later, in preference to mounting actions of its own, the Pentagon stated its support for the CIA program. Kennedy approved the establishment of covert bases and harassment inside North Vietnam, authorizing Americans and third-country nationals to fly the necessary air missions.

In Saigon the CIA's Combined Studies Group (CSG) managed this program from a facility separated from the U.S. Embassy. Colonel Gilbert Layton, CSG chief, procured aircraft and boats for missions to the North. The CIA got its own hardstand for planes at Tan Son Nhut and opened a forward boat base at Da Nang. It also employed a paramilitary force of tribal Nung, eventually the equiva-

Smoke rises above the presidential palace in Saigon during the November 1963 coup that ended in the death of President Ngo Dinh Diem and his brother Nhu.

lent of two small battalions (later passed on to Special Forces). But the agent teams conducted CIA missions mainly in enemy-controlled areas in the South, as President Kennedy occasionally prodded for more action.

The CSG air detachment initially consisted of three planes, unmarked and painted black, which the agency later upgraded to newer C–123s. William Colby added ostensibly private aircraft of a Vietnamese proprietary he helped form, then enlisted the services of the Vietnamese Air Force to fly the planes. There were more than a dozen aircraft by 1964. Nguyen Cao Ky, later air marshal and prime minister, commanded the air transport squadron that furnished crews for the CIA program. Ky pioneered new visual techniques for low-altitude night flying to evade North Vietnamese radar. Once Ky took Colby on a flight so low over the South China Sea that the CIA station chief talked of bringing his fishing rod along the next time. On at least two occasions the planes did not return from their missions.

CSG also conducted boat operations using Swifts, very fast armed boats that could creep in to shore and land parties of agents. Layton delegated control of the boat base to Tucker Gougelman, a colorful CIA paramilitary specialist who had served as a Marine in the Pacific, lost a foot in Korea, and run agency missions into Eastern Europe. U.S. Navy craft called Nasties later augmented the CIA boats.

The air and sea programs brought little success in 1961–1962, only frustration for CSG. The few teams inserted into the North were quickly captured. Intelligence could not supply adequate identification documents for the infiltrators, while North Vietnamese villagers were constantly vigilant against penetration. Whenever a mission did establish itself, CSG faced the dilemma of whether to use it to build an espionage network or to start guerrilla operations. Lack of basic intelligence fed the failure of the whole effort.

The CIA submitted a reinvigorated covert action plan to Kennedy in January 1963. McGeorge Bundy told JFK it was worth approving, although "there is every reason to think that the execution of this plan will encounter all the difficulties of an operation in a denied area." Kennedy agreed, but again the results were sparse. Eleven months later NSC staffer Mike Forrestal reported to a new president that, despite considerable effort, "very little has come of these operations, partly because of the tight police control in the North and partly because of their very small size."

Increased size could most easily come from the military. Already available was a suitable Vietnamese unit, the 300th Special Detachment with a strength of 388 men, which the South Vietnamese general staff intelligence branch had created in 1962. For joint U.S.-Vietnamese operations the Americans required better air and sea capabilities. In May 1963 the Joint Chiefs of Staff (JCS) directed the Pacific commander to prepare for nonattribut-

able raids against the North using U.S. materiel, training, and advisory assistance. At a November conference in Honolulu, CIA's Colby, together with MACV, received orders to prepare a plan for a twelve-month, three-phase covert offensive against the North. Secretary McNamara reviewed the completed plan in December, and President Johnson approved it for implementation beginning on January 16, 1964. Drawing heavily on the Pacific commander's OPLAN 34–64, the new plan became OPLAN 34–A.

The air operations plan called for inserting psychological warfare/sabotage teams along North Vietnam's main roads, with one team specifically aimed at the Hanoi–Yen Bay rail link that ran up the Red River Valley to China. There were also to be leaflet and gift-kit drops, as well as radio broadcasts. In February 1964 the North Vietnamese claimed to have shot down a transport aircraft at night. From April to late July there were eight 34–A airdrops. Bundy judged the program "very moderately successful" with high casualty rates but continued radio contact with about half the groups that landed. Station chief Peer de Silva's analyses of radio traffic convinced him, however, that the operators were working under North Vietnamese control.

On January 16, 1964, MACV activated the Studies and Observation Group, with staff section Op 31 to control maritime operations (MAROPs). The CIA relinquished its responsibility for the boat effort, and the Swift force, augmented by eight heavily armed assault boats (Nasties) from the Navy, came under Op 31 control for missions. The Navy assumed control of Da Nang base, adding a boat support unit, SEAL Team 1, and a maintenance detachment with 100 tons of spare parts.

The first 34–A boat mission occurred on February 16, soon after arrival of the first Nasties. Vietnamese frogmen tried to sabotage a ferry and some North Vietnamese patrol boats at Quang Khe. This MAROP was a failure, as were several further missions. Concerned at the early losses, Ambassador Lodge protested on April 5, "I do not believe any of these missions can be justified except as part of a well thought out diplomatic maneuver." Later Lodge dismissed the MAROPs as good training perhaps, but having no impact on Hanoi. Pacific commander Admiral U.S.G. Sharp blamed inadequate intelligence and an increased state of North Vietnamese alert, making sabotage targets "more difficult to reach than was visualized at the time."

On May 27, MAROPs boats captured a North Vietnamese junk at sea. In June, landing parties successfully demolished a storage facility and a bridge on Highway 1, plus a water pumping station. In the last of these missions, on the night of June 30–July 1, the North Vietnamese discovered the landing in progress and two Nasties shelled their defenses to enable the shore party to escape. Two men were killed and several 57MM recoilless rifles abandoned.

In July, MAROPs captured several more junks and conducted psychological warfare actions against the North Vietnamese naval bases at Binh Thuy and Quang Khe. In Saigon, MACV approved an August MAROPs schedule providing increases in the number of operations of 283 percent over July and 566 percent over June levels. On the night of July 31, four Nasties bombarded the islands of Hon Me and Hon Nieu.

Unknown to the Nasties or their American MAROPs advisers, a U.S. Navy destroyer was in the Gulf of Tonkin the night of August 1–2, on a regular DeSoto patrol designed to intercept North Vietnamese radio and radar transmissions. In any case, the North Vietnamese ordered torpedo boats to sea after the MAROPs shelling, and these boats attacked the destroyer U.S.S. *Maddox* on the afternoon of August 2. The ship retired, the destroyer U.S.S. *Turner Joy* joined her, then both returned to the gulf to complete the patrol and assert their presence.

The first of the August MAROPs called for four Nasties to shell a radar installation at Vinh Son and a post on the south bank of the Ron River. One boat suffered a mechanical failure seventy miles east of the demilitarized zone and aborted the mission. The others carried out a twenty-five-minute bombardment on the night of August 3–4. Although Navy officers had discussed over several months coordination of MAROPs with DeSoto patrols, cooperation was ruled out, and the missions during the early morning of August 4 were independent of the DeSoto patrol. That night, however, both destroyers experienced a series of events they interpreted as a second North Vietnamese attack in international waters.

President Johnson ordered retaliatory air strikes. The Gulf of Tonkin incident became an important milestone on the American road to war in Vietnam. MAROPs contributed to the initiation of the incident. The SOG-Op 31 planners recognized as much at the time—the Swifts and Nasties moved farther south to shelter at Cam Ranh Bay, returning after five days to Da Nang base. MACV temporarily suspended MAROPs; a few days later President Johnson ordered a halt to all 34–A operations.

In September LBJ approved resumption of MAROPs and another DeSoto patrol. Nasties patrolled off Vinh Son in the first week of October, and three returned on the twenty-seventh to bombard it. There were other missions too, including the final bombardment on December 8, when four Nasties hit the Mach Nuoc radar installation. But MAROPs lost the momentum acquired before the Tonkin Gulf incident and were subsumed in the general war effort, as both sides escalated with the deployment of regular ground forces. The Vietnam War acquired an unmistakably military cast.

Army Lieutenant James S. Bowers, flying out of Qui Nhon, saw this change in front of his helicopter on the morning of February 16, 1965. As Bowers crossed Vung Ro Bay he glimpsed an unfamiliar ship in its unprotected waters. On second look he indentified it as a camouflaged 100-ton steel vessel unloading supplies. Bowers radioed Nha Trang, which summoned an air strike. The ship was sunk, then inspected. A U.S. investigation showed that the craft was a Vietcong supply ship. The Johnson administration then used the incident as evidence of North Vietnam's escalation of the war to help justify the commitment of American ground forces.

Vung Ro, however, was too far south along the Vietnamese coast for a North Vietnamese supply vessel to reach in an overnight run. Where the North Vietnamese could have gotten such a ship, and why they would use it in preference to their thousands of disguised junks, remained unanswered questions. There are unconfirmed reports that the CIA staged the Vung Ro incident, that the Soviet and Chinese weapons captured there came from the agency. No final judgment on Vung Ro is yet possible, but the event seems typical of psychological warfare methods. As always, many questions in the Vietnam conflict remain unanswered. Vietnam might have become the military's war in 1965, but the CIA remained very much in business.

Soon after the controversial Vung Ro incident, Special Forces Sergeant Edward Spinanio examines enemy weapons discovered hidden in a nearby cave on February 20, 1965.

Edward G. Lansdale

Edward G. Lansdale was one of the most influential and controversial intelligence agents in the post–World War II era. Born in 1908, Lansdale worked for an advertising agency after graduating from UCLA. He joined the Office of Strategic Services in 1941, and served with the U.S. Army in the Pacific during World War II. Afterward, as an Air Force officer, he helped rebuild the Philippine army's intelligence service.

Lansdale returned to the Philippines in 1950 as a USAF officer assigned to the CIA's Office of Policy Coordination. As adviser to Philippine defense minister Ramon Magsaysay, Lansdale helped weaken the Communist-led Hukbalahap rebellion. His success propelled Magsaysay into the presidency of the Philippines and prompted CIA director Allen Dulles to send Lansdale to South Vietnam in 1954 to help strengthen that country's fledgling government. Lansdale succeeded by bolstering the political position of President Ngo Dinh Diem and implementing a program of unconventional warfare, one that included sending sabotage teams into North Vietnam, and social reform.

Until his departure from South Vietnam in 1968, Lansdale pressed his conviction that the means to success were good will and concern for the "little guy," bolstered by an effective counterinsurgency program.

After several years of increasingly obscure retirement, Lansdale died in February 1987 in McLean, Virginia.

Colonel Lansdale (left) meets with Cao Dai leader, Trinh Minh The (center), in 1954. Lansdale bribed The and other religious sect leaders with CIA money to win their support of the shaky Diem government.

Lansdale relaxes with his Philippine protégé, Defense Minister Ramon Magsaysay (top), and later finds his name in a headline announcing his departure from the Philippines (above).

King Maker

Lansdale was a major force in the rise to power of Ramon Magsaysay in the Philippines and Ngo Dinh Diem in South Vietnam. He shared a bungalow with the Philippine defense minister in the early 1950s and served as his friend, adviser, and even public relations agent during Magsaysay's successful campaign for the presidency. When Lansdale was transferred to Saigon in 1954, he quickly became Diem's chief advocate and confidant. He shifted the weight of CIA support behind Diem and helped the young premier weather threats from disgruntled generals and South Vietnam's powerful Hoa Hao, Cao Dai, and Binh Xuyen sects. Lansdale's skill in promoting these leaders was immense, and his superior officer was correct in saying, "This officer was a king maker."

Lansdale (left), Diem (back turned), and Diem's brother, Ngo Dinh Nhu (third from left), enjoy a restful weekend at Long Hai beach in late 1956.

Counterinsurgent

After his early successes against the Huk rebellion in the Philippines, Lansdale became a persuasive proponent of counterinsurgency operations. He was especially fond of psychological warfare techniques, many of which drew on advertising gimmicks he had learned in his first profession. False rumors, propaganda pamphlets, and anti-Vietminh slogans were all tools in Lansdale's efforts to sway the Vietnamese population.

Right. *Lansdale (center) poses with friends in the Philippines in 1946.* Below. *Lansdale (second from right) meets with Philippine counterinsurgency officers in the early 1950s.*

Social Reformer

Lansdale knew, however, that counterinsurgency techniques alone could not decide a struggle. Civic action programs were also a necessary component. In his tours in the Philippines and South Vietnam, Lansdale called on officials to visit the countryside and learn the needs of the villagers. He pushed for initiatives such as land reform, road repair, and school construction that would endear the government to the population.

Right. *Lansdale and a team of students construct houses at Liberty Camp, a settlement for South Vietnamese refugees, in September 1965.*

Below. *Lansdale, now serving as special assistant to the U.S. ambassador and attempting to coordinate various pacification programs, leads an inspection tour in the South Vietnamese countryside in 1967.*

Operation Phoenix

In the fall of 1966, General William Westmoreland, Secretary of Defense Robert McNamara, and other important American leaders formulated a division of labor between U.S. and Vietnamese military forces. American ground soldiers, with their air support, would engage Vietcong and NVA Main-Force units since superior U.S. firepower, air mobility, and communications could most effectively be brought to bear against a technologically inferior foe. After one or two years of intensive combat, enemy casualties would reach the "crossover point," where dead and wounded exceeded the Communists' capacity to field replacements.

Behind this "shield," as Westmoreland called it, ARVN soldiers could fight smaller VC detachments and provide security for Vietnamese villagers while the government of South Vietnam attempted to "pacify," or win the political allegiance of, the rural population. U.S. officials thought that it was absolutely essential for the government of South Vietnam (GVN) to establish a strong political base in the

countryside to prepare for the crucial period following a negotiated peace settlement. American political and military leaders believed such negotiations would culminate in an agreement once the U.S. reached the "crossover point" and Hanoi realized that it could not defeat the United States. They thought this settlement would include the withdrawal of U.S. and North Vietnamese Army (NVA) forces and a truce between Vietcong and ARVN soldiers. The military conflict would then be transformed into a political struggle between the South Vietnamese government, the Lao Dong (Communist) party, and other political groupings. Without popular support, the GVN would lose this final phase of the war.

The pacification problem

At the same time American officials thought that the United States needed a new, centralized management structure for coordinating its many civilian and military aid programs assisting pacification. Such an organization would increase efficiency and provide far more leverage in helping American advisers influence South Vietnamese civilian and military officials to concentrate on pacification problems. In April 1967 President Lyndon Johnson announced the formation of Civil Operations and Revolutionary Development Support (CORDS) to fill this role. CORDS was placed under General Westmoreland's command in MACV with a civilian deputy commander serving as chief administrator. Robert W. Komer, Johnson's personal representative in South Vietnam, received the appointment as deputy commander MACV-CORDS and held the rank of ambassador.

CORDS's own budget was relatively small, an estimated $4 billion from 1968 to 1971. Most of its funding came from other U.S. government agencies. CORDS simply provided the management structure for administrating various pacification programs. Its personnel came from both the military and civilian agencies. By 1971 some 3,000 servicemen assigned as advisers to Vietnamese ARVN officers were placed under the command of CORDS. In civilian personnel, CORDS grew from 800 in 1968 to 1,200 in 1971. The U.S. Agency for International Development, responsible for both delivering material aid to millions of Vietnamese refugees and for economic development programs in Vietnam, staffed most civilian positions. A few U.S. State Department foreign service officers and a few public relations–psychological warfare specialists from the United States Information Agency added to the CORDS roster.

But from the beginning, personnel from the Central Intelligence Agency played the most crucial role in designing CORDS programs. Komer, himself, had served for years on the agency's National Estimates Staff. Komer's chief assistant, William Colby, first served as the deputy chief of the CIA station in Saigon in 1959, then became chief of station from 1960 to 1962. He headed the CIA's Far East Division for the Directorate of Plans (the office that supervised clandestine intelligence collection and covert action) until 1968, when he went on leave without pay from the Central Intelligence Agency and joined Komer at MACV-CORDS as an employee of the Agency for International Development.

Placing in charge experienced personnel who had once served in the CIA made sense because CORDS administered both "overt" and "covert" programs as part of its pacification strategy, and the agency had a long history of paramilitary operations, psychological warfare, and rural development programs. Edward Lansdale had pioneered many techniques of counterinsurgency in the Philippines during the war against the Hukbalahap guerrillas (1950–1953). A few years after his principal Philippine ally, Ramon Magsaysay, won the 1953 presidential election there and the rebellion atrophied, Lansdale moved to Saigon where he helped Ngo Dinh Diem consolidate his power base as prime minister of the new southern Republic of Vietnam.

Lansdale persuaded Diem to establish a "Civic Action" program for rural pacification based on his Philippine experiences. Low- and middle-level government bureaucrats—often refugees from the North who had come south after the 1954 Geneva accords—received basic training in manual skills that would help villagers develop wells, roads, bridges, and other public services. Dressed in black pajamas like the peasantry, these teams spent several weeks in each village trying to win the peasantry's political allegiance through propaganda and public works projects. They were augmented with Civil Guard policemen and ARVN troops to provide protection against the Vietcong.

CORDS reinstated the Civic Action teams under the new name of Revolutionary Development Cadres. Active duty CIA personnel assigned to CORDS retained close control. One U.S. Army history of the pacification effort states, "Just how jealously the CIA guarded its prerogatives was apparent from a memorandum of understanding which gave the CIA station chief and the chief of the Revolutionary Development Cadre Division, a CIA official, wide authority and veto power over planning, programming, funding, and operating the Revolutionary Development Cadre program."

Revolutionary development teams were composed of fifty-nine South Vietnamese, divided into three eleven-man security squads and twenty-five Civic Action cadres. Each team was assigned to spend six months in a village to fulfill the "Eleven Criteria and Ninety-Eight Works for Pacification:

1. Annihilation of the Community Underground Cadres
2. Annihilation of the Wicked Village Dignitaries
3. Abolishing Hatred and Building Up a New Spirit
4. The Administration of People's Democratic Organizations
5. To Organize and Struggle Against VC
6. Illiteracy Campaign
7. Health
8. Land Reform
9. Development of Agriculture and Handicraft
10. Development of a Communication System
11. A Meritorious Treatment of the Combatants"

Some of these goals were readily met. New strains of "miracle rice" and fertilizers increased agricultural productivity. A communications system placing 40,000 two-way radios in the villages was developed. Basic health care helped people. The illiteracy campaign often translated into building schools that at worst became storage sheds and sometimes actually were staffed as functioning schools. "Meritorious treatment of the combatants" trans-

CIA station chief William Colby, who later became the director of CORDS and coordinated the controversial Phoenix Program, visits a market near Hue in January 1961.

lated into helping veterans and survivors of fallen ARVN soldiers receive the benefits to which they were legally entitled, including medals honoring their sacrifices.

Other RD efforts faced major social and political obstacles. The GVN did not engage in serious land reform until 1973. Much of the government's support came from the landlord class, and the return of ARVN troops and GVN officials to a formerly "unpacified" area meant that the landlords could safely return to collect back rent. Attacking corruption—the "annihilation of the wicked village dignitaries"—proved extremely difficult because graft had become pervasive in the Vietnamese government. As one former U.S. adviser to pacification found in his interview with an RD cadre in Long An Province: "This is the most difficult task of all. They are all tied in with one another from the generals right down to the hamlet. We report them, but nothing ever happens."

NHÂN DÂN TỰ VỆ CHỐNG GIẶC

NG GIỮ LÀNG

The Propaganda War

The Phoenix Program was just one effort among many designed to undermine Vietcong support in the South Vietnamese countryside. The CIA also spent large sums on a propaganda campaign, complete with pamphlets and posters, that attempted to woo South Vietnamese villagers and montagnard tribesmen to the GVN cause.

A U.S.-produced poster (left) shows popular forces protecting their hamlet against the Vietcong, while the cover of a news pamphlet (below) features a Rhade tribeswoman executing a captured Vietcong soldier.

RD teams and U.S. military advisers assigned to CORDS could, however, help build paramilitary forces in the hamlets. The "aboveground" efforts focused on creating local militia units called Regional and Popular Forces (RF/PFs). These units were designed to help solve the desertion problem in ARVN. From 20 to 30 percent of ARVN soldiers deserted each year; most returned home. Since Regional Forces (company-strength units with up to 140 men) were deployed in their home provinces and Popular Forces (platoon-strength units of at most 40 to 50 men) stayed close to their native hamlets, the former deserters could be regrouped along with new recruits to provide a regular military presence at the local level. One of Komer's and Colby's major programs in 1968 was to provide these Territorial Forces with new M16 rifles and other modern infantry weapons.

RF/PFs, or "Ruff-Puffs," as they were sometimes called by Americans, suffered high casualties. Because they were responsible for village defense they were a high-priority target for Vietcong and NVA units attempting to destroy the pacification program. While they represented at most half of the Republic of Vietnam armed forces, they suffered from 55 to 66 percent of South Vietnamese military deaths. In return, they inflicted an estimated 30 percent of the total casualties suffered by the Vietcong and North Vietnamese forces. Some American analysts, such as Thomas C. Thayer of the Defense Department, contend that since these regional forces took less than 20 percent of South Vietnam's military budget they were "dollar for dollar, the most effective large force in killing VC/NVA troops in South Vietnam."

Other close observers of the RF/PF forces developed more critical views. Marine Colonel William R. Corson noted that the high casualty rates of these militia units resulted from "the fact that the great bulk of the RF casualties are incurred because of their timidity and unwillingness to seek out the enemy. It may be bad form to shoot 'sitting duck' in England, but the VC are under no such a compunction when they attack the RF."

This timidity resulted from morale problems. Once attacked, local militia often did not receive assistance from senior province officials and ARVN commanders who felt little allegiance to low-ranking peasant soldiers who lived far from the cities and province capitals. Stories of province officials pocketing salaries designated for Regional- and Popular-Force soldiers also point to the persistent social barrier faced by CORDS in trying to pacify those in the lower classes when part of the Vietnamese leadership did not understand their importance for the long-term survival of South Vietnam.

The "underground" paramilitary effort instituted by

CORDS and the Revolutionary Development Cadres was known as the Phoenix Program. When the RD cadres left each village, one team member stayed behind to fill a new GVN position called "Census Grievance." The public function of this cadre was to perform census tasks and to listen to complaints about corrupt officials. Beneath this cover the Census Grievance man reported on villagers whom he suspected were members of the Vietcong political apparatus, or "infrastructure" (VCI).

These reports became part of an extensive Central Intelligence Agency program initiated in 1967 that called for all U.S. military and civilian intelligence agencies to pool information on the organization and membership of the National Liberation Front. This effort, at first called Intelligence Coordination and Exploitation Program, was assumed by Robert Komer when CORDS was established. He created the new name Phoenix, or *Phung Hoang* in Vietnamese, meaning "all-seeing bird."

In this approach to counterinsurgency and pacification,

The cover of the Phoenix Program's 1969 year-end report displays the MACV insignia and the Phung Hoang, the legendary Vietnamese bird remotely similar to Western mythology's phoenix. The image of the Phung Hoang also appeared on wanted posters and even on "kill cards" left on dead VC.

South Vietnamese regional troops and their American advisers examine the body of a Vietcong political leader killed in action in 1965.

Strangler II

Disrupting South Vietnam's shadow government—the Vietcong infrastructure—was a massive task that was not restricted to the Phoenix Program and that sometimes employed traditional military ground units. In February 1969, for example, the U.S. Army's 199th Light Infantry Brigade, along with several ARVN units, conducted a three-day cordon-and-search operation called Strangler II in the Tan Nhut Triangle, fifteen kilometers southwest of Saigon. While brigade troops cordoned off a region of the triangle, GVN units herded villagers to a makeshift tent city called the combined holding and interrogation center (CHIC). There, members of the 199th entertained, fed, and provided medical care to civilians. Most important, they checked identification papers and made photographic records. In three days the 199th processed 2,500 civilians and uncovered 21 confirmed Vietcong and 11 ARVN draft dodgers.

Above. A South Vietnamese family poses for a picture after passing through the CHIC intelligence section. Right. Soldiers and civilians mill about a CHIC tent during Operation Strangler II.

the political powers of the Vietcong were viewed as more important than their military strength. Vietcong political strength *creates* Vietcong military strength. By identifying and "neutralizing" members of the Vietcong infrastructure, the Communists' efforts at mass organizing could be crushed and they would lose the support of Vietnamese peasants. At the same time, the destruction of the Vietcong political apparatus would cripple their ability to persuade Vietnamese villagers to join the revolution as armed guerrillas, thus leaving their combat units with no means to field replacements. The destruction of the Vietcong infrastructure was designed to defeat the Vietcong on both the political and military fronts. Pacification and the creation of popular allegiance to the GVN could then proceed without sustained opposition.

Moreover, Phoenix did not require that the GVN conduct major political and economic reforms to achieve success; a coordinated intelligence and targeting program against the VCI did not *seem* to require changing the Vietnamese power structure very much.

In July 1968 Komer persuaded President Thieu to issue a presidential decree ordering Vietnamese intelligence agencies to participate in the program. The resulting Phoenix network was highly elaborate and complex. In Saigon, the Vietnamese established a national staff as part of the National Police Command. CORDS and the CIA personnel responsible for coordinating intelligence reports on the VC infrastructure coming in from all American military intelligence programs also had their controlling headquarters there.

Most of the actual intelligence gathering and apprehension of suspected members of the Vietcong infrastructure took place at the province and district levels. Intelligence reports came from a variety of sources. Some came from the Census Grievance officials. Various Vietnamese intelligence, military, and police units had their own paid networks of local agents, as did the CIA and U.S. military intelligence personnel. Operation Phoenix collected and cross-referenced the names and reports generated by these diverse networks. According to the official rules governing Phoenix, only after a VCI suspect had been reported from three independent sources could that person be arrested.

Several different paramilitary units were available for apprehending suspects. The CIA financed, controlled, and often directly led elite Vietnamese commando squads called Provincial Reconnaissance Units (PRUs), which included recruits from Vietnamese prisons and Vietcong defectors. Regional-Force militia units were also available at the province level and Popular-Force platoons at the district level. Large police formations with military weapons called Police Field Forces could be deployed, as could the regular National Police.

Assuming the VCI suspect was captured rather than killed resisting arrest, he or she was then taken to a Provincial Interrogation Center. These prisons, along with a regional prison in each of four military regions and a national center, were financed by the CIA, and CIA advisers to the Vietnamese Special Branch (National Police) served in each one as part of the CORDS Pacification Security Division.

Suspects could be legally held there and interrogated for thirty days, after which the suspect's interrogation report was forwarded (along with the rest of his or her dossier) to the Provincial Security Committee (PSC), the governing body responsible for both judging the guilt or innocence of the suspect and passing sentence. The PSCs, composed of the province chief, the public prosecutor, the chairman or member of the Province Council, and various local security officials, had sixteen additional days to judge and sentence or release a suspect from custody.

These proceedings followed very different rules from criminal trials. The accused did not have the right to examine the evidence against them or appear before the committee in self-defense or have a lawyer or appeal a conviction or ask for International Red Cross intervention as a prisoner of war.

Instead, the law prescribed that the PSC could classify a guilty suspect as a "leader," a "cadre," or a "follower" on the basis of the intelligence and interrogation reports found in his or her dossier. Leaders could be sentenced for up to two years, cadres up to a year, and followers for up to six months. At the end of each prison term, a convict's dossier was examined again. A new "finding" could result in resentencing.

Field reports differ on how well this complex network of intelligence operatives, paramilitary forces, and administrative-judicial bodies functioned. In his memoir, Captain John L. Cook suggested that the Phoenix Program enjoyed considerable success. Cook arrived in Vietnam in May 1968, a second lieutenant recently graduated from the U.S. Army School of Intelligence at Fort Holabird, Maryland, as a counterintelligence specialist trained to neutralize the enemy's intelligence apparatus. He was assigned to Bien Hoa Province, Di An District, as a district intelligence officer under CORDS supervision with the mission to assist the Vietnamese in identifying and dismantling the Vietcong infrastructure.

Success at Di An

Cook found both a coherent American advisory effort and a determined Vietnamese district team. His Vietnamese allies immediately began to test him, putting him through rituals to measure his ability to work with them and his determination to succeed in his mission. Some appeared innocuous, such as an invitation to the district chief's home to meet his wife and children. Capt. Cook remembered, "Major Chau introduced me to the young Chaus—four girls and two boys—who gave me a careful going over, trying to determine if I was suitable for being in their district.

Apparently I passed their test, for after a few minutes' scrutiny, they disappeared."

Immediately after the afternoon repast, though, Cook's Vietnamese counterpart in the Phoenix Program, Lieutenant Hau of the District Intelligence and Operations Coordination Center, announced, "Tonight we go on ambush. Here is very good information. Can you come with me, Thieu Uy (second lieutenant)?" Cook well understood the issue: "It was more than a question or a simple invitation to participate in some nighttime activity; it was more of a direct challenge." He accepted, "It will be an honor for me to go."

In the early evening Hau, Cook, and his commanding officer, Colonel Anderson, and twelve Vietnamese members of the Provincial Reconnaissance Unit boarded their battered three-quarter-ton truck (nicknamed Claymore, from the battle damage it had received from Vietcong-detonated claymore mines) and departed for the ambush site. Shortly after ten o'clock the PRUs sprang the ambush with their own claymore mines and M60 machine-gun and M16 rifle fire. U.S. artillery immediately covered the area with illumination rounds. Seven Vietcong members of a suspected assassination unit died that night during Cook's initiation. Lt. Hau collected what documents they carried while the PRUs collected weapons and ammunition for bounties as well as the enemy's rings, watches, and personal effects—the spoils of battle.

Beginning with this auspicious evening raid, Cook became an effective intelligence officer. He secured additional file cabinets for Hau, which permitted him to separate dossiers containing little evidence against an individual from those containing several reports of a person's participation as a Vietcong political official.

More dramatically, he helped raise 100,000 piasters (1,000 dollars) from the U.S. Army's 1st Division intelligence unit to post as a reward for information leading to the capture of To Van Phoung, first secretary of the district Communist party organization. Phoung was already well known to the Phoenix operatives, but all of their previous attempts to capture him found "that Phoung had slipped away once again, vanishing into thin air."

But in May 1969, two months after the wanted posters and leaflets announcing the bounty on Phoung had been distributed, a young woman walked into district headquarters demanding to speak with Major Chau. After their lengthy conversation, the major told Cook her story. For the past year she had been To Van Phoung's lover and was now pregnant with his baby. When she informed Phoung, he replied that "he had more important things to worry about than a pregnant girl," and besides, he had a new girlfriend.

The spurned lover informed Major Chau that the next day Phoung would be meeting with a local party official in a tunnel near Binh An Village. He would arrive there around three in the afternoon to avoid the ongoing military operations in the district that usually began early in the morning and ended before one in the afternoon.

This time the Phoenix intelligence operatives and the Provincial Reconnaissance Unit and National Police assisting them changed their normal operating schedule. They arrived late in the afternoon and quickly identified the tunnel entrance. After their demands for Phoung's surrender went unanswered, a smoke grenade thrown into the tunnel elicited a plea for assistance. Two Communist operatives declared the smoke had made them too sick to move on their own. A police officer was then lowered into the tunnel on a rope but had to be withdrawn quickly when a brief firefight wounded him in the shoulder. Lieutenant Hau then threw a hand grenade into the tunnel and Phoung's former lover identified the bodies. She had been brought along on the operation in the event she was springing an ambush on Hau and Cook.

Cook concluded: "It had been a valuable lesson, this tracking down business of Phoung. It had taught me a great deal, and for this I had my Vietnamese friends to thank. But even more important, our idea of tracking Phoung down systematically had worked—the Phoenix concept was far more than theory (we had proved that over and over again)—and the Vietnamese had accepted advice. I could ask for nothing more." Facing the end of his one-year tour, Cook decided to extend his service. He soon was promoted to captain and became the district security adviser in Di An, an unusual accomplishment for a twenty-four-year-old.

The problem of Phoenix

But Di An was more of an exception than the rule in the execution of Phoenix operations. Frequently, Vietnamese province chiefs and Vietnamese intelligence agencies were reluctant to participate fully because they had their own, different political goals. There was no such thing as an apolitical Vietnamese intelligence agency or province chief; fighting the Vietcong and struggling with other South Vietnamese officials for political and economic power within the GVN occurred simultaneously. According to CIA analyst Douglas S. Blaufarb, the political interests of rival Vietnamese intelligence agencies took precedence over cooperation: "They had more urgent priorities, including the goal of advancing their own positions in competition with rival services. Pooling of effort in a center where service identity was merged in a larger whole did not serve that purpose."

Conversely, although President Thieu had ordered the intelligence agencies to cooperate at Komer's request, he feared that their active cooperation, as opposed to the norm of interservice competition, could create potential political rivals in his bid for continued rule. As U.S. military analysts at MACV headquarters in Saigon noted, "The Phoenix–Phung Hoang program is looked upon by many

Vietnamese as having been forced upon the GVN by the Americans" and was thus resented as an unwanted intrusion into Vietnamese affairs.

A third difficulty concerned the very objective of the Phoenix Program: targeting specific individuals and attempting to arrest them in their native hamlets. Many Vietnamese families had members on both the GVN side and in the National Liberation Front forces. As the MACV analysts assigned to study GVN reluctance to participate in Phoenix said, "There are ways that are accepted to kill your brother and there are other ways such as 'breaking his rice bowl' which are not. Further, an attitude of 'if I don't bother his home, he won't bother mine' is sometimes prevalent, particularly at the hamlet level."

To overcome this inertia, Robert Komer instituted a system of *numerical quotas* detailing how many VCI members needed to be eliminated each month in every district and province in order for the Vietnamese officials to re-

ceive full CORDS financial support for pacification operations and economic development assistance.

Resorting to quotas was not a new development in the Vietnam War. On the contrary, U.S. ground force commanders were under considerable pressure to report high enemy body counts as indexes of their unit productivity and contribution toward reaching the "crossover point." According to Professor Francis West of the Naval War College, if a battalion commander did not achieve a satisfactory body count "he had a 30 to 50 percent chance of being relieved of command." Air Force and naval air units in turn measured their productivity in terms of how many sorties they flew each month. And even before CORDS was formed, Komer had written that pacification was like

---

In this artist's rendition, a member of Captain John Cook's Phoenix team pulls To Van Phoung's body from a tunnel as Cook and Phoung's former girlfriend look on.

a business and that "management of our pacification assets is not yet producing an acceptable rate of return for our heavy investment." Putting Phoenix on a production quota basis thus refocused the program along the same managerial strategy by which much of the war was conceptualized and run.

Although the quota system certainly did increase motivation among CORDS personnel and Vietnamese officials dependent upon CORDS funding, this shift toward managerial strategy also created severe problems for Phoenix. Frequently Vietnamese province chiefs ignored the official procedures designed to determine who was a suspected member of the Vietcong infrastructure. Alan Goodman, a social scientist studying the problems of rural Vietnamese, summarized his findings from extensive discussions with several hundred rural political and religious leaders:

During 1969, the primary problem faced by the rural population involved the injustices suffered under the administration of the "Phoenix" program. Often "Viet Cong" are arrested on the basis of anonymous denunciations received by the police from those who bear personal grudges against the "suspect." Of greater concern, however, are the large numbers of persons arrested in connection with the efforts of each provincial security agency to fulfill the quota assigned to it, regardless of a suspect's political affiliation, and it has not been unknown for province or police chiefs to seek each month to exceed their quotas in order to demonstrate competence.

Congressional hearings in July 1971 revealed the use of different techniques of dubious validity in generating Vietcong infrastructure suspects. Congressman Pete McCloskey of California examined Phoenix dossiers on a trip to Vietnam: "We found one of an individual who was accused of being a potential VCI because while his village was occupied by the Vietcong he had paid taxes to the Vietcong and his son had been drafted into the Vietcong forces. There was nothing to indicate that this man was engaged in making war against his own country." If his village was occupied by the Vietcong, the man in question had little or no choice but to pay taxes and watch his son be drafted.

Testimonies by former intelligence agents raised similar questions. Lieutenant Michael J. Uhl arrived in Vietnam in November 1968, assigned to the 1st Military Intelligence Team, 11th Infantry Brigade, American (23d Infantry) Division. As Supervisor of the counterintelligence section, he was responsible for suspected VCI members. Uhl reported two methods of generating suspects. First, regular search and destroy operations conducted by the American Division detained scores of unarmed Vietnamese. These people were turned over to 1st MIT for interrogation. Intelligence personnel then classified the Vietnamese as either "innocent civilians" (ICs) or "civilian defendants" (CDs). According to Uhl, "There was an extraordinary degree of command pressure placed on the interrogation officer to classify detainees turned over to Interrogation, Prisoner of War, as civil defendants (CDs)," because, "the way the

brigade measured its productivity was not only by its 'body count' and 'kill ratio' but by the number of CDs it had captured." All CDs in turn were classified as VCI and from there sent to the Province Interrogation Centers.

Uhl's second counterintelligence method involved supervising Vietnamese agents who listed people as VCI. These names were then forwarded to the Phoenix centers. In retrospect Uhl noted that the information they provided could not be checked: "We had no way of determining the background of these sources, nor their motivation for providing American units with information. No American in the team spoke or understood Vietnamese well enough to independently debrief any 'contact.' None of us were sufficiently sensitive to nor knowledgeable of the law, the culture, the customs, the history, etc." Vietnamese agents were paid for their work, and those who did not provide names were not retained.

In theory, whatever errors were made in arresting suspected Vietcong infrastructure members could be corrected at the Province Interrogation Centers. The innocents would be released after interrogation. CIA analyst Douglas Blaufarb indicated that the questioning and requestioning of suspects was intended as "psychological pressure" to "emphasize the prisoner's helplessness and dependence on his captors" and thus tell the truth, but that "physical duress" was not "part of the concept." Nevertheless, the CIA advisers did not control the centers, and "there is no doubt that torture was employed."

Interrogation reports in turn were forwarded to the Provincial Security Councils for use in judging and sentencing suspected VCI. Komer's successor, William Colby, testified before Congress in 1971 that the confessions obtained at the PICs "used to be used exclusively" by the security councils in passing judgment.

Under torture or the threat of torture, suspects often reported what they thought the interrogator wanted to hear. If they had the means they did anything to win their freedom, including offering bribes. Alan Goodman continued his report on Phoenix: "With large numbers of helpless persons detained in province or district jails, opportunities for corruption have proliferated. In some provinces the Phoenix Program has been turned into a money-making scheme through which a villager's release can be obtained for payment of a bribe, usually about $25 to $50." Once bribery was institutionalized, both the innocent and the guilty could bribe their way out, or rather those who could raise the money. Phoenix advisers estimated in 1969 that only 30 percent of those detained were sentenced to jail terms.

In response to the problems generated by arrest quotas, Colby changed the policy to require provinces to meet a 50 percent *sentencing quota* of VCI suspects. Congressman Ogden R. Reid of New York asked Colby if this was not begging the question: "As I read the current report, there is a quota or goal, if you prefer, relative to sentencing which

The Legend of Phoenix

by James William Gibson

The controversy surrounding the Phoenix Program did not end with the fall of Saigon in the spring of 1975. Instead, the word *Phoenix* became a special metaphor for what happened in Vietnam. Hollywood movies, television shows, and pulp novels have all used Phoenix as a symbol of the war and the strategic and moral lessons to be learned from it.

The first important appearance of Phoenix in the popular media came in October 1977 with the première of director Ted Post's film *Good Guys Wear Black*. Chuck Norris starred as the leader of the "Black Tigers," a special commando unit also called Phoenix. The film opens with scenes from the Paris peace talks in 1973. Undersecretary of State Conrad Morgan is concerned that 150 CIA men held prisoner by the North Vietnamese—a fiction—will probably be executed once the treaty is signed. With only forty-eight hours remaining until the treaty is signed, Captain John T. Booker (Norris) and a small commando force stage a rescue mission on the prison camp where the CIA men are thought to be held. The Black Tigers destroy the camp but find no prisoners. Nor do their helicopters return to pick them up at the landing zone. A wounded Capt. Booker tells his men, "Everything went wrong by the numbers. And that takes planning. I'm saying we've been set up."

The film then cuts to Riverside, Califor-nia, in 1978. Booker is now a history professor and race-car driver. A reporter mysteriously appears asking him questions about the Black Tigers. She somehow has learned that only five Phoenix operatives survived the rescue mission, while none of the 150 CIA men returned. As the story unfolds, the viewer learns that Conrad Morgan, now nominated to be secretary of state, has ordered the assassination of Booker and the other survivors from his team because the Vietnamese are blackmailing him. Unless he eliminates the survivors, the Vietnamese will reveal that he was involved in the deaths of the CIA prisoners. Booker eventually kills Morgan by kidnaping him in his car and then driving off a pier into the ocean. Booker swims out alone. The movie earned $22 million on a $600,000 investment; its success propelled Chuck Norris toward a long string of *Missing in Action* and other commando films in the 1980s.

Phoenix became a metaphor for the true American warrior, the warrior who could have won in Vietnam if he had not been restrained by corrupt and cowardly politicians and bureaucrats. Phoenix men—like their namesake, the mythical Egyptian bird that could resurrect itself in a new life as its corpse burned on a funeral pyre—cannot be destroyed. Instead, Phoenix men can be reborn, and warrior rebirths have become a common feature of war romances.

In Don Pendleton's series of pulp novels, *The Executioner*, his original hero, Sergeant Mack Bolan, is called home from Vietnam to confront a family crisis. His father has lost his job because of heart problems and then borrowed money from the Mafia. After seeing his father beaten by the mob, Mack's sister becomes a prostitute to repay the family debt. When Dad finds out, he kills his daughter, his wife, and then himself.

Bolan, an Army sniper with more than 100 credited kills in Vietnam, attacks the Mafia, easily killing 30 to 50 men per book. Each killing is described inch by inch: bullets, knives, and grenade fragments enter the body and sensuously destroy flesh, releasing fluids in orgasmic deaths. The first thirty-eight volumes of this series sold 25 million copies. In the thirty-ninth book, Bolan is recast as a U.S. government special agent:

Mack Bolan no longer existed, of course, in the official sense. He had been recreated in the government computers as one John Macklin Phoenix, Colonel, U.S.A., Retired. And the entire Phoenix Program was a covert operation, unrecorded in the official records and forever obscured by several levels of bureaucratic smoke screen.

Bolan/Phoenix is joined by two commando teams under his command, *Able Team* and *Phoenix Force*. Together they fight the forces of evil in the world: Central Americans, Palestinians and Arabs of all nationalities, drug dealers, neo-Nazi groups, and most of all, the KGB. Phoenix men redeem defeat in Vietnam through their victories over all these contemporary enemies.

Although the popular media largely portray Phoenix warriors as incarnations of American individualism and courage, there are significant exceptions. In the spring of 1987, the television series "Miami Vice" presented an episode in which a Phoenix operative, code named "Savage," is identified as an assassin under the control of an ex-CIA case officer, Coleman, who now targets prominent international liberal and leftist leaders for death. Castillo, the Miami Vice commander, receives assistance from a Texas detective named Nguyen Van Tranh, a former Saigon policeman whom Castillo knew during the war.

Castillo and Tranh entrap Savage with a prostitute named Gina, actually a Miami Vice policewoman. In the ensuing battle Castillo is wounded while Tranh kills Savage in combat and then murders Coleman in his hotel room. Tranh flees Miami but later sends a letter to Castillo revealing that he is actually a North Vietnamese intelligence officer who has been tracking Savage and Coleman for years. In his letter he writes, "I dream of a more perfect world in which we could all be comrades."

What these episodes share is the use of Phoenix as a metaphor for an uncontrolled warrior who acts outside the bureaucratic chain of command. In the conservative interpretation, Phoenix represents what went right in Vietnam, where "self-imposed restraints" were abandoned. The left views this same absence of restraint as a symbol of the war's corruption. Phoenix serves as a reminder of this immorality and a warning against future covert actions. Of course, the real history of the Phoenix Program is missing in all the action.

is roughly half of the total by each military region that are supposed to be captured. How can you, as a concept, administratively, legally, or otherwise, set up a quota for what we might think are some kind of judicial proceedings? If you set a quota, is not that almost automatically saying we are setting a quota irrespective of the facts, the evidence or justice?"

Colby avoided the question by shifting the frame of reference. Rather than answering the question of whether one can legitimately set a quota for judicial proceedings ostensibly searching for the truth, he replied that meeting quotas this way was preferable to "filling the quotas by those who happened to be killed in the course of battle."

Colby's response raised what was perhaps the most controversial dimension of the Phoenix Program. From January 1968 through May 1971, CORDS reported 20,587 VCI killed. The Republic of Vietnam reported a much higher figure of 40,994 killed from August 1968 through mid-1971. In his testimony Colby said that in the Vietcong military forces "there are some individuals who are both military commanders or guerrilla commanders and VCI. In the course of the military fights with a lot of those troops, a lot of people are killed who are revealed as, and identified as, VCI." That is, the corpses of armed Vietcong were somehow identified as men and women who were also political cadres. Once identified as having come from the ranks of the VCI, their deaths were recorded in the Phoenix operational centers.

According to CORDS statistics, from January 1970 through March 1971, 87.6 percent of those VCI killed met their deaths in routine combat operations conducted by Main-Force U.S. and ARVN units. Only the remaining 12.4 percent of VCI deaths could be attributed to operations initiated by Phoenix in its systematic search for political cadres.

Colby thought live VCI suspects obtained through the Phoenix identification program constituted the best way to defeat the Vietcong infrastructure. Prisoners could talk; corpses could not provide any information on Vietcong organization and activity. Hence he thought assigning provinces and districts a "sentencing quota" based on the arrests of serious suspects was an improved management technique in contrast to either mass arrests of virtually anyone (to fill the previous arrest quota) or filling the Phoenix quota through dead Vietcong guerrillas who were later identified as being political cadres. However, as his statement before Congress indicated, Colby did not question the accuracy of identifying dead guerrillas as VCI counted in the Phoenix quotas.

Inevitably, Phoenix operatives disputed the accuracy of these statistics. After Lt. Cook and Lt. Hau received their briefing on the quota system in August 1968, shortly after their successful neutralization of Phoung, they joked, blaming each other's superiors for coming up with the idea. But Cook's attitude became more serious:

It was far from being funny. Some of the obvious shortcomings of such a plan were immediately visible. For starters, it would now be a tremendous temptation to claim that regular Viet Cong guerrillas, killed in combat, were actually members of the infrastructure. This was sure to happen if the powers above us insisted on a certain number of eliminations. The actual status of such people could be easily falsified by switching their identity with that of a known member of the infrastructure.

Lt. Michael J. Uhl reported that in the American Division's 1st Military Intelligence Team, VCI deaths, which became part of the Phoenix statistics, were fabricated because the commanding officer had ordered that no military intelligence personnel go on routine combat patrols. The commander told Uhl that he was afraid he would not be able to get replacements for casualties incurred on such patrols: "He further informed me that the only purpose for MI people to be on patrol was for the purpose of hunting down VCI. From that point on, any 'body count' resulting from an MI patrol was automatically listed as VCI. To my knowledge, in fact, all those killed by 1st MIT on such patrols, were classified as VCI only after their deaths. There was never any evidence to justify such a classification."

Uhl indicated that this list of dead VCI included both Vietnamese found with weapons and unarmed Vietnamese whose corpses contained no documentation linking them with the Vietcong. The latter may well have been Vietnamese civilians. Either way, both his testimony and Cook's indicate that Phoenix thought it was eradicating far more VCI than it actually was.

Critics of Phoenix also frequently raised a darker allegation about the count of dead VCI. They questioned whether Phoenix operatives ordered the deliberate assassination of suspected VCI on a routine basis. In his autobiography Colby wrote that when he first took command of CORDS in 1969 he "issued a directive on the subject of assassination and other equally repugnant activities." The memo stated that Phoenix operatives "are specifically not authorized to engage in assassinations or other violations of the rules of land warfare." MACV issued a similar order forbidding assassination.

Congressman Ogden Reid asked Colby, "Do you state categorically that Phoenix has never perpetuated the premeditated killing of a civilian in a noncombat situation?" Colby replied, "No, I could not say that, but I do not think it happens often. I certainly would not say never. Let me distinguish. Phoenix, as a program, has not done that. Individual members of it, subordinate people in it, may have done it. But as a program, it is not designed to do that."

But some Phoenix operatives disagreed with that description. Kenneth Osborn, another graduate of the U.S. Army's intelligence school at Fort Holabird, Maryland, supervised forty to fifty Vietnamese agents and subagents out of Da Nang under his cover as a U.S. Agency for

International Development refugee worker. Osborn received additional funding for his projects from the district Phoenix center when he began forwarding to them names of suspects provided by his Vietnamese agents. He also worked with members of the Combined Studies Group, a CIA organization, and with their Vietnamese commandos for Phoenix operations, the Provincial Reconnaissance Units. Osborn describes the dynamics between American advisers and Vietnamese commandos:

I never saw it codified; that is, I never saw an official directive that said the PRU's will proceed to the village and murder the individual. However, it was implicit that when you got a name and wanted to deal effectively in neutralizing that individual you didn't need to go through interrogation. It was good enough to have him reported as a suspect and that justified neutralization. It became a sterile depersonalized murder program.

Upon hearing Osborn's testimony, Congressman McCloskey asked him, "How far up in the command structure does the intelligence collection procedure—how far up in the command structure is the torture, the brutality, the assassinations fully known to those in command and in charge of completing the mission? Does it go up to the captains, the majors, the colonels, the generals, the Ambassador?" Osborn did not have a concise answer to this question. He instead indicated that superior officers had a "real reason not to know," that completing their assignment of collecting information and neutralizing VCI suspects outweighed concern over how it was done. In Osborn's experience, superiors rarely questioned the reports submitted by subordinates as long as the goals were met. Finding out how many Vietnamese were killed deliberately by Phoenix operatives is thus not possible.

However, using official Phoenix records, Thomas C. Thayer, a systems analyst for the Department of Defense, found that 616 suspected VCI who were specifically targeted by Phoenix were killed by Phoenix forces from January 1970 through March 1971. His data do not indicate if those killed were assassinated or if they were killed resisting arrest. He noted that the 616 represented less than 2 percent of all VCI killed, captured, or "rallied" to the GVN during this period. From this low percentage he concluded: "There is no way of telling from the data whether any political assassinations were taking place, but the data do suggest that such activity was not the primary aim of the program."

Thayer also analyzed the rank of all VCI killed, captured, and defected through the Phoenix Program. Although Phoenix was supposed to neutralize high-level political officials of the National Liberation Front, very few high-ranking officials were ever caught. Only 3 percent of VCI "neutralized" in 1970 and 1971 were Communist party members above the district level. Around 75 percent of those killed, captured, or rallied operated at the lowest organizational levels—villages and hamlets—and less than half of the total were Communist party members.

Lt. Cook foresaw this outcome when the quota system was instituted in 1968:

Wouldn't we be far better off if we had the party secretary for Bien Hoa Province than a whole sackful of hamlet-level cadres? This business about numbers would be acceptable if we were dealing with apples or automobiles, but people were different. Some are simply worth more than others. If they insisted on concentrating only on numbers, then no one would have time to go after the higher-ranking members of the political structure. All of our time would be spent on satisfying this silly-ass requirement, which could be done quite simply by eliminating unimportant members of the organization.

Cook inadvertently provided a second explanation for the concentration by Phoenix on low-level functionaries. Many of the examples he offered of successful Phoenix operations began with information obtained from a Vietcong defector or a close personal associate of the VCI member. The reasons given for betrayals were personal,

The body of a Vietcong cadre targeted by the Phoenix Program lies on public display after he was shot down in a South Vietnamese marketplace. Lying next to him is a bystander, probably innocent, shot in the volley.

like the spurned lover, or another case in which a VC defected after he was passed over for promotion to squad leader and informed Phoenix where his unit was located. Higher-level Vietcong infrastructure members, operating among other dedicated party members, were more insulated from those with shaky ideological commitments. Certainly the traditional Leninist cell-structure, where each Communist activist only knows the few party members in her or his own cell, is designed to provide more protection to cadres at each successively higher level of the party.

A 1970 CIA analysis of successful Vietcong infiltration of the Republic of Vietnam offered a third explanation for the limited success of Phoenix. By the spring of 1970, the Vietcong had infiltrated an estimated 30,000 agents into South Vietnam's military, police, and intelligence agencies. Of these, about 3,000 belonged to the Vietcong security service; they "permeated the South Vietnamese police intelligence service, the army intelligence service and military security service, and the Central Intelligence Office, the South Vietnamese counterpart of the CIA." A summary of the CIA report appearing in the *New York Times* continued: "The chief mission of its 3,000 agents in the South Vietnamese structure is to keep the communists informed of how much the Government knows about them and to block any penetration by the Government. The Vietcong security service is so efficient that none of its important agents had been apprehended, the study says." The U.S. officials who leaked the study to the *Times* thought that it provided the "most plausible explanation" for the failure of Phoenix.

With its core intact, the National Liberation Front was often able to replace VCI casualties. In July 1971 Colby told Congress, "There is no contention that the total of VCI goes down together with the number of those neutralized because there is replacement going on." Successful replacement was a function of both NLF organizational strength and the persistence of social conditions in the countryside that made revolutionary war appear to peasants as the only possible path to major social change.

While virtually all assessments of Phoenix by American observers, including high-level participants like Colby, acknowledge its limited success, more recent statements from Hanoi have challenged that prevailing view. Journalist Seymour Hersh reported an interview with North Vietnamese foreign minister Nguyen Co Thach in the early 1980s:

The Central Intelligence Agency's assassination program in South Vietnam, had slaughtered far more than the 21,000 officially listed by the United States. "We had many weaknesses in the South," Thach said, "because of Phoenix." In some provinces, 95 percent of the Communist cadre had been assassinated or compromised by the Phoenix operation.

Thach's comments, however, might well be the result of

a misunderstanding. Vietcong political cadres were indeed suffering heavy losses in 1969 (some province committees could only meet safely in Cambodia), and Phoenix certainly played a part in inflicting those casualties. However, CORDS statistics indicate that routine combat operations were killing far more VCI than was Phoenix. Thach would not have been in a good position to distinguish between the sources of these casualties.

These Vietcong losses in turn led the Communist party to accelerate its infiltration of the GVN. The party even used one CORDS pacification project, the Chieu Hoi amnesty program, as a means to give its agents legal cover, in their terms "the transformation of party cadres into innocent people." CORDS and their Vietnamese counterparts offered peasants financial rewards for persuading members of the National Liberation Front to surrender. The higher the rank of the defector, the more lucrative the payment to the third party who induced the defection. These former Vietcong spent a month and a half in relatively pleasant camps and received political indoctrination by leaflets and special television programs. After the six-week indoctrination, they were given two sets of clothes, some money, and were released. Of the 47,000 VC and VCI defectors who won amnesty through the Chieu Hoi program in 1969, the CIA estimated that several thousand remained Vietcong political operatives. Other observers suspected that many of the rest were never hardcore Vietcong to begin with but were instead, at best, recruits who had quickly become disillusioned when confronted with the severe hardships of guerrilla life.

How then does one evaluate Phoenix when confronted with the conflicting reports? Robert Komer, after leaving CORDS and joining the Rand Corporation as an analyst, concluded that Phoenix was a "poorly managed and largely ineffectual effort," while his final summation on the pacification war concluded, "As this study suggests, the U.S. did not get comparable value for its massive aid to the GVN." From Komer's managerial and business approach, pacification was a bad investment to be written off.

His answer does not reveal why Phoenix and the other paramilitary programs in pacification, despite some significant local successes, failed on the whole. As CIA analyst Douglas Blaufarb suggested, the U.S. offered *techniques* to the GVN but did not analyze the social and political structure of that society and government: "The essence of the rural political problem of the GVN was the cultural gap between the apparatus and the population, the lack of communication across the gap, and the resultant sense of insecurity of the peasant who saw the ruling power as arbitrary, capricious, and inscrutable when it was not nakedly exploitative." It should be emphasized that the "cultural gap" Blaufarb points to was simultaneously a difference in class position. South Vietnam was a highly stratified class society and most GVN political and military leaders, despite their internal struggles for

HỘ. TRƯỜNG

control of the political system, wanted to retain that class hierarchy.

The GVN leadership was not willing to conduct the major reform efforts that many in CORDS and others in the U.S. government thought were necessary to win popular allegiance. As the highest-ranking foreign service officer in the State Department, U. Alexis Johnson, analyzed the weakness of U.S. hopes for GVN reform in a memorandum for President Johnson: "In some cases only radical reforms will obtain the necessary results. Yet the measures we advocate may strike at the very foundations of those aspects of a country's social structure and domestic economy on which rests the basis of a government's control."

Consequently, an entrenched GVN elite found Phoenix quota requirements and rules—a system of paper reports or production indices—imposed upon them by the Americans. Filling in these reports was necessary for the GVN officials to obtain the material aid they needed to stay in power. But they subverted the program to meet their own

Hoi Chanhs, Vietcong who have accepted amnesty under the GVN's Chieu Hoi ("open arms") program, line up to be interviewed by U.S. government agents on July 23, 1970.

needs, sometimes by relatively harmless fabrications, at other times by jailing even non-Communist political opponents, or by bribery schemes that clearly created numerous enemies among the same rural populace CORDS was trying to pacify. Men like Cook and his Vietnamese associates in Di An, who were able to complete their mission by overcoming these obstacles, remained lonely exceptions.

The U.S. premise that there were technical solutions to deep social and political problems proved wrong. If the GVN elite was isolated from the peasant majority, the Americans were at least twice removed. Rarely able to speak the language, knowing little of the history and social structure, they were ready targets for both GVN corruption and the extensive Vietcong counterintelligence efforts.

Special Military Operations

The United States waged a frustrating struggle in Vietnam. Large U.S. Army and Marine units, stationed in secure bases, operated throughout the countryside at will, but Vietnam remained unpacified. NVA and VC units fought confidently despite numerous battlefield defeats, sophisticated American weapons failed to ensure success, and normal measures of military progress did not guarantee victory. Fleets of helicopters were subject to a hail of gunfire at any landing zone, tank-escorted convoys faced destruction on many highways, and entire battalions of troops could still be ambushed and threatened with heavy losses. Senior American officers, trained to fight according to World War II and Korean War tactics or concepts of nuclear supremacy, were unable to eliminate the elusive bands of peasant guerrillas and light infantrymen of the jungles.

The United States Central Intelligence Agency, however, was determined to strike hard behind the lines at North Vietnamese and Vietcong resources

and had initiated a clandestine campaign of special activities designed to undermine NVA effectiveness. In December 1963 this highly classified unconventional warfare program came under the command of the military, which formed a joint service high command to direct such operations on January 16, 1964. The title, MACV Studies and Observation Group, was chosen as a cover designation. Its existence was explained as a staff group studying combat lessons learned in Vietnam. The staff, in reality, was a hand-picked collection of crack U.S. special operations experts who operated on the premise that it takes a guerrilla to catch a guerrilla. Few rules of political restraint applied.

MACV-SOG was a joint command encompassing all branches of the U.S. armed forces and some civilian agencies, with vast responsibilities that extended throughout Burma, Cambodia, Laos, North and South Vietnam, and even included the southern Chinese provinces of Yunnan, Kwangsi, Kwangtung, and Hainan Island. Within this large geographic area, MACV-SOG mission commanders struck at the entire NVA command structure and logistical network. The organization conducted an array of special operations, but as a military unit with a creed of inflicting maximum destruction while gathering strategic intelligence, most MACV-SOG objectives were aimed at achieving direct combat results: tracking down and disrupting North Vietnamese, Khmer Rouge, and Pathet Lao forces within their own territories.

SOG: its men and operations

The most important MACV-SOG assignment was to locate and interdict NVA infiltration routes and their sources of supply—wherever they might be found. This quest routinely took SOG operatives into neutral countries bordering South Vietnam, a technical violation of both international law and America's own professed rules of engagement. Sometimes, but not often, this task carried the far-ranging SOG strike teams deep into nations not directly connected to the Southeast Asian conflict. The planning and execution of such far-flung missions are among the most closely guarded secrets of the Vietnam War, and their nature can only be hinted at. For example, teams might be dispatched to sabotage installations responsible for the manufacture or shipment of ground-to-air missiles potentially damaging to U.S. helicopters, if actual shipment to North Vietnam was deemed imminent.

SOG operations against NVA troop lines and depots extended well beyond simple raids to demolish convoys or direct B–52 bombing runs against NVA/VC base staging areas. Working imaginatively with the shrewd armaments

experts available within MACV-SOG, its commanders used secret Navy funds to develop one of the most cunning programs executed in modern warfare. Faulty or "rigged" ammunition was inserted by commando teams into selected North Vietnamese depots, with the express purpose of undermining the NVA munitions system.

The effect was often devastating. The carefully planted rounds soon found their way into front-line units, where exploding weapons maimed mortar crews, machine gunners were killed because their weapons jammed in firefights, and snipers began to lose faith in their rifle bullets. The program was so secret that the codes were regularly altered: Eldest Son, Italian Green, and Pole Bean were among the code names used to describe this effort.

The Joint Chiefs of Staff abruptly stopped this program on February 23, 1970, with no official explanation ever given. High-level MACV-SOG personnel who possessed the "need to know" about the program, and were aware of its effects, grumbled sarcastically that the operation was probably too successful. But there might have been other concerns. While MACV-SOG ensured that their own personnel using NVA items had "clean" ammo, there were rumors that several American and South Vietnamese Ranger teams were wiped out while equipped with captured weapons. The real reasons for halting the program may never be fully revealed, because like many other SOG projects, the circumstances surrounding this effort are in classified Pentagon vaults under the tightest security possible.

Other MACV-SOG endeavors centered on intelligence, information analysis, and monitoring responsibilities for a host of crucial war-related purposes. One component, SOG–80, searched for crashed aircraft and missing or captured personnel as the Recovery Studies Division, an office that exists to this day. SOG–36, the Airborne Studies Group, parachuted intelligence agents and psychological warfare teams across several borders in a drive to confuse and destroy enemy forces.

Some examples of SOG–36 teams demonstrate the remarkable diversity of this one MACV-SOG agency. In the North, Earth Angel teams composed of an intelligence network of NVA turncoats and mixed American-Indochinese STRATA (Short-Term Roadwatch & Target Acquisition) detachments saturated large regions in both Laos and North Vietnam. SOG–36 later fielded Pike Hill intelligence collection teams dressed in Khmer Rouge uniforms and Cedar Walk Cambodian guerrilla units to the south. A wide range of individual agents supplemented these detachments. "Oodles" clandestine national agents, "Borden" diversionary NVA agents, and "Singleton" agents were among an array of highly trained male and female paracommandos, whose proficiency at silently landing and carrying out vital assignments insured that no NVA/VC sanctuary was truly safe.

MACV-SOG engaged in myriad other tasks, much more

Preceding page. *Montagnard troops march past the bagged bodies of soldiers killed in fighting near the beleaguered Special Forces camp at Bu Prang, South Vietnam, in November 1969.*

Special Forces Captain Ken Nauman of Project Delta, an organization similar to SOG that operated within South Vietnam, calls in an air strike while on an operation in the A Shau Valley in 1968.

sinister in nature, including numerous "black" psychological operations. Sophisticated transmitter stations and antenna arrays, stretching from the "octopus" site near Saigon to the northern radio relay towers outside Hue–Phu Bai beamed false North Vietnamese broadcasts and hampered NVA/VC tactical message traffic. Navy SEAL interception teams using fast patrol boats kidnaped North Vietnamese fishermen and coastal residents, brainwashed them, and returned them to their native areas as unwitting agents. Roads and trails throughout Laos and North Vietnam were doused with counterfeit money, propaganda leaflets, and promises of large financial reward for the identification of key targets.

The blackest MACV-SOG projects were premised on concepts of absolute denial if ever exposed. These included the initiation of resistance movements, encouragement of bandit activity, and the hiring of assassination teams that stalked through the countryside of neutral nations to hunt their prey in a campaign justified only as "counterterrorism." This was the no-holds-barred style of warfare that MACV-SOG fought best, by its own rules and on its own terms, a war in which questions were rarely asked but prompt results were often obtained.

MACV-SOG acted in accordance with the highest national authority. Although the command was structured on paper to report to the MACV commander, a top-secret section of the Joint Chiefs of Staff at the Pentagon was established to watch over the organization and even to direct SOG in fulfilling additional assignments. This section was headed by the Special Assistant for Counterinsurgency and Special Activities (SACSA), and its very existence and connection to MACV-SOG was known only to a few officials during the entire Vietnam War. The section contained three divisions—for Special Operations, Counterinsurgency, and Psychological Operations—and each division could harness the entire military special warfare power of the United States for any task anywhere on the globe.

The presidential decree of December 1963, which transferred MACV-SOG–type operations from the CIA to Pentagon control, established a unique system of mission accountability. To ensure utmost flexibility under wartime circumstances, the system gave considerable latitude to senior SOG officers in determining actual operations. However, every plan for a patrol or other activity involving SOG was sent seven days in advance via ultrasecret electronics channels directly to the secretary of defense and SACSA in the Pentagon. Copies of these messages were also sent for presidential consideration to the National Security Council and the commander-in-chief, Pacific (CINCPAC), Office J–46, which monitored SOG activities at that command level.

This secure, limited-distribution satellite communications link allowed the Joint Chiefs of Staff or the president seventy-two hours to stop or modify a pending SOG action. If MACV-SOG did not receive any further instructions or response, the mission was considered approved. There were important exceptions to this process. The system allowed MACV-SOG to launch strikes immediately and delay informing higher authorities, if immediate response was deemed crucial in a combat situation. Also, local SOG force commanders sometimes undertook actions on their own responsibility, without the cognizance or approval of anyone higher in the chain of command.

One example of the use of unilateral emergency power took place in late 1971. Lieutenant Colonel Roger M. Pezzelle, the SOG ground commander, learned from intelligence agents inside Laos that a captured Air Force pilot, a lieutenant colonel named Butcher, had escaped from a jeep carrying him to a northern prison camp and was evading NVA search parties. Col. Pezzelle immediately dispatched several raiding teams into Laos to find the downed aviator. For two weeks a series of skirmishes exploded as the heavily armed SOG commandos tried to locate the pilot while forming a shield between him and his NVA pursuers. Unfortunately, after a sixteen-day search, the pilot was recaptured by the NVA.

Throughout the MACV-SOG structure, the watchword was secrecy. In developing situations, such as the attempt to save Col. Butcher, the discovery of SOG landing sites or interception of SOG transmissions could prove fatal. On any given day, some thirty small, isolated teams performed ventures of great risk "across the fence," far from friendly support, and any compromise could bring sudden, violent death. The need for strict secrecy surrounding the methodology of SOG operations was also considered crucial. During the war, the knowledge of how teams were inserted, what gear they carried, and every detail of their operating procedures was classified.

The vital importance of this confidentiality became more obvious as the years passed. North Vietnam apparently raised several Soviet-advised counterraider teams, which were designed to surprise and eliminate the MACV-SOG recon teams. The counterraiders became increasingly proficient at adapting SOG techniques and uniforms and eventually even acquired appropriate helicopters.

Communist tribesmen impersonated the indigenous SOG commandos, while either Russians or renegade Americans, whose existence, even, is classified, imitated white and black patrol members.

This counterraider effort was very limited—probably because the Russians feared international complications if their involvement became known—and never amounted to more than a nuisance. However, SOG suffered adverse effects beyond occasional loss of personnel, especially where counterraider forces randomly committed terrorist acts and destruction that was incorrectly attributed to SOG activity. The clever counterraider campaign was ultimately a failure because it did not reduce MACV-SOG's overall effectiveness. Many of the special methods and operating principles that the SOG organization employed are still highly valued in contemporary covert activities.

MACV-SOG included personnel from the CIA, the Defense Intelligence Agency (DIA), the USIA, and other selected branches of the U.S. government, as well as citizens of other nations. Nationalist Chinese crewmen manned SOG's own "Gray Ghost" aircraft squadron, Turkish Air Force officers flew helicopter couriers, and Australians piloted the Red Kangaroo–painted Caribou aerial delivery planes. MACV-SOG worked in close conjunction with the crack South Vietnamese Special Exploitation Service, a band of ruthless agents and intelligence officers who could be counted on in the most dangerous undertakings. The primary fighting arm of MACV-SOG consisted of small teams of courageous Americans and trusted Asian mercenaries, equipped with highly classified weapons and other specialized items, who conducted a series of top-secret missions across international borders.

The military personnel within MACV-SOG represented all branches of the service. Marine reconnaissance commandos, Air Force aircraft crewmen, Navy SEAL combat swimmers, and even Coast Guard communications experts served in a variety of roles. However, the majority of personnel came from the ranks of Army Special Forces, an elite group of guerrilla warfare experts given their green berets by President Kennedy in 1963 as the front line in his crusade against Communist "wars of liberation." Although most senior Pentagon officers were determined to fight a war of big battalions in Vietnam, the Joint Chiefs of Staff were fortunate to inherit President Kennedy's Green Beret troopers as the vanguard of their behind-the-lines war against the major arteries of North Vietnamese military power.

All Special Forces soldiers assigned to MACV-SOG were posted to the organization under ultrasecret orders, which made them appear to be mere reinforcements for the 5th Special Forces Group at Nha Trang inside South Viet-

While on a mission against the Vietcong, a Navy SEAL commando captures for interrogation a South Vietnamese boy who had been hiding in a canal.

nam. The recruiting for MACV-SOG was conducted on such a secret basis that often the personnel themselves were unaware of their ultimate assignment. Sergeant Bob "Baron" Bechtoldt of Belleville, Illinois, was one of only eighteen Special Forces candidates chosen from a 1,000-man parachute course at Fort Benning in 1968. He did not know at the time that he was being assigned to SOG.

Sgt. Bechtoldt completed demolitions expert school in accordance with his wishes to be a combat engineer. When he was sent to advanced military intelligence analysis training, his inquiries into the reason for this unusual schooling were politely brushed aside. After graduation, he was given coded orders to the 5th Special Forces Group in Vietnam and learned he was in MACV-SOG only when he was whisked instead to an isolated airstrip at Ban Me Thuot. As Bechtoldt and seven other new engineer–intelligence specialists debarked from the Caribou aircraft, a rugged sergeant major approached them. He said bluntly, "You've been hand-picked for an extremely high-risk special mission unit, but participation is strictly voluntary. If you want out, you only have to raise your hand."

Bechtoldt felt like raising his arm as high as he could reach but kept motionless because no one else moved a hand in response. He later found out that the others felt the same way; if only one person had raised his hand they all would have quit that instant. He also discovered that he was part of a sudden influx of new replacements sent to MACV-SOG at the beginning of 1969, because the ranks of Command & Control South (CCS) had been decimated in action just weeks earlier.

CCS was one of three field commands established during 1968, as MACV-SOG expanded and consolidated its previous six smaller, numbered forward operating bases. MACV-SOG was structured in conformity with specific project targets. The largest project was Prairie Fire, originally known in 1965 as Shining Brass. Its goal was to curtail NVA infiltration through eastern Laos. Command & Control North (CCN), based at Da Nang, shared responsibility for Prairie Fire missions along with Command & Control Central (CCC) at Kontum. CCN also handled missions into North Vietnam, which were first initiated on February 1, 1964, under Operation Plan 34–A. However, the smaller CCS was fast gaining a fearsome reputation of its own as MACV-SOG became active on a newer project, Daniel Boone (renamed Salem House in December 1968).

Project Daniel Boone, the top-secret Special Forces reconnaissance campaign across the Cambodian border, started on June 27, 1966. President Johnson did not grant formal permission to use Daniel Boone teams until May 1967, and even then only a small slice of the northern "tri-border" area of Cambodia was opened to MACV-SOG

Two buildings of Command & Control South (CCS) headquarters, MACV-SOG's field command for southern South Vietnam, lie in ruins following a June 1969 Vietcong rocket attack.

scrutiny. The recon teams began identifying so many NVA base camps and roadways that by October they received presidential permission to expose all of the Cambodian frontier, up to a depth of twenty (later thirty) kilometers, to MACV-SOG operations. Two lettered zones divided the southern Cambodian portion of Project Daniel Boone at Snuol (Zones Alpha and Bravo), but the largest sector of the Cambodian target area was so ravaged by SOG teams that it was officially nicknamed "The Wasteland."

Into the Fishhook

One of the most dangerous regions within the Project Daniel Boone area of operations was the Fishhook, a sharp bend in the Cambodian border north of Saigon. Throughout late 1967, SOG recon teams reported a menacing NVA/VC buildup in the Fishhook, but the Pentagon turned down General Westmoreland's urgent appeals to bomb that portion of Cambodia. The Fishhook staging area proved instrumental in enabling the Communists to attack Saigon during the Tet offensive of 1968. Thereafter, a chagrined MACV-SOG took special vengeance against the Fishhook, which in its own peculiar jargon became coded as the "Golf–80 series targets."

In that sector, Bob Bechtoldt would soon face one of his most harrowing ordeals, but first he completed MACV-SOG's strenuous recon team-leader course at the restricted base of Long Thanh. The mini–Ranger-school was designed to test the will power and stamina of potential cross-border raiders, while introducing them to the grim fact of SOG survival: There was no margin for error on the part of any team member inside enemy territory. The course ended with a "training operation" into a suspected VC base near Kontum. The MACV-SOG instructor noted that the test on South Vietnamese soil was merely preparatory to their real cross-border job but cautioned them with typical gallows humor: "Remember that MACV has lost over 40,000 soldiers so far in these in-country training courses."

Upon successful completion, Bechtoldt was assigned as a radioman, one of two Americans on a six-man CCS recon team, the number that could be transported in a single helicopter. The other four members were montagnard ("yard") tribal warriors hired on the basis of their jungle expertise and loyalty to Special Forces. They usually wore ordinary tropical fatigues and carried no identification, except that the point man and tail gunner were dressed to resemble enemy troops in the area. NVA or VC soldiers stumbling across a team would hesitate upon seeing a yard dressed in khaki, complete with an AK47 rifle and ammo pouches, and this often gave the team an extra edge in responding.

Recon teams within CCS were named after tools; Bechtoldt was on Team Auger. Teams were ideally suited for missions lasting five to ten days, followed by a five-day

"stand down" rest period. However, Bechtoldt recalled that so many teams were being shot up in 1969 that there weren't enough Americans to go around. Missions were run almost continuously, back to back, and we were getting pretty shaky. MACV-SOG was deliberately trying to stir up trouble in the Golf-80 zone, and the area was so hot that we felt like suicide squads. Our hatchet forces were supposedly reaction elements for other teams in distress, but actually they were just larger units that killed whatever was around—to let the NVA know we were pissed. SOG had a vendetta down in the Fishhook, and the NVA/VC knew it. So the ops we ran there were like blood feuds.

On June 6, 1969, exactly twenty-five years after the Allied invasion of Normandy Beach in World War II, Sergeant John "Buff" Costello of Winchester, Virginia, led Team Auger into Cambodia on a MACV-SOG strike mission. The helicopters leapfrogged across the triple-canopy rain forest, as door gunners threw mats filled with bomblets and fireworks into clearings, creating the sounds of firefights to throw off North Vietnamese spotters. By using this tactic, the team was able to land without incident and started to zigzag through an assigned ten-kilometer patch of the Golf-80 zone. The weather was relatively dry, and on the second day the team reached a two-lane road with heavy truck and bicycle traffic. After recording data on the road, they patrolled the area and found an unattended bamboo hut that was being used as a classroom.

Sgts. Bechtoldt and Costello realized that they were on the edge of a large base but could not resist quickly entering the empty structure and taking photos of themselves beside the podium with their Nikon intelligence camera. That night was strangely quiet, and the team members slept with rucksacks on, only their web gear unsnapped for comfort. The next morning Mang-Kwa, a yard, was serving point for the team as it patrolled up a small hillside. As he was crossing the knoll, a volley of gunfire erupted, punctuated by loud whistle blasts.

Sgt. Costello raced back down the hillside as Bechtoldt yelled out, "Where's Mang-Kwa?" but Costello hastily signaled to reverse direction and retreat at once. The team rapidly redeployed in reverse order as Mang-Kwa, who happened to be delayed trying to take a dead man's automatic weapon, suddenly appeared. Dozens of North Vietnamese gunners charged into sight behind him, but the team members opened fire and blasted apart the leading ranks. They exploded delayed charges to upset the NVA pursuit as the team ran to a dry creek bed and radioed for immediate extraction.

As the North Vietnamese closed in on their positions, Costello was able to flash his emergency mirror and contact the forward control OV–10 aircraft. Four Air Force Huey helicopter gunships of the 20th Special Operations Squadron came in low over the treetops, their miniguns blazing. Bechtoldt knew that the squadron would do anything to get them out, because the Air Force often relied on MACV-SOG teams to rescue their downed air crewmen, and "no differences in race, creed, or branch of service existed at the SOG ground level."

One helicopter caught two NVA companies running toward the skirmish in tidy formation, with weapons held rigidly at "port arms," and mowed them down with a combination of rocket and machine-gun fire. Another set of helicopters shattered an NVA company assembling on line to charge the creek. The NVA fire slackened, enabling Air Force Huey "slick" helicopters to hurl ropes and harnesses known as McGuire rigs to the beleaguered recon troops. The montagnard commandos were pulled out first.

The chase helicopter raced overhead to rescue the three Americans on this mission. In the haste to extract the team, medical specialist Ken Quackenbush tossed out a parachute harness along with two McGuire rigs, all lashed to a jungle penetrator that crashed the extraction equipment down through the trees. Bechtoldt and Morris seized the bundle and got into the McGuire rigs, while tossing the parachute harness to Costello. The helicopter promptly lifted them through a hail of NVA gunfire and the snarl of bamboo as the trio returned fire.

In breaking through the jungle canopy, "Buff" Costello, who was hanging in the parachute harness several feet lower than Bechtoldt and Morris in their McGuire rigs, constantly slammed into the boots and equipment of the other two. The long half-hour flight back became very painful because of the injuries all three had sustained and the impairment of blood circulation that extraction rigs cause after about twenty minutes. That "Buff never forgave me for giving him the parachute harness," was the most vivid memory Bechtoldt has of the mission. The official record states simply: "Team Auger was extracted successfully, having identified a new base camp and putting an estimated battalion out of action."

SOG finds a cook

Another CCS veteran, Staff Sergeant Robert J. "RJ" Graham, of Ontario, Canada, was among the numerous foreign volunteers accepted into MACV-SOG. His father was a Canadian armored corps hero of World War II and the regimental commander of Lord Strathcona Horse. Graham gave up a chance of completing Canadian officer candidate school and accepting a commission in his father's old outfit when he crossed into Buffalo, New York, and joined the United States Army Special Forces. During his training, he was dismissed from radio code school because, as a foreign national, he was technically ineligible for classified communications courses. Instead, the Special Forces sent him through an intelligence operations course where he became an expert at setting up multinational intelligence agent nets. Soon afterward he received orders to the 5th Special Forces Group in Vietnam and was shocked to find out at Nha Trang that he was under top-secret orders to MACV-SOG.

Chinese Nung commandos operating with a U.S. Special Forces unit apply one of their interrogation methods to a VC suspect captured in June 1966 in Duc Phong, South Vietnam.

When Graham arrived at Ban Me Thuot CCS headquarters in March 1969, the officers were aghast over his unfamiliarity with radio codes. "You can't operate without knowing the code book!" they exclaimed, and the first order he received was to learn the codes denied him stateside. Although Graham served as the leader of Recon Team Pick until November 1970, his most adventurous assignment involved a parachute commando raid carried out by Staff Sergeant "Foul" Frank Oppel's team.

Some of the most hazardous MACV-SOG missions involved parachuting behind NVA lines, and when Sgt. Oppel's team was selected for such an assault, his radioman quit rather than make "an insane jump." Oppel was desperate to find a new radio operator but could not talk anyone into joining. Finally, one night he stumbled drunk and dejected into Graham's hootch, and Graham, equally drunk, agreed to go along. In the morning Oppel came back to Graham's room and smiled, "You're on," but Graham could not remember what he had volunteered for.

Sgts. Oppel, Graham, and David "Zack" Paul were teamed with three Chinese Nung paratroop-qualified commandos, given football-style helmets with wire cage masks, and trained to land through the trees at night. On one nocturnal practice jump they were accidentally dropped near an outpost of Korean soldiers and were almost shot as NVA sappers. The Koreans were notorious for taking few prisoners, but the paracommandos managed to surrender. Only after they were marched through the camp gate, with hands held high, did the SOG members realize that the Koreans thought they were Soviet or Chinese agents and were probably anxious to torture information out of them. Fortunately, a phone call to a special number in Saigon quickly cleared up the confusion.

The purpose of a MACV-SOG parachute strike was usually to conduct a very important mission, such as seizing a North Vietnamese prisoner for interrogation after helicopter raiding parties had failed. The parachutist commandos relied on stealth in making a high-altitude 7,000-foot jump, which was as high as the helicopters could drop them without the need for oxygen masks. Steerable chutes were used to insure the men's ability to land on a small field surrounded by dense jungle, and the parachutes were quickly buried.

A prisoner snatch was always a chancy business. This particular mission was further complicated since the area of Cambodia about which MACV wanted intelligence was some distance from the border. It lay north of Svay Rieng, far beyond the range of friendly artillery and prompt air support. The men in the team were all dressed in standard khaki Communist uniforms with pith helmets and AK47 ammunition pouches. Oppel carried his favorite .45-caliber, silenced grease-gun, while Graham carried a CAR15 and the others used AK47 rifles. Each man also had a high-standard, silencer-equipped .22 pistol.

The patrol required a week to march to the site of the prisoner snatch and carefully set up an ambush along a well-used trail. They jumped out and caught the first NVA soldier ambling along the route and led him off into the woods. Unfortunately, they failed to realize that the prisoner had stepped out of his sandals and left them on the trail. His NVA comrades quickly found the empty sandals and initiated a large-scale pursuit.

The SOG team carried a radio and usually made short situation reports only once a day in the evening. However, as the lead North Vietnamese troops overtook them, Graham keyed the handset and radioed simply, "Contact." The Air Force armed helicopters arrived overhead an hour later and quickly used up their ammunition. Because the flight into Cambodia was unusually long, their fuel supply had been diminished and the helicopters could remain overhead only a short time. Radio transmission was minimal and the pilots signaled that they were leaving by circling the team, firing their personal weapons, and tossing out empty ammunition boxes. Still, the sudden velocity of this concentrated air strike enabled the team to break contact, and the men evaded subsequent NVA search parties.

Two Huey slicks arrived and extracted the team. Sergeant Paul got on the first helicopter with the prisoner and sat on him so he would not jump off. Once they landed, MACV-SOG intelligence personnel began the interrogation and quickly learned that the captive was only a cook, unlikely to know anything important. The team was soon ridiculed throughout the CCS compound. Oppel was heartbroken; all that danger and trouble just to catch a cook.

Soon afterward, CIA officials found reason to applaud the ingenious parachute commando effort. The cook was proving to be one of their most valuable sources of information. He was intimately familiar with his regimental organization—a previously unidentified unit—and his regional trading of foodstuffs made him an unparalleled expert on the NVA logistical system inside Cambodia. In addition, the poor cook was so afraid and eager to talk that the CIA was able to get this information with relatively little effort. Inevitably, the command was soon directed to make a special attempt to capture more cooks.

Staff Sgt. Graham typified the diversity of the MACV-SOG effort, both as a foreigner and as a soldier of great accomplishments. He recalled his highest tribute: "As far as the recon team leaders were concerned, the ultimate award for SOG service was not the medals, of which there were plenty, but the simple presentation of a 9MM Browning high-powered Silver Pistol, given with the earnest gratitude of the colonels in charge, which came carefully inlaid in velvet within a mahogany box, purchased by funds donated from all members of the command."

MACV-SOG reconnaissance team missions involved much more than searching areas and routes for NVA/VC activity and capturing personnel. Other teams planted mines along roadways, ambushed vehicles and foot units, conducted wiretapping, assessed the effects of bombing runs, directed air strikes and heavy artillery against troop concentrations, and performed heroic rescues.

Legends of SOG

In an organization like MACV-SOG, where routine missions took teams well beyond the range of PRC–25 radios, into the misting primeval rain forests that marked the very edge of civilization, some stories became the stuff of legends. Colonel Rolf W. Utegaard, the commander of Project Sigma, fondly recalled the "SOG patrol member who suffered a broken foot when a passing elephant stepped on him. I was told that authorities determined that

Special Forces Sergeants Robert Graham and David Paul return from a week-long mission in Cambodia with an unlikely source of valuable information, a North Vietnamese cook.

it had to be a Viet Cong elephant, since the area inhabitants were all rated as VC. After the elephant's allegiance was determined in this fashion, the patroller received the Purple Heart."

Several SOG leaders became particularly famous within the small circle of their comrades. Lieutenant Colonel LaMar's Project Omega contained a number of brave men, and Utegaard related that during 1967 "one of Pappy's key recon people was Sergeant First Class Jerry M. "Mad Dog" Shriver, who was so gung ho that they literally couldn't keep him out of the field. Once, after Shriver had completed a series of consecutive missions, Colonel Bill Johnson [MACV-SOG ground commander] issued a direct order that Shriver would take a well-earned, ten-day R & R and relax in some place like Saigon or Da Nang, doing whatever he pleased. During the period of the R & R order, the colonel visited a forward operating base in the northern part of South Vietnam. During this visit a team had an emergency extraction and arrived back at the airstrip. When he went out to meet the returning team, of course it included Shriver." Shriver's idea of having fun on R & R was simply running more missions in a new area.

Over the course of several years, Mad Dog Shriver's exploits became so notorious that Radio Hanoi began taunting him by name. Shriver reportedly became infuriated and, knowing the Communist radio channels, switched to their frequency and either arranged a personal duel of some kind or told them where he was coming and dared the NVA to stop him.

On the morning of April 24, 1969, Captain Paul R. Cahill air-assaulted into Cambodia with a reinforced platoon of several Special Forces members and twenty-five montagnard special commandos. Among them was Mad Dog Shriver. The North Vietnamese were waiting and unleashed withering machine-gun and rocket fire against the platoon almost as soon as it landed. Most of the SOG troops scrambled for cover in the cratered earth and desperately radioed for helicopter support and fighter-bombers.

Sergeant Shriver led a commando charge against the nearest machine-gun bunkers and disappeared into the trees. Cahill at first maintained radio contact with Shriver, but the transmissions ceased. In the raging battle that followed, Cahill was temporarily blinded, his assistant platoon leader and medic both killed, and the platoon all but wiped out. Ten air strikes, napalm, and nearly 2,000 rockets covered the helicopters as they dashed in to retrieve bodies and the few survivors.

The Army later declared Sgt. Shriver missing in action. But such was his reputation that some believed Shriver had made it through the NVA wall of resistance to perform a mission yet to be revealed by government censors. For years, unconfirmed reports even placed Mad Dog Shriver "moving north to settle old scores with the Communists." Many MACV-SOG veterans, however, sadly believe that he had finally met his fate in that fight.

One of the greatest mysteries of MACV-SOG involves the case of another MACV-SOG hero, Major Larry A. Thorne, the most admired member of that elite organization. Thorne was born in Viipuri, Finland, in 1919 and entered the Finnish army in 1938. His first experience in unconventional warfare came in World War II, when he led his commando company twelve miles deep into Soviet lines during 1942 and wiped out a 300-man Russian convoy without suffering a single casualty. Captain Thorne refused to quit after Finland surrendered in 1944 and completed the German School for Sabotage and Guerrilla Warfare in January 1945. Still eager to fight the Russians, he joined a group of German marines who resisted for nearly a week after the Nazi government capitulated. By the time Thorne was captured by American paratroopers, he had fought against the Russians for six years, was wounded three times, and received the highest award Finland could bestow, the Mannerheim Medal, equal to the U.S. Medal of Honor.

Thorne was placed in a British prison inside occupied Germany but quickly escaped and returned to Finland after a perilous 200-mile journey on foot to the Danish border. The Soviets coerced the Finnish government into preferring charges against Thorne for his wartime collaboration with the German armed forces, and he was imprisoned again. Thorne attempted two escapes, then reached Sweden on his third try. He left Sweden as a merchant seaman on a ship bound for Venezuela and eventually reached the United States. He contacted a former Finnish diplomat in New York City, who arranged for Congress to approve his enlistment in the American Army, along with U.S. citizenship, effective January 28, 1954.

Sergeant Thorne served as a mountain climbing and winter warfare instructor at Fort Carson, Colorado, before his assignment to the 77th Special Forces Group. He received a commission as a 1st Lieutenant of Special Forces in 1956. In November 1963 Thorne commanded a Special Forces A–team sent to Vietnam, where he was decorated for valor and earned a Purple Heart. The next year the Army promoted him to major, assigned him to the intelligence staff of the 5th Special Forces Group, and transferred him to MACV-SOG as a special project operations officer.

Brigadier General Donald D. Blackburn, then a colonel and commander of MACV-SOG, related, "On the evening of October 18, 1965, he was to launch a combined reconnaissance patrol of ten personnel into an area of heavy Viet Cong activity to search out and confirm suspected targets for attack by air. As the hour for launch approached, it became apparent that the weather would be marginal at best. Based on the prevailing weather conditions and the likelihood of heavy ground fire en route to the landing zone, it was determined that a third H–34 helicopter should trail the troop lift aircraft as chase ship. In the event of mishap, the aircraft would attempt recovery of

Lieutenant Kenneth Bowra, who earlier led a successful raid against the command post of the 222d NVA Transportation Regiment, poses with his team of Bru montagnards in February 1972.

downed personnel. In view of the extremely hazardous conditions under which this mission was to be conducted, and to ensure maximum control, Larry volunteered to fly this mission himself."

The aircraft formation flew through the cloud-covered mountains and successfully inserted the patrol west of Kham Duc despite fog and VC antiaircraft fire. As nightfall approached, and a heavy cloud bank closed in, Maj. Thorne remained in the area above the team in case they needed assistance. The rest of the helicopters climbed to 8,500 feet, topped the clouds in the waning twilight, and returned to base. When the patrol informed Thorne that it was safely on the ground, he started back. By now visibility was zero. The last radio contact heard from Thorne's helicopter was a constant keying on the FM frequency used by his aircraft, lasting about thirty seconds.

Extensive searches of the region failed to reveal any trace of Maj. Thorne or the helicopter. Major Clyde Sincere, the MACV-SOG executive officer of Forward Operating Base 1 at Phu Bai, related, "Given Larry's background and the extreme interest the Russians always exhibited in getting him, it is quite possible that Major Thorne was intercepted, or forced down, and taken alive back to the Soviet Union." In October 1966, the Army adjutant general summarily declared that Thorne was deceased, even though no debris from the aircraft or evidence of his demise was found. As late as 1975, the last Special Forces teams returning from Southeast Asia reported intelligence information, all with varying degrees of substantiation, that Thorne was being held inside either China or Siberia.

Vietnamization

In March 1971, MACV-SOG was restructured as part of the Vietnamization program. By that point in the war, United States policy concentrated on turning the brunt of the fighting, including special missions, over to the South Vietnamese. MACV-SOG's three command-and-control units (CCN, CCC, and CCS) were renamed Task Force Advisory Elements 1, 2, and 3. This change reflected the political goal of subordinating SOG components to the Special Mission Service of the Vietnamese Strategic Technical Directorate, itself a redesignation of the old Special Exploitation Service.

In reality, the activities of the SOG task force advisory elements, which were shrouded in the highest secrecy, represented a further escalation of American special warfare policy. This policy favored hitting more targets in an effort to slow down NVA buildups and make the South Vietnamese more efficient in their own special missions. A new generation of specialized equipment, developed in response to battlefield experience, was now arriving in MACV-SOG stocks. Advanced Stabo extraction gear replaced the older McGuire rigs, exotic night-vision devices became widely available, and highly modern electronics material included a new family of emergency radios and automatic sensors. MACV-SOG developed increasingly effective strike tactics using these new capabilities.

In one fierce battle, MACV-SOG destroyed a large North Vietnamese troop convoy in southern Laos. Previously, recon teams reported on such lucrative targets, ambushed a few vehicles, and directed air raids. In July 1971, a SOG recon team found hundreds of trucks threading their way through a series of narrow, heavily forested mountain passes. An exploitation force, armed with mortars, 90MM recoilless rifles, and light antitank weapons was immediately dispatched into the area. In a running series of sharp clashes fought over the next seven days and nights, MACV-SOG attacked on the ground while Air Force Specter gunships demolished the stalled convoy from the air.

After a week of steady combat, all traffic flowing into the tri-border area was temporarily stopped; only lack of ammunition forced the exploitation force to withdraw. Based on reports of the damage inflicted, the Joint Chiefs of Staff started to chastise the MACV-SOG command for sending unauthorized numbers of men into Laos. They were amazed to discover that the entire engagement required a minor commitment of only sixteen Special Forces troops. The close MACV-SOG–Air Force relationship displayed in this engagement was estimated to have been as effective as two battalions of regular American infantry.

As the MACV-SOG campaign of active interdiction intensified, the North Vietnamese Army took extra precautions to safeguard their lines of communication. The SOG teams faced greater danger with each passing year. Recon Team Kansas, commanded by 1st Lieutenant Loren D. Hagen, landed on a strategic hilltop in a critical area of the demilitarized zone on August 6, 1971, with orders to reconnoiter increased NVA troop movement and take a prisoner if possible. The team consisted of six Americans and nine indigenous commandos.

Throughout the night, the team strengthened its rocky mountain position. Early next morning hundreds of North Vietnamese attacked, charging uphill. During the savage fighting, which was often hand to hand, the team was forced back into a smaller perimeter. Lt. Hagen repeatedly crawled under intense fire to reach the positions of fellow team members and to repel the repeated NVA battalion assaults. When one of the team's few bunkers was de-stroyed by a B40 rocket, Hagen decided to check the burning position for survivors. He turned to Australian Sergeant Anthony C. Anderson, the assistant team leader, and yelled, "If I don't come back, get the rest of the team out and make sure you get my body!" He then raced through a shower of grenades, firing his CAR15 into the advancing waves of NVA shock troops. He was killed before he could reach the bunker, but his gallant sacrifice enabled the other men to get out, and his effort was later recognized with the Medal of Honor. Lt. Hagen was one of seven MACV-SOG members awarded the nation's highest decoration.

Another mission late in the war involved a daring High Altitude, Low Opening parachute mission carried out by Recon Team Idaho, commanded by 1st Lieutenant Kenneth R. "El Cid" Bowra. On November 19, 1971, the team dropped into the southern portion of the A Shau Valley with orders to knock out the command post of the 222d NVA Transportation Regiment. Three MACV-SOG teams had already been annihilated in the area, two of them before they could even send a radio transmission, but these forays had pinpointed the NVA regimental headquarters.

Senior SOG officials decided that the opportunity to eliminate this key target, which would severely impede infiltration traffic, was worth great risk. Such an assignment was a reflection of the extreme sophistication of new MACV-SOG operating techniques. Past teams had often been put behind the lines to cause as much random destruction as possible, but seldom were the logistical commanders and technicians in a headquarters unit singled out for elimination.

Team Idaho caused crippling damage to the regimental headquarters, destroying equipment not easily replaced and stockpiles of spare parts, before regular NVA infantry surrounded it and forced the men to flee back to the landing zone. The team called for extraction as the North Vietnamese began pounding the ridge with mortar fire. Cobra gunships arrived overhead and rocketed the NVA lines, as recovery helicopters darted between the explosions to retrieve the men. The pilots knew that Bowra's men must have hit a sensitive target: "We never saw so many NVA, or so much ground fire!"

When the third and last helicopter dropped its ladder, the remaining Americans prepared to lift out. Lt. Bowra attempted to hook up but noticed two NVA riflemen running toward the field. He realized that they might be able to get into position to shoot down the helicopter and stayed on the ground until he killed both. Bowra later became the commander of 2d Battalion, 5th Special Forces Group.

The success of Team Idaho was part of the final chapter of MACV-SOG history. On April 30, 1972, the organization was closed down as America withdrew from Vietnam. However, the military's secret wars in Cambodia and Laos outlived MACV-SOG. The personnel of MACV-SOG were transferred to a new unit, Strategic Technical Directorate

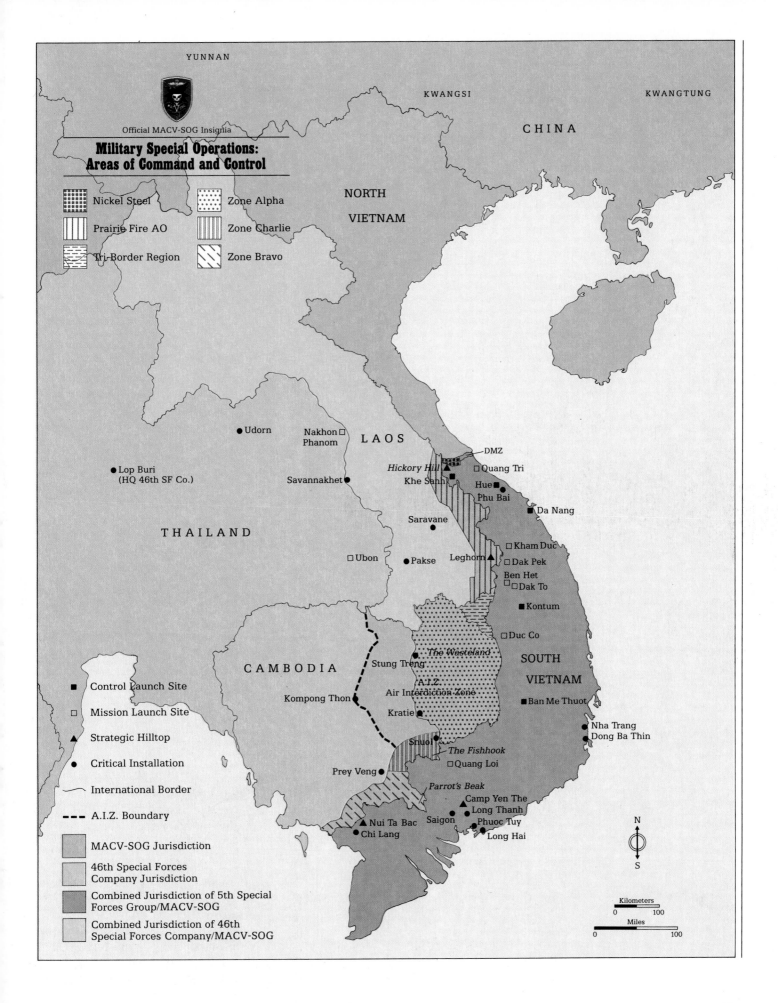

Official MACV-SOG Insignia

Military Special Operations: Areas of Command and Control

▦ Nickel Steel	▦ Zone Alpha
▥ Prairie Fire AO	▥ Zone Charlie
▤ Tri-Border Region	▨ Zone Bravo

YUNNAN

KWANGSI   KWANGTUNG

CHINA

NORTH VIETNAM

LAOS

● Udorn   Nakhon □ Phanom

● Lop Buri (HQ 46th SF Co.)

Savannakhet ●

THAILAND

● Saravane

□ Ubon   ● Pakse

DMZ
Hickory Hill ■   □ Quang Tri
Khe Sanh   Hue ●
Phu Bai ●
■ Da Nang

□ Kham Duc
Leghorn ▲   □ Dak Pek
Ben Het
□ Dak To
● Kontum

□ Duc Co

The Wasteland
Stung Treng ●
A.I.Z.
Air Interdiction Zone
Kratie ●

CAMBODIA

Kompong Thon ●

Snuol ●
The Fishhook
□ Quang Loi

Prey Veng ●

Parrot's Beak
▲ Camp Yen The
▲ Nui Ta Bac   Long Thanh
Chi Lang   Saigon ●   ● Phuoc Tuy
Long Hai

SOUTH VIETNAM

● Ban Me Thuot

● Nha Trang
Dong Ba Thin

■ Control Launch Site

□ Mission Launch Site

▲ Strategic Hilltop

● Critical Installation

— International Border

- - - A.I.Z. Boundary

▦ MACV-SOG Jurisdiction

▦ 46th Special Forces Company Jurisdiction

▦ Combined Jurisdiction of 5th Special Forces Group/MACV-SOG

▦ Combined Jurisdiction of 46th Special Forces Company/MACV-SOG

N
S

Kilometers
0   100

Miles
0   100

Special Warfare Weapons

The Special Forces and special warfare contingents of MACV-SOG and other top-secret programs used a wide variety of weapons in Southeast Asia. The regular military establishment deliberately limited the number of its weapon types for reasons of economy. Special warfare agencies with access to liberal operating funds, however, acquired expensive weapons and ammunition specifically tailored to their requirements. These weapons were usually more accurate, more powerful, and quieter than Army general-purpose weapons. The selection of weapons shown on these pages represents the diverse weapons used by special warfare personnel operating throughout Southeast Asia.

Smith & Wesson's M76 9MM submachine gun, shown here with sionics silencer, was fabricated mainly of stampings with a folding steel stock and was mechanically similar to the Swedish K. The weapon benefited from the favorable combat reputation gained by Smith & Wesson's superb Model 39 military pistol, used by SEAL teams, and was used by Navy clandestine teams operating in North Vietnam.

Bell Laboratories developed the "grease gun," the M3A1 .45-caliber submachine gun (shown here with silencer) for OSS use during World War II. The weapon was still being used by Special Forces reconnaissance teams in Southeast Asia during the early 1960s becuase of its availability and its relatively quiet discharge—less than the crack of a .22-caliber pistol shot.

The M45 9MM Karl Gustaf "Swedish K" submachine gun was considered one of the best-silenced submachine guns available during the Southeast Asian conflict. Because of its high rate of fire, large numbers of this model without silencers were supplied to Rhade tribal warriors by the CIA.

The XM 177E2 5.56MM "Colt Commando" submachine gun, shown here with an improvised foregrip, had a thirty-round-magazine capacity and high-velocity killing impact. One soldier who used it, Sergeant Robert Rothwell of CCS, normally placed green tape over the ejection port to keep out dirt and used a montagnard bracelet to hold the strap.

The M16 5.56MM rifle, here equipped with a Honeywell Nightscope (giving it the nickname "Black Widow") featured an infrared thermal imaging system employing a detector array of mercury cadmium telluride cooled to seventy-seven degrees Kelvin.

The High-Standard HD .22-caliber pistol with silencer was the standard sidearm of the Central Intelligence Agency despite the fact that it was only moderately silent. This was the weapon reportedly used by Captain Robert F. Marasco to kill double agent Thai Khac Chuyen, resulting in the arrest of the 5th Special Forces Group commander during the infamous Green Beret murder case of 1969.

Assistance Team 158, but its power rapidly eroded through drastic cuts in manpower.

Beyond SOG

The major responsibility for classified missions in Southeast Asia was shifted to the Pentagon, which increasingly relied on the Thailand-based 46th Special Forces Company (itself renamed U.S. Army Special Forces Thailand as a cover for its true designation, the 3d Battalion of the 1st Special Forces Group). This unit worked in close conjunction with its parent 1st Special Forces Group to cover the special mission assignments of the 5th Special Forces Group, which departed Vietnam in March 1971. The closure of MACV-SOG completed the transition of the regional center of special warfare from Vietnam to Thailand.

The Army Special Forces in Thailand had been active in the CIA-sponsored covert Laotian wars since 1967 and possessed a strong cadre of special operations experts. They also trained the Cambodian Special Forces as part of Operation Freedom Runner and regularly escorted the Thai Rangers and border patrol police across the Thai border into Laos. One of the largest requirements for this unit was to send selected personnel on detached duty to Project 404, which operated as an extension of the Defense Attaché Office in Vientiane, Laos.

The Defense Attaché Office was limited by law to a small staff assisting the Royal Laotian Army, which was mostly concentrated in bases along the Mekong River. Since the office's sphere of influence did not extend far into the mountains and plains of Laos, where the war was being fought by CIA-financed tribesmen, Project 404 became the umbrella secretly used to field Special Forces troops from Thailand. This was always an important adjunct to MACV-SOG missions, because the latter organization was politically restricted to a small presence in either Thailand or western Laos.

Project 404 missions became especially important to military special operations once MACV-SOG was terminated. Perhaps the largest and most dangerous 404 assignment took place at the very end of the conflict, when the DIA sent numerous Special Forces teams into remote Chinese-held and NVA-occupied sectors of Laos and other countries to saturate suspected infiltration routes with durable, ground-planted sensor detection instruments (see sidebar, page 93). This particular operation ended by presidential order in March 1973.

There were numerous other military special operations conducted outside the MACV-SOG command itself. The most famous of these was the Pentagon-directed Son Tay raid, controlled directly by SACSA, which used personnel from Special Forces units within the United States (see Chapter 8). Another example was the highly classified joint Special Forces–SEAL strike against a SAM missile storage depot inside China that took place shortly after

May 1972, when the Soviet Union began shipping supplies over Chinese railroads to avoid the mined harbors of North Vietnam. This raid probably prompted the Chinese to complain on June 13, when they protested that their border was violated by U.S. activity.

One of the final and most secret missions conducted during the Vietnam War occurred shortly before the Communists took final control of South Vietnam in 1975. The U.S. had financed the construction of a nuclear research reactor near Da Lat in Vietnam's central highlands under America's "atoms for peace" program. The United States, fearful that certain very sensitive enriched uranium products and other ultrasecret equipment would fall into NVA hands, sent experts to remove the most sensitive components. A Special Forces team, escorted by young Vietnamese women who were atomic equipment specialists, was also dispatched in case the reactor had to be destroyed. The details of this raid remain strictly classified, but apparently the reactor was sufficiently disabled to render it useless.

The operations of MACV-SOG and associated military special operations in the Vietnam conflict were the foundation for America's present special warfare programs. A recent history of the Special Forces in Vietnam, *The Green Berets at War*, summarizes its effects:

Demolished convoys, blazing ammunition dumps, slain guards, and kidnapped personnel highlighted the most sustained American campaign of raiding, sabotage, and intelligence-gathering waged on foreign soil in U.S. military history. By 1970, when 441 recon missions included commando forces up to company strength, MACV-SOG had already earned a global reputation as one of the most combat effective deep-penetration forces ever raised.

MACV-SOG did not accomplish all that it hoped. High casualties, the handicaps induced by limited tours of duty for its personnel, and political restrictions caused it a number of setbacks. The ultimate MACV-SOG dream of establishing a lasting resistance movement inside North Vietnam never materialized. The need for absolute secrecy often hampered the swiftness of MACV-SOG response, and there are still nagging questions about the direction and control of SOG-type actions.

More fundamentally, no war has ever been won by commando raiders alone, but such operations did cause significant damage to the North Vietnamese war machine. SOG's major problem, like other successful American military activities in Vietnam, was that its operations were not undertaken in the context of a winning strategy. However, the actual bravery and accomplishments of a few special warfare experts "with ice in their veins and hot weapons in their hands," as Major Sincere described them, operating beyond all reasonable expectations of ordinary military duty, exhibited the great potential of American special operations.

With Project 404

by Shelby L. Stanton

In late 1971 I was serving as a lieutenant in the 82d Airborne Division's 1st Battalion, 508th Infantry, supply section at Fort Bragg, North Carolina. Part of my job was securing hard-to-find items, like the rubber boats we needed for lake-crossing exercises. To get them I swapped parachutes and other gear with the 5th Special Forces Group. The group had just returned from Vietnam and was anxious to rebuild its own stock. This bartering transpired outside normal supply channels, and in the process I gained some friends among the Special Forces NCOs. When I was summoned one day to their headquarters, I thought it was just for another trading transaction.

A well-known lieutenant colonel in special warfare was waiting when I arrived on Smoke Bomb Hill. He was an old hand from Southeast Asia, and I thought to myself, "What in the hell could this guy, with all his connections, possibly need?" I quickly found out that he wanted me.

"You're just the right size and ranger qualified," he said with a grin. "We need small Americans like you for a special recon mission overseas. After all these years fussing with camouflage, we finally realized that the VC were getting our teams because they could spot tall Americans." I was only five feet, five inches, and the Army had insisted on a waiver of my height before commissioning me. The colonel's invitation was too beguiling to turn down.

Although I was not told, I knew where I was going. With the air filled with talk of peace between the U.S. and North Vietnam, the Defense Intelligence Agency was planning to send a few Special Forces teams deep into Laos on one of the last missions of the war. My top-secret training included mastering the latest electronics surveillance devices. These were permanent, sophisticated instruments designed to last years, not the kind the Air Force dropped and then bombed to pieces whenever they hit the target. We would carry sensors and implant them along the Ho Chi Minh Trail network. These would monitor the flow of NVA traffic and troop levels after the truce.

The only Special Forces unit left in Southeast Asia was the Thailand-based 46th Special Forces Company, a unit that no one knew much about. The unit's deliberately fuzzy cover, that it worked on the Thai railroad—"laying Thais," they liked to say—was suspiciously low profile. Upon assignment to the company, I realized it was run like SOG in Vietnam. We were on the unit's roster, but we worked elsewhere.

I was attached to Project 404, which paired with a secret Thai operation called North Star. This combination permitted the fielding of joint recon teams. My eight-man team was composed of two Americans—myself and a Special Forces master sergeant who, because of his experience, actually led the patrol—a few Thai special warfare experts who could call in artillery from CIA-sponsored Thai Special Guerrilla Unit howitzers, and Meo hill-tribal warriors who knew the countryside.

A myth has grown around such Special Forces operations, that we usually carried Communist weapons. But when I showed up at the launch site with an AK47, my sergeant slapped it away with a sneer that underscored his disgust toward officers, especially new ones. In close firefights in the jungle, it was too difficult to distinguish between sides if both were blazing away with similar-sounding weapons.

We went to our launching positions in huge Air Force HH–3 Jolly Green Giant helicopters, which had the fuel capacity and the range to cover the distance. Once inserted, we remained on the ground for two or three weeks. We were resupplied by sophisticated triangular parachutes called parawings, which could be dropped from 30,000 feet during any kind of weather. Their electronic homing devices locked onto our radio signals, and they always landed within 100 feet of us.

After two decades of tropical combat, Special Forces had acquired the guerrilla expertise and equipment needed to infiltrate enemy territory without being detected. In any case, the North Vietnamese were too busy fighting and building to comb the Laotian jungle looking for our small teams. The NVA were more careful along the periphery of their supply lines, and there they routinely scoured the rain forests at night with flashlight crews.

The NVA searchers were of two kinds: brave and timid. The brave ones would stab through foliage and underbrush with probing beams of light. If detected, you could douse their light with one quick rifle burst, but the racket would alert an entire guard battalion. The timid ones would amble around, making plenty of noise, and shine their lights up through the trees and everywhere else. Those soldiers did not want to die in any sudden exchange of fire.

If the presence of the team was compromised by enemy contact the entire mission failed, since the NVA or Chinese would then uproot the surrounding jungle until they found our sensors. After chasing Special Forces recon teams for two decades, the North Vietnamese had learned to close in for the kill with overwhelming firepower. Most teams that got discovered were wiped out completely. Those of us who returned without incident had the satisfaction of knowing that our safely emplaced surveillance gear would keep the United States government fully aware of North Vietnamese activity after any truce.

The NVA-led Pathet Lao assaulted our Laotian launch sites in a concerted effort to destroy our teams before we could "disappear" into the wilderness. I was wounded by 122MM rocket shrapnel during a night rocket barrage in February 1973. One month later the final American withdrawal mandated by the Paris peace accords took place, and our war was officially over.

The purpose of reconnaissance is to gather intelligence, and this mission exacted a high price both in lives and expensive equipment. The sensors we planted accurately recorded the North Vietnamese buildup in Laos in 1974 and 1975 as the NVA prepared its final offensive against the South. That meant little, though. The United States government made no use at all of the volumes of intelligence those devices sent back.

A Project 404 team rescues a downed Air America pilot inside Laos. The team defended the site against Pathet Lao troops until the Air Force 56th Special Operations Wing arrived and extracted them and the pilot.

South Vietnamese Special Agents

The South Vietnamese regime raised several expert counterguerrilla units during the war, which were paid and equipped outside the regular military system. These units became known as "special warfare" elements because they served in a role that depended upon stealth and cunning rather than firepower to detect and destroy Vietcong targets. The Vietnamese National Police became specialized in using advanced police tactics to crack the Vietcong insurgent movement. Highly trained police detectives interrogated suspects while large police field forces went into the countryside searching for guerrilla hide-outs. Many VC and NVA who surrendered were paid to use their guerrilla expertise for the American side and became known as Kit Carson scouts. The U.S. Army Special Forces organized many native tribes and militant dissident factions into special warfare units as an adjunct to the Civilian Irregular Defense Group (CIDG). These "road-runners" and other strike teams patrolled remote areas and raided VC bases. The most sophisticated special warfare operators served on Phoenix Program Provincial Reconnaissance Units, which employed only the most skilled and trusted people recruited from all Vietnamese special warfare organizations.

A soldier from the Civilian Irregular Defense Group runs for cover at the perimeter of the besieged Plei Me Special Forces camp in October 1965.

A member of a South Vietnamese "roadrunner" team dressed in peasant garb reconnoiters an enemy trail network.

The largest South Vietnamese special warfare group was the National Police Field Force, which used heavily armed men to search and destroy enemy villages and fight guerrilla bands, much like regular soldiers. However, the police normally wore uniforms and could not infiltrate into the actual Vietcong jungle bases. This task was performed by Special Forces–trained strike units of the Civilian Irregular Defense Group. Some of their bravest men were disguised in Vietcong clothing and carried special weapons. They were known as roadrunners because they performed many of their missions by moving along secret VC trail networks. Roadrunners and Kit Carson scouts were paid very well to serve in American units and find enemy booby traps and tunnels, marching in the vanguard of U.S. patrols to help them avoid danger at the hands of the Vietcong.

Left. *A member of the South Vietnamese Police Field Force, known for its ruthless interrogation practices, inspects a VC suspect's papers while forcing him to keep his teeth clenched on a detonating fuse found in his clothing. Below. Kit Carson scouts, former Vietcong, demonstrate enemy sapper techniques at Long Binh in late 1969.*

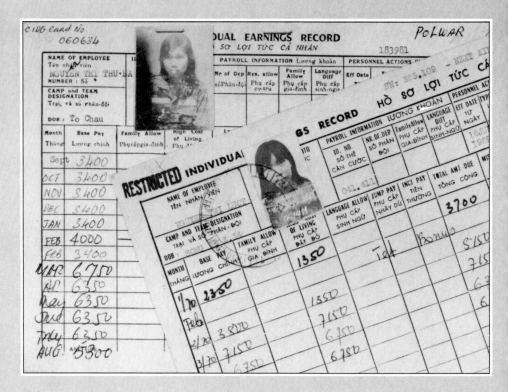

Right. *Pay cards identify two female Special Forces agents, Corporal Nguyen Thi Thu-Ba and Master Sergeant Nguyen Thi Luot.* Below. *The bodies of female Special Forces agents who were executed by Vietcong raiders on April 16, 1967, lie at the Special Forces base at Sour Chan.*

A South Vietnamese Military Security Service officer frisks an employee at the U.S. installation at Dong Tam in 1968.

Most South Vietnamese special warfare units employed female agents. The majority of these women served as air equipment riggers, photographic reconnaissance analysts, or intelligence specialists. These jobs involved actual combat risk only if their work sites came under direct NVA or VC attack. However, some women were sent through advanced agent and parachutist training and performed vital missions behind enemy lines.

The Military Security Service used female officers to safeguard South Vietnamese installations throughout the country. These women were used primarily to detect Communist infiltrators by searching female workers and visitors at large base camps.

The U.S. Army Military Intelligence and Special Forces units also hired large numbers of Vietnamese female special agents. They were used as interpreters, liaison personnel, escorts, and clandestine agents within their forward operating base areas. Their work was very dangerous because collaboration between Vietnamese women and American Special Forces troops merited automatic death sentences by the VC National Liberation Front.

The Making of a Clandestine Army

It was October; it was hot and it was wet. There had been six of them out there. They had gone into northern Laos more than a month earlier and, despite all of the training and absolute assurance that their communications equipment worked, they had been unable to send any reports. Major Nicol Smith leaned over the radio receiver once again as he had done for the past month. It was contact time, but once again there was nothing but static. Nick Smith's thoughts returned to New York. . . . There all you had to do was to pick up the phone. Here, in Southeast Asia, hot, dirty, and humid Southeast Asia, nothing seemed to work. And what did it matter? No one actually cared. This was not where the real war was. News from Laos was no news at all. People at home did not even know where. . . . First, there was a clear and distinct dot. Then a dash. The radio receiver, silent for a month, suddenly sprang to life. The identity code was correct. The message started coming across with growing clarity and strength. Sweating and increasingly excited,

Major Smith went to work. Two of his men had been caught and executed. One had died from sickness. The other three were alive, well, and finally in the right place. The decoded message contained a bombing target. Smith quickly scratched out a message, powered up his transmitter, and relayed the target location to headquarters. Within hours, U.S. bombers were on their way for the strike. The airplanes were B–25s. The target was a Japanese airfield in northern Thailand. It was October—October 1944.

Nicol Smith, an officer in the United States Office of Strategic Services (OSS) during World War II, was one of the first Americans to direct and support a clandestine war in Southeast Asia. He would certainly not be the last. Some of his fellow officers in the OSS would return to Southeast Asia after the war and participate in a new clandestine war, this time against the North Vietnamese. There would be pilots, Americans who had flown for Claire Chennault's Flying Tigers in China, who returned and flew for Chennault's postwar commercial enterprise, Civil Air Transport, and its offspring, Air America. Other World War II veterans, Army officers and tough battle-wise sergeants, would lead U.S. Special Forces teams into the mountainous regions of Laos to train and assist Lao, Thai, and hill tribesmen in their fight against the Lao Communists, the Pathet Lao. There would also be Americans devoted to more peaceful pursuits: doctors and agricultural specialists, who would help the friends of the United States. It takes many skilled men to make a clandestine war. Major Nicol Smith was one of the first. In the next thirty years, there would be many more.

Smith was right. His effort was a side show. The main U.S. thrusts against the Japanese in 1944 were led by MacArthur in the Southwest Pacific and Nimitz in the Central Pacific. Later, in 1945, OSS began arming Lao to fight against the Japanese, sending Americans into the jungles to help them. They did not walk in as had Smith's agents; they were delivered by parachute. One OSS officer, Jim Thompson, organized a guerrilla unit in southern Laos and was probably the first American to support a clandestine war in that country. Major Smith's efforts had been centered on Thailand. Thompson extended the program to Laos.

The key to Indochina

Laos is shaped like a key, and in the history of Southeast Asia, it has been used like one. The key handle, or northern part of Laos near China, is a heavily forested, mountainous region that contains a crooked, winding valley corridor running east-west and connecting North Vietnam with Thailand. Invading armies have often used this path. The narrow shaft of the key points south and has the great Mekong River Valley corridor as its western edge, a traditional invasion route from China to Cambodia. In the south, near the Vietnamese border, is the Nape Pass, and a little farther south, the Mu Gia Pass. These important terrain features have been used over the centuries as short cuts between the populous Red River Delta and the Mekong Delta. The quickest way from Hanoi to Saigon is not the coastal route, but through one of these passes, taking a direct path through Laos.

There are three relatively flat areas in Laos. The first, in the north, is the Plain of Jars, lying along the corridor linking Thailand and North Vietnam. The second is the Mekong corridor, the level land along the great river's banks and much of the surrounding countryside. Finally, there is the Bolovens Plateau, hilly territory at the southern tip of Laos. These areas have often been used by invaders because they provide quicker passage than the tortuous routes through the mountains. Geographically and strategically, Laos is a key.

At the time of the Vietnam War, the population of Laos numbered about three million, but only two-thirds could be described as Lao people. The Lao are similar to their neighbors to the south, the people of Thailand. The Thai and Lao languages are closely related, the customs of the two peoples are almost the same, and the two nationalities even look alike. But the Lao, like the Thais, are lowlanders and Laos is a mountainous country. The extensive mountain region of the country contained only about one-third of the population, and these people, the montagnards, were quite different from the Lao and Thai. Many of the hill tribes were of Chinese origin, rarely spoke Lao, and were noted fighters. The largest tribe, the Hmoung, lived in the northern part of the country. Generally, the hill people did not get along with the lowlanders and insisted on living a separate life. In the southern and narrow part of the country lived a people known as the Kha. Believed by many to be the original inhabitants of Laos, the Kha were a very poor people and did not live at the high elevations that the montagnards favored. Although there were many disputes among the peoples of Laos, they paled before the strength of a common dislike, a widespread distaste for the people of northern Vietnam, the Tonkinese.

When the Vietnamese Communists, under Tonkinese leadership, defeated the French in the First Indochina War, they did not achieve their goal of controlling all of Indochina. The agreement concluding that war established two independent states, Laos and Cambodia. The two Vietnams were temporary administrative zones, their ultimate status to be decided by a plebiscite. The northerners were, however, in a position to continue the conflict; they controlled about 1,500 to 2,000 Lao Communists, called the Pathet Lao. In addition, the Vietnamese forcibly transported 6,000 Lao youth into North Vietnam for training. Finally, Hanoi did not withdraw all of its troops from

Laos as it had agreed to do in 1954. Although the U.S. had not signed the agreement ending the First Indochina War, American officials kept a close eye on the area and knew that there were 87 radios in Laos transmitting coded messages to Hanoi well after the treaty had been signed.

The new leaders of free Laos knew of North Vietnamese designs and took measures to prepare a defense of their country. The fledgling Royal Lao Army was a French-trained force that had sustained 3,000 casualties during the First Indochina War out of its strength of about 20,000. But, the Lao had virtually no leadership capability for the French had insisted on supplying most of the officer positions in the Lao army. Lao negotiators at the peace conference therefore obtained an amendment to the agreement that permitted them to have French forces stationed in their country. In addition, the Lao secured the right to import armaments, munitions, and items of military equipment "necessary for the defense of Laos." Although Laos was not permitted to enter into any military alliances "so long as its security is not threatened," it was permitted to welcome foreign military instructors for the effective defense of Lao territory. Even before one war was over, the groundwork for the next was laid.

The attempt of the newly independent Kingdom of Laos to maintain its freedom and territorial integrity was not successful. Both Pathet Lao and North Vietnamese combat units contested Vientiane's control of the northeast and extreme southeast portions of the country. The latter area appeared to be very important to the Vietnamese, especially around the Lao town of Tchepone, near the Mu Gia Pass. That region contained one of the gateways to South Vietnam, a path later called the Ho Chi Minh Trail.

After directly confronting the North Vietnamese with their treaty violations and calling on the United Nations for assistance—all to no avail—the harried Lao leaders appealed to the United States. Meeting with President Eisenhower in Washington during 1956, the Lao detailed Hanoi's aggression and appealed for American support. At that time, U.S. efforts to assist the Lao were minimal. There was a small American military presence in Vientiane, but this twenty-two–man contingent was only funneling U.S. materiel to the Lao army through its French instructors.

Hmoung tribesmen gather at their headquarters at Padong in northern Laos in 1961. Known for their aggressive spirit, the Hmoung were recruited to fight Laos's Communist Pathet Lao.

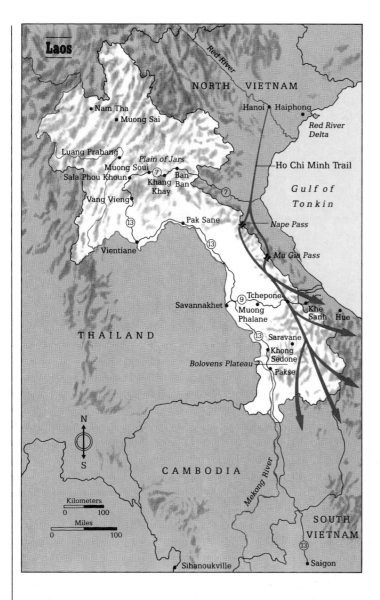

Called the Program Evaluation Office, its members wore civilian clothes. Unlike Cambodia and South Vietnam, where there was open, uniformed U.S. military support to the governments and obvious American backing, the U.S. policy in Laos centered on neutrality. Laos was considered a buffer state between the Chinese and North Vietnamese and the U.S. allies to the south and west: Thailand, South Vietnam, and Cambodia. Then too, Washington was particularly concerned about China. The United States had just concluded a war with Peking in Korea and saw no need to antagonize China. Buffer states often are subjected to some outside violence, and the president was not convinced that Laos was about to fall. The men of the small American military supply team could remain in civilian clothes, flags were not to be flown, and symbols were not to be displayed. The U.S. was not enticed into the argument between Vientiane and Hanoi. The Lao delegates received little satisfaction from their appeal.

All of this changed three years later. In January 1959, the North Vietnamese Army moved into the southern panhandle of Laos and seized three towns in the vicinity of Tchepone. By May, Hanoi had begun a major engineering effort in the construction of a trail, eventually capable of supporting truck traffic, to transport men, weapons, and ammunition into South Vietnam. At first, the trail was used by agents and Hanoi-trained South Vietnamese guerrilla leaders. The trail was carved through Lao soil.

With the French increasingly absorbed in the struggle to retain their colony in Algeria, the U.S. decided to bolster the Lao's ability to defend themselves and their land. The U.S. increased its small military contingent in the country in order to supplement the French military instructor cadre, and the American role expanded from supply to training as well. But the U.S. presence remained low key and indirect; civilian clothes remained the order of the day. Washington was still concerned about Chinese perceptions.

Enter the Green Berets

The new training task was given to U.S. Special Forces. While Nicol Smith and Jim Thompson were conducting their clandestine endeavors in Laos during World War II, Captain Arthur "Bull" Simons was seizing one of the Japanese-occupied islands off the Philippines with his Ranger company. In July 1959, in command of 107 Special Forces officers and men, Simons, now a lieutenant colonel, retraced Smith and Thompson's path into Laos. Five years earlier, American Special Forces teams had trained a similar Thai special operations organization, and some of these Thai soldiers joined Simons's effort in Laos, working as interpreters. The Thai government was concerned about North Vietnamese aggression in Laos but did not want to advertise its military presence in "neutral" Laos. Simons and his men lived with the Lao, sharing their food and primitive accommodations, a new experience for the Lao who were accustomed to foreign advisers who insisted on living in luxury. The Americans in Laos were assigned for only six-month tours of duty, but this was offset by the frequency of the tours. Within two years, many of the Special Forces troopers were on their third time around in Laos and brought considerable knowledge, experience, and skill to their tasks.

In August 1960, a coup overthrew the Lao government, paving the way for the Soviet Union to exert its power in the small country. Captain Kong Le, a battalion commander of a Royal Lao parachute unit, seized control of Vientiane, pushed right-wing elements out of the city, and proclaimed "true neutrality" for the nation. While the young captain was sincere in desiring neutrality, his power did not reach beyond the city limits of the capital. The North Vietnamese and Pathet Lao took advantage of the power vacuum to start grabbing territory, especially around the Plain of Jars and in the south, near Tchepone. When the United States, Thailand, and Lao rightist factions protested the new form of "neutrality," Moscow began an airlift of Pathet Lao and North Vietnamese troops into

Vientiane itself using Russian military aircraft and crews.

The Thais, Americans, and Lao military authorities devised a plan to install a new government under a friendly Lao general. The Special Forces teams cast aside their trainer status and assumed the role of advisers to the Royal Lao Army. In December 1960, a Thai artillery unit arrived near Vientiane to support an assault on the Communist-controlled capital. Parachuting into the city, the U.S. Special Forces teams aided the 1st and 3d Lao Parachute Battalions in driving Kong Le's 2d battalion of paratroopers and their Communist allies from the capital. A right-wing government took control, but Kong Le was driven into the arms of the Pathet Lao, the Vietnamese, and the Russians.

As Kong Le fled north toward the Plain of Jars, the Pathet Lao and their North Vietnamese mentors gained control of the plain itself. This area was Hmoung country, and the military leader of the tribe, Lieutenant Colonel Vang Pao, a well-respected officer holding a commission in the Royal Lao Army, persuaded the Hmoung village chiefs in the surrounding area to evacuate the plain. The tribesmen needed little encouragement. Their previous experience with the Pathet Lao and the Vietnamese had been a sad story of forced labor, conscription of the young, and food taxes. Seventy thousand Hmoung fled to the mountains during December 1960 and January 1961.

While the U.S., Thai, and Lao military orchestrated the elimination of Soviet and Vietnamese influence from the capital, the Communists were gaining control of much of the countryside. The American embassy set about the task of contesting that control. Operatives of the Central Intelligence Agency contacted Vang Pao in his mountain lair. An informal agreement was reached with the new Lao government, the Hmoung, and the Thais. The government of Thailand had an understandable concern about the Vietnamese and Russians reasserting control over Laos and offered to assist in the training of American-equipped Hmoung guerrillas near the Plain of Jars. The Lao government agreed to recognize the Hmoung right to regain control of their land and offered to uphold the traditional status of semiautonomy for the displaced tribesmen. The Americans agreed to support the operation through the CIA, provide Special Forces trainers and advisers to the Hmoung, and use Air America to supply Vang Pao's people on their mountaintop bastions. This complex arrangement lasted for more than ten years with little change. Although the agreement was not officially acknowledged by the U.S. government, it was an open "secret." The substantial Thai role, however, remained one of the best-kept secrets of the Vietnam War.

The Hmoung project was conducted in secret for a variety of reasons. First, although the Soviets had publicly criticized the U.S. role in Laos, they had been careful to keep their own military efforts in the country masked as much as possible. Both Washington and Moscow found it

White Star team member James Powers—a soldier in mufti—uses a wooden replica of a rifle stock to instruct recruits of the Royal Laotian Army in Pakse in 1959.

convenient to downplay media speculation about a military confrontation between the two superpowers. Neither side wanted its prestige to be on the line. Second, public acknowledgment of U.S. support to Lao and Hmoung armed soldiers could provoke China into taking official notice and possible action. Washington could not accurately predict Peking's reaction, but the Chinese had done nothing during the period of intense activity around Vientiane, and it was thought that if the new arrangement was kept as quiet as the old, the Chinese would continue to ignore American efforts on their southern border. In addition, the Thais favored a behind-the-scenes approach to minimize their image in Asia as a military power. Finally, there was the matter of risk. U.S. control of events in Laos was so marginal that setbacks could easily be foreseen. If the American role was hidden from the public, popular opinion would not demand more forceful action in the event of failure. In other words, the low-visibility approach permitted a toleration of reversals. A secret war was far preferable to a crusade.

Supporting the Hmoung effort was a relatively easy task and soon began to bear fruit. Near one of the villages, the tribesmen were asked to clear a short airstrip or, if that was not possible, a helicopter landing zone. One or two trainers arrived and an Air America parachute drop brought weapons and ammunition. Since the Hmoung had

At his headquarters at Padong in May 1961, Lieutenant Colonel Vang Pao, leader of the CIA-backed Hmoung army, informs his troops of recent Pathet Lao cease-fire violations.

left their own rice fields, they required rice drops. The rice was double-sacked and an Air America C–47 flew a figure-eight pattern over the drop site at an altitude of 500 feet. A "kicker" in the aircraft pushed the rice sacks out of the plane on a bell signal from the cockpit. It was not long before the Hmoung constituted a considerable armed force, contesting many of the Communist positions and roadways in the valleys of the Lao countryside.

The Special Forces personnel who served as advisers in Laos had all undergone the rigorous training that earned them their green berets. In addition, Special Forces required that most officers who volunteered for advisory duty in Laos be fluent in French since almost all of the officers in the Royal Lao Army and many of the Hmoung village chiefs spoke French. An American could learn to converse in French after a six-month course at the Army's Language School in Monterey, California. After graduating from the Language School, some of the officers had to spend endless hours coaching their sergeants in French so that their entire teams were bilingual.

A knowledge of the Lao language was considered as a further requirement, but rejected. However, as soon as the teams arrived in Laos, they followed a time-honored Special Forces practice of seeking every opportunity to learn the native tongue and local customs. This tenet of Special Forces lore not only ensured a rudimentary ability to survive in unexpected situations where no one spoke

French but also thoroughly pleased the Lao and Hmoung, who enjoyed watching the tall, husky Americans show an interest in learning how to talk with their hosts. When it came to social relations, the Lao and Hmoung got along very well with the Green Berets.

Trouble arose, however, whenever a situation required professional competence in Lao officers. At times, advisers felt as if there were no decent Lao officers in the entire country. The problem stemmed from a number of deeply rooted factors. First, the French had not concentrated on selecting and training Lao officers. Their colonial system was based on creating a dependence on the leadership of French officers. Second, Laos had been at war for many years, and military resources were naturally focused on field operations and essential security tasks, not on the building of a competent corps of officers. Third, in a divided society such as Laos, the premium is placed on loyalty, not competence. All of these factors and more contributed to a weak Lao military leadership.

Attempts to overcome the Lao leadership problem failed consistently. For example, more than 200 Lao lieutenants were shipped to the U.S., trained to speak English, and put through a six-month course of infantry training. To the anguish of the Americans, when the lieutenants returned the Lao high command assigned them largely to rear-area jobs. Later, the reason for the placement became obvious. The Lao generals and colonels had selected their sons and relatives to go to the U.S., not their promising young combat leaders.

It was far different among the Hmoung. Vang Pao or Hmoung village chiefs themselves selected the tribal leaders. Ever at the scene of battle, Vang Pao did not tolerate an incompetent leader. It was much the same with the village chiefs. If they selected a leader, it was certain that the man had the respect of his peers, was the proud representative of his village, and had a talent for getting things done. The Hmoung, a relatively classless society, emphasized merit and prized the hunter and warrior. If there was a problem between an American and a Hmoung leader, U.S. authorities looked first to the American as the source.

The American role was not only limited in the selection of leaders, it was also highly restricted in the conduct of operations. The basic tenet of U.S. field procedures in Laos was that Americans were to train, advise, and assist—not fight. The standard order was: "Keep your head down. It's their war, not ours." Army and CIA field advisers trained the Lao and Hmoung in handling weapons, communications, logistics, and tactics. Although there were consistent orders against direct U.S. participation in combat, on some occasions it could not be avoided. It happened most often

One of the aircraft of the CIA-owned airline Air America drops rice to the Hmoung in 1968. The airline acted as the life line to Hmoung villages situated in Pathet Lao territory in eastern Laos.

among the Special Forces teams assigned to an outlying Lao unit or Hmoung village in close proximity to the Pathet Lao or North Vietnamese forces.

The birth of White Star

By the first few days of 1961, the Communists had been driven from the valley of the Mekong River and were now in a precarious position near the Plain of Jars. The Thai government was involved in supporting both the Royal Lao Army and the Hmoung guerrillas in northern Laos. All this was accomplished with minimal U.S. involvement: a few men from Special Forces, the CIA, and Air America. The physical danger for the Americans was greatest among those men living with the Hmoung, behind North Vietnamese and Pathet Lao positions, but there were only eighteen CIA and Special Forces personnel serving there. Then too, the Hmoung were high up in the mountainous jungles, areas that the Communist lowlanders shunned. There was no order from Washington to clear Laos of the Communists. That would require too many resources, too many Americans. The U.S. had to be content with a partial solution.

When John F. Kennedy assumed the duties of the presidency, he inherited this ambiguous situation in Laos. After a setback occurred on the battlefields of the tiny country, JFK reacted with decision: On March 28, 1961, he delivered a nationwide address. A map of Laos prominently displayed behind him, Kennedy stated that a Communist takeover would "affect the security of the United States." He warned that in such an event, the U.S. response would be "selective, swift, and effective," code words for an American military deployment. Later, the president took Andrei Gromyko, the Soviet minister of foreign affairs, into the White House Rose Garden. He told Gromyko, "The United States does not intend to stand idly by while you take over Laos."

The setback that provided the impetus for the stern threat from the young American president began with a Communist counteroffensive led by Kong Le. Aided by daily Soviet supply flights, the paratroop captain had struck west from the Plain of Jars in early March. By the time President Kennedy made his speech to the American people, the Lao paratroop leader, with his Pathet Lao and Vietnamese allies, had retaken Route 7 from the Plain of Jars to the intersection of that road with Route 13, an important link between the royal capital of Luang Prabang and the political capital, Vientiane. The lofty promontory overlooking the junction of Routes 13 and 7, Sala Phou Khoun, was in Kong Le's hands. Undeterred by the American warning, Kong Le turned south and pressed his attack toward Vientiane, seizing the small road town of Vang Vieng.

JFK responded to the new threat by raising the stakes. On April 19, the United States announced the formation of a full-fledged military advisory group in Laos. The Program Evaluation Office members in Vientiane put on their uniforms, and the Special Forces detachments in the field, now dubbed the White Star Military Training Team, donned combat fatigues. The president directed the U.S. Marine Corps to turn over fourteen H–34 helicopters to the CIA and its proprietary company, Air America. A Marine Corps maintenance contingent of 300 men was sent to Thailand to maintain the helicopters and train their Air America replacements. The authorized strength of the Lao army was raised from 25,000 to 40,000, the increase to be paid for by U.S. military assistance funds.

The Communist response was swift and effective. On April 22, two Communist battalions attacked Captain Walter Moon's U.S. Special Forces team. Moon had three Special Forces sergeants with him, John Bischoff, Gerald Biber, and Orville Ballenger. The mission of the small team was to advise and assist the Lao 6th Infantry Battalion in its defense of Route 13, north of Vang Vieng. In the early morning hours, two Pathet Lao battalions attacked the battalion and quickly overran the defenders' positions. Moon was last seen trying to steady his Lao charges amid a Communist infantry assault. The 6th Battalion rapidly crumbled into a disorganized mass fleeing south on the road. Bischoff and Biber jumped on an armored car in an attempt to head off the deserters. Running into an ambush on the road, Bischoff grabbed the machine gun on the turret of the vehicle and began firing into the Pathet Lao attackers. Biber made a futile attempt to rally the cowering Royal Lao infantrymen and was killed by a grenade in the process. Then Bischoff was shot dead.

Sergeant Ballenger found himself with a group of survivors in the jungle, surrounded by the Pathet Lao victors. Silently, he led the soldiers through several groups of the Communist attackers and reached a river crossing. Finding a boat, the American sergeant placed the Lao in the craft and began drifting downstream. Ballenger's luck did not hold out. Seven days later, he and his companions were surprised and captured by the Pathet Lao. He spent more than a year in captivity before his release and return to the United States.

Walter Moon's tragic fate was not known until sixteen months later. He had tried to rally the 6th Infantry Battalion but was soon captured by the Pathet Lao and hustled to a primitive prison. Attempting escape, the Special Forces captain was recaptured. He tried again and was badly wounded in the chest and head. Moon's head wound and brutal tormenting by his guards caused him to lose his senses. In the meantime, an NBC correspondent, Grant Wolfkill, was taken by the Pathet Lao when engine failure caused his helicopter to crash-land. He was placed in the same prison that held Moon, where, unknown to his captors, Wolfkill witnessed the maltreatment and eventual execution of Captain Moon by a Pathet Lao officer.

While the battle raged along Route 13, the North Vietnamese were expanding their control of eastern Laos. Hanoi had already seized Tchepone, but not content, the North Vietnamese Army also seized Nape Pass to the north. Hanoi now held the two prime geographic entry points leading from the Red River Delta into the traditional north-south invasion route ending in South Vietnam and Cambodia. Reports of these North Vietnamese moves were confirmed between May 4 and May 8 when Washington authorized U.S. Navy photo reconnaissance flights over Laos. Ho Chi Minh had secured the shortest path between Hanoi and Saigon.

The new administration in Washington started a concerted diplomatic effort to conclude a cease-fire, neutralize Laos, and free it from all foreign military contingents: Russian, American, Thai, and North Vietnamese. In order to impress Hanoi with the seriousness of the U.S. concern, the administration continued the show of military activity. U.S. Air Force pilots began to fly supply missions directly into Vientiane's airfield. In July 1961, the size of the White Star complement doubled from 154 to 300 men. Bull Simons returned to Laos and began a fresh recruiting campaign among the Kha in the southern part of the country. Beginning in December, Simons's program sent ten eight-member Special Forces teams to raise and train twelve Kha "shock" companies. The goal was to clear the Bolovens Plateau of Communist forces. By the end of May 1962, Simons's force was ready and the men began to move toward the Ho Chi Minh Trail. Pathet Lao resistance was light as there had never been great enthusiasm for the Communist cause in the south.

While Bull Simons's progress in the south was encouraging, the Special Forces teams in the far north ran into trouble. Air America had given the Americans a decided advantage since their unique, short takeoff and landing aircraft were capable of supporting forces in the most inaccessible mountain areas. Despite Communist control of the roadway directly north of the capital, Special Forces teams and Lao battalions were able to position themselves well north of the Pathet Lao and the Vietnamese, near the Chinese border. Two Green Beret teams assigned to assist Royal Lao units in this new area found them to be commanded by incompetent officers. One of the Lao battalions there made several halfhearted attempts to seize Muong Sai between December 1961 and April 1962. Each attempt was characterized by poor leadership and failure. It was the same at Nam Tha, west of Muong Sai. The Lao massed nine battalions by March, but at the first sign of resistance, the operation ended in an ignoble rout that did not stop until the fleeing soldiers reached the Thai border.

Despite these failures, the operations served the purpose of challenging the North Vietnamese in the northern part of Indochina. Although the guerrilla war, aided by Hanoi, was heating up in South Vietnam, Simons's effort might disrupt the link between Ho Chi Minh in Hanoi and his followers to the south. The modest efforts in Laos afforded some protection for Cambodia and Thailand and they gave some hope for South Vietnam.

However, in Washington, Laos had become a troublesome subject. To the new administration, it appeared to be a contest with no end in sight. Despite the pleas of President Diem of South Vietnam, the advice of former President Eisenhower, and the warnings from U.S. negotiators of Hanoi's probable duplicity, Washington reached an accord with North Vietnam and the Soviet Union in July 1962. It required the Special Forces contingent, now numbering 512, to depart Laos in October. As few as 40 North Vietnamese went through the checkpoint established by an international control commission, only a fraction of those stationed in Laos. So the American military was largely out of Laos, whereas the North Vietnamese remained with unchallenged use of Nape Pass, Mu Gia Pass, Tchepone, and the Ho Chi Minh Trail.

President Kennedy confers with Vice President Johnson and others in May 1961. The new president devoted much energy in his first months in office to the widening war in Laos.

Kong Le

by Col. Rod Paschall

Kong Le (with back toward camera) holds a strategy session with some of his officers at his mountain command post at Ban Na on May 27, 1964.

In August 1960, a military coup took place in the capital of Laos. The citizens of Vientiane, accustomed to such things, wisely did not expect much change and went about daily chores in their usual, relaxed fashion. But soon, an amazing story emerged, a tale that spread around the town with great speed and considerable excitement. It seemed that a woman on the way to market had stopped before a wall, looked at a freshly placed poster, and went into a trance. Snapping out of the spell suddenly, she screamed, "Setthathirath has returned!" and fainted. That was enough to set the city buzzing

for some time. King Setthathirath is the Laotian version of King Arthur, mostly legend, somewhat fact. He is supposed to have disappeared in the jungle sometime during the sixteenth century and is expected to return, saving the country during an ill-defined crisis. The Lao people are deeply superstitious and put great stock in both legends and mystical stories. The coup would not have been notable in the war-weary capital's gossip except for the event at the wall. On the poster was a picture of the officer who had led the coup: the paratrooper Captain Kong Le.

Although the residents of the Lao capital knew little about Kong Le, several officers in the United States Army did. He was born in Phalane, southern Laos, in 1931. His parentage was significant: a Lao mother and a Kha father. The Kha are the most humble of the Lao peoples, the term *Kha* meaning *slave*. Kong Le had already disproved the Lao belief that the Kha could not fight by his service in the French army during the First Indochina War against the Vietminh. The French promoted him to sergeant, unusual for a Lao private. He gained a commission in the Royal Lao Army in 1954. Even for the Lao,

In order to pressure the Lao government into signing the agreement with the Communists, Washington ended all economic aid to Vientiane in February 1962. The Lao generals had initially attempted to thwart Washington's will and raise their own funds by resorting to legalized gambling, high rates of inflation, and the production and sale of opium. When the generals finally yielded to U.S. desires and aid resumed, they continued their lucrative side business (see photo essay, page 22).

The new agreement left Vang Pao and the refugee Hmoung tribesmen almost defenseless against the Pathet Lao and North Vietnamese soldiers. The agreement did allow for the continued resupply of rice and medical support for the Hmoung even though they were cut off from all road contact with the capital. The U.S. Agency for International Development (AID) placed "Pop" Buell, a retired American farmer, along with other AID personnel

with the tribe, in an attempt to make the Hmoung agriculturally self-sufficient. U.S. contact with the tribe still existed.

Toward the end of 1962, reports from the North reached American ears that Kong Le and the Communists were coming to a parting of the ways. The dispute arose over Kong Le's belief that his paratroopers were not getting their fair share of the supplies from Moscow and the conviction that his Marxist companions had no real interest in a neutral Laos. On hearing of the dispute, the U.S. Embassy dispatched occasional Air America supply flights to Kong Le and his troops.

In the spring of 1964, with Lyndon Johnson now in the White House, the dispute between Kong Le and the Communists erupted into fighting on the Plain of Jars. Badly outnumbered, the young captain led his men to the high rain forests and contacted the Hmoung. News of this event he was small: five feet, one inch tall and weighing only 115 pounds. Kong Le earned a reputation as an effective leader in combat against the Pathet Lao in the 1950s. In 1957 he was picked by the U.S. Army to receive Ranger training in the Philippines. He possessed a magnetic personality, an ability to gain the intense loyalty of his men. Becoming a battalion commander with the Royal Lao Army parachute troops, he began to draw the attention of foreign military observers. The problem with Kong Le was that he was politically naive.

When Kong Le overthrew the Lao government, the U.S. Embassy found that his speeches and pronouncements were being written by a Moscow-trained public information specialist. Shortly after his troops seized the capital, Russian military aircraft and crews, as well as North Vietnamese troops, began arriving at the Vientiane airport. The captain had only about 3,000 Lao troops loyal to him. The great majority of the Royal Lao Army—with U.S. support—began to organize a countercoup. As plans were being prepared for a concerted U.S. and Lao initiative, the American embassy decided to take care of the Kong Le "problem" by sending a message to Washington. It contained a proposal to assassinate the young paratroop leader.

The plan was to use a mine. Picking an ambush site was easy; almost every evening Kong Le visited a "lady of the night" at a spot in town. He could be killed en route. The commander of the U.S. Special Forces in Vientiane was given the mission. That officer refused to be responsible for the deed, but his direct participation was not essential to the plot. All that was lacking was approval from Washington. The Eisenhower administration considered the assassination proposal, and the response was not long in coming: No. The United States would have to live with Kong Le, but not with the government that he had installed.

After a successful countercoup backed by the Americans, Kong Le fled the capital with the Communist forces and remained with them until 1963. That year his deputy commander was killed by the Pathet Lao, and Kong Le reconsidered his association with the Communists. He decided to switch sides once again. In 1964, he was fighting the Communists and receiving U.S. support.

Kong Le was not "pro-U.S."; he was antiforeign. He explained his brief power grab in Vientiane as an attempt to achieve neutrality for his country. He said that he had believed the Communists were sincerely interested in a Laos controlled by Lao. When he came to know the real Communist goals, he realized the true intent of Hanoi. He described his subsequent change of allegiance as the best hope to get the North Vietnamese out of Laos. He knew that could be accomplished only with force and American support. He said, "Whether we win or lose, I'm afraid there is not much choice except to fight until we can fight no longer."

Kong Le was much like the people he fought for: superstitious. He wore cotton strings around his wrists, a Lao custom believed to prevent the soul from leaving the body, and a small stone tied to his waist to ward off bullets. His soldiers described him as "chai di"—man with a gentle heart. To the Lao, the phrase combines two meanings: compassion and generosity. He was given to periods of depression, particularly when his fortunes on the battlefield appeared to be slipping. In those times, he would often threaten to leave his country and to go "anywhere that has pretty girls."

Kong Le's band of followers was named the Neutralist Army. His army was supposed to represent a middle ground between the pro-U.S. "rightists" and the Communists. In fact, the right and middle combined to fight the Communists. Kong Le's Neutralist Army was a small force, loyal to the Lao politician Souvanna Phouma, a man who tried in vain to find a path to independence for his people. The Neutralist Army fought for many years. As the head of this army, Kong Le became a general, but his reputation as a charismatic leader always went back to his exploits as the young paratroop captain who had stormed Vientiane.

Perhaps he sensed his fate. His army fought until it could fight no more. Before the Communist triumph, Kong Le left his country. He went to France and later returned to Southeast Asia, settling in Thailand. Both nations are noted for their "pretty girls."

caused the Johnson administration to seek military contact with Kong Le and his paratroopers. A Special Forces officer was hurriedly sent to Laos to report on Kong Le's situation.

The secret war heats up

As more and more North Vietnamese infiltrators and supplies arrived in South Vietnam via the Ho Chi Minh Trail, the U.S. president and his advisers became increasingly suspicious of Hanoi's activities in Laos. The war was not going well for Saigon, and although the full magnitude of the North Vietnamese use of Laos was not known in Washington, there had been a number of clues. Both the U.S. and the Thai governments were coming to believe that the Geneva accords of 1962 jeopardized the security of Cambodia, South Vietnam, and Thailand. Concerns also arose in Vientiane. There, the neutralist government of Souvanna Phouma began to realize that it could not maintain itself or any degree of independence as long as the North Vietnamese continued their military efforts. Reluctantly, Souvanna Phouma, a man who had long worked for the neutrality of Laos, asked for U.S. military assistance. When it was learned that Kong Le was now willing to join Vientiane in the fight against the Communists, Washington and Bangkok decided to increase their support of the Lao government.

Souvanna Phouma authorized low-level U.S. photo reconnaissance missions over his country in mid-May 1964, and the U.S. government was eager to learn the extent of North Vietnamese activities in Laos. The flights by both USAF RF–101 and U.S. Navy RF–8 aircraft began on May 19. By early June, more than 130 flights had been completed. Most of the missions flew over the Plain of Jars, but about 50 passed over the Ho Chi Minh Trail, the latter gaining information on the extensive use of the route into South Vietnam. The North Vietnamese antiaircraft batteries on and around the Plain of Jars responded to these flights with increasing fire, but little damage was sustained to the speedy U.S. aircraft.

All went well until June 6. On that day, Lieutenant Charles F. Klusmann was launched from the deck of the U.S.S. *Kitty Hawk*, piloting his RF–8A. His mission was to photograph an area between Khang Khay and Ban Ban, Laos. The region had recently been nicknamed "lead alley" by his wingmates because of North Vietnam's numerous rapid-firing 37MM weapons located there. Reaching the target area, Klusmann dived in for the camera run. Making a low pass, the Navy aircraft was hit and the lieutenant lost control. The pilot ejected out of the crippled aircraft and parachuted into the jungle. Klusmann was captured just as an Air America helicopter arrived for the rescue.

The young naval officer was held under close guard and subjected to several days of interrogation before he was thrown into a prison compound with a number of Lao and Thai captives. His new prison was very loosely guarded, and Klusmann was able to lead an escape with five Thai and Lao companions. Four of his fellow escapees drifted away from the American during the trek through the jungle, but Klusmann and one other reached a Hmoung village on August 21, three days after their breakout. The tribesmen quickly passed the word to American friends and Air America brought the pilot to safety.

Meanwhile, the U.S. Embassy in Laos and the Lao military leadership were preparing a plan to get Kong Le's forces into a defensible position, one that could seriously challenge the Communist hold on northern Laos. In mid-1964, a scheme was hatched, code named Operation Triangle, to move Kong Le's paratroopers from their hilltop camp on the southern rim of the Plain of Jars to the western entrance of the plain, a mountain pass called Muong Soui. The pass contained Route 7, and occupation of the pass would block Communist road communications between the plain and the strategically important intersection of Routes 7 and 13 at Sala Phou Khoun. So that Kong Le would not be sandwiched between two Communist forces, one on the plain and the other at Sala Phou Khoun, the plan included an attack on the Communist position at Sala Phou Khoun coinciding with the Air America airlift of Kong Le's forces into Muong Soui. With success, all Communist forces in northern Laos west of the Plain of Jars could be cut off and the road from Luang Prabang to Vientiane, Route 13, freed for the first time since 1961.

The main attack on Sala Phou Khoun was to be delivered by a regimental-size force that had to march several

Pathet Lao soldiers hold a meeting in a cave on the Plain of Jars. By the early 1970s, the Pathet Lao and their North Vietnamese allies controlled most of eastern Laos.

North Vietnamese forces move to the battlefield in southern Laos in the early 1970s. Their drive westward permitted the expansion of the Ho Chi Minh Trail.

days through the jungle in order to attack the key intersection from the west, an unlikely avenue of approach. The American Special Forces officer who had been sent by the embassy to contact Kong Le was placed with this column, and CIA operatives with the Hmoung were assigned to coordinate a fire attack on the Communist position at the road junction coinciding with the Royal Lao regiment assault from the west.

Hot, tired, and thirsty, the Lao regiment arrived at a small, forested hill one mile west of and overlooking the Pathet Lao position of Sala Phou Khoun. It had taken three days to traverse the thick jungle terrain. The attack was due to begin on July 22—with considerable support. At 10:00 A.M., artillery fire was heard in the distance, both north and south of the road intersection. Above, an Air America C–47, flying at a high altitude, soon radioed to the Special Forces officer that two feints, mock attacks on Pathet Lao positions along Route 13, had worked. Trucks were departing Sala Phou Khoun to reinforce garrisons above and below the intersection. The Lao regimental commander ordered the assault on the depleted garrison. With the Hmoung hitting the rear of the Communists and the Royal Lao infantry streaming out of the jungle, the contest was soon over. Operation Triangle was a success. Air America had moved Kong Le's forces to Muong Soui without incident, and the roads linking Luang Prabang, Vientiane, and Muong Soui was free of enemy forces.

By late 1964, the U.S. government had become painfully aware of the consequences of Hanoi's use of southern Laos. The South Vietnamese army began to lose an average of one battalion per week in battles with the North Vietnamese and Vietcong regulars. In August, Congress gave President Johnson a "blank check" when it passed the Gulf of Tonkin Resolution. The administration interpreted it to permit the use of American forces throughout Indochina. Johnson took full advantage of his authority. He authorized a number of initiatives separate from the overt conflict in South Vietnam. The activities of the Central Intelligence Agency, the use of Air America, and an increasing employment of the U.S. Air Force, all in Laos, were examples of what later became known as "a secret war."

There were a number of reasons to continue keeping the war in Laos hidden from the public. First, there was the involvement of Thailand. The Thais still desired anonymity for their efforts in assisting the Lao and Hmoung. They wanted to maintain diplomatic relations with all of their Asian neighbors, and acknowledged belligerency could threaten regional communications. An official disclosure by the U.S. of Thai activities risked a withdrawal of

Bangkok's aid. Second, the strategy of the Johnson administration hinged on changing Hanoi's mind. Openly castigating Hanoi for its efforts in Laos would create another issue dividing the North Vietnamese and the U.S., one that would be added to the agenda of the hoped-for agreement ending the war in Southeast Asia. The final resolution of the conflict would then involve not only South Vietnam but Laos as well. By keeping quiet about the war in Laos, the U.S. gave Hanoi one less item it would only deny at the conference table. Of course, the North Vietnamese had no more desire to acknowledge the war in Laos than the Americans. Thus, all the foreign participants, whatever the Lao people might feel, could agree that the "secret war" should be kept secret.

Air power was a key component of the secret war. The aircraft utilized included an odd mixture of World War II cargo airplanes flown by the jungle-wise civilian air crews of Air America, Thai and Lao pilots at the controls of Royal Lao Air Force propeller-driven fighters, high-performance jet aircraft of the U.S. Air Force and Navy, and an assortment of other craft operated by Lao and Americans. Some U.S. spotter aircraft and USAF pilots were stationed with the Hmoung and operated out of the rough, mountaintop airstrips. They were used to mark targets and coordinate bombing missions by USAF and Navy aircraft based in Thailand and in the Gulf of Tonkin. The Thai government, ever wary of the North Vietnamese, offered their own pilots in the same way they had offered the use of their artillery units to the Lao government—in secret. This hodgepodge of an air force with its peculiar mix of airplanes and air crews operated for eight years in the crowded skies over Laos.

The Thais also helped in Laos on the ground. Thai artillery units were employed initially in the north with Kong Le. Not trusting the ability of the Lao to provide adequate security for Thai gunners, the Royal Thai Army stationed a small security detachment of infantry with the artillery. In addition, the Thai leadership recruited volunteers to serve in Special Guerrilla Units that were employed alongside their Lao neighbors and against the North Vietnamese and Pathet Lao. By 1967, all of this had achieved a measure of stability in Laos. But, it was not enough to cut off North Vietnamese use of the Ho Chi Minh Trail.

The conflict was characterized by small, seesaw battles against the North Vietnamese and their Lao allies in control of the Plain of Jars, with the Hmoung, Thai, and American air crews harassing their adversaries around the flanks. This dreary scenario was repeated month after month until the North Vietnamese mounted an all-out effort in 1968. Aiming at a final victory in both Laos and South Vietnam, Hanoi directed the Tet offensive against Saigon but also committed eleven battalions of its regulars against Vang Pao's Hmoung in northern Laos. As in Vietnam, the attack in Laos was quick, spirited, and effective.

Thirteen Americans were killed, along with an unknown number of Thais, Lao, and Hmoung. But the great majority of the Hmoung escaped to their jungle lairs in the mountains. Vang Pao gathered his battered survivors and planned a campaign that was broad in scope and aimed at revenge. It was a difficult campaign, for in 1969, the North Vietnamese brought an entire division, the 312th, into Laos in an attempt to consolidate their gains.

Preceded by a massive U.S. bombing of the North Vietnamese beginning in March 1969, the Hmoung streamed down from the hills in June, cutting Route 7 between the North Vietnam border and the Plain of Jars. Groggy and badly wounded from the U.S. air attack, the North Vietnamese were no match for the Hmoung. The eleven North Vietnamese battalions, even with their invading division, were rapidly pushed out of the Plain of Jars, leaving behind many dead and prisoners. For the first time in the long war, the fortunes of Vientiane looked promising. However, U.S. policy was changing once again.

"Laotianization"

In Laos, as in South Vietnam, President Nixon's policy had as its prime goal the withdrawal of American forces. The fighting continued, but every effort was made to turn over the war to the Lao, Thais, and Hmoung. The policy unfortunately worked to undercut the morale of the American allies and only encouraged Hanoi to continue the war. The northerners massed their forces for yet another attempt to secure the now-pockmarked Plain of Jars. This time, they brought two divisions: the reinforced and revived 312th and the 316th Division.

A crushing assault by the North Vietnamese in February 1970 was too much for the fatigued Hmoung. Once again, the tribesmen herded their women and children into march columns for a fighting withdrawal into the mountains. Most of Vang Pao's brave legions never returned to their sacred valleys of northern Laos. They eventually fled across the Mekong, and many of them later began a new life in the United States as refugees.

While the Hmoung were fighting a losing battle for their homelands, an entirely different sort of war was under way in the southern, or panhandle, area of Laos. Beginning in the late 1960s, the Lao and Americans organized another arm of the clandestine army. Composed of Lao and Thai volunteers, small units of well-paid soldiers were trained in guerrilla tactics to interdict North Vietnamese use of the Ho Chi Minh Trail. Marking targets for U.S. air strikes and staging classic ambushes, these units soon attracted heavily armed North Vietnamese units that were forced to conduct counterguerrilla sweep operations, much like American infantry units in South Vietnam. In Laos, the tables had been turned. But soon, the Thai and Lao guerrilla units had to change their tactics.

The abandonment of guerrilla operations in the pan-

handle and the acceptance of more conventional combat methods came about because of Hanoi's desperate need to widen the geographic corridor containing the Ho Chi Minh Trail complex. The overthrow of Prince Sihanouk in Cambodia had eliminated the Communist use of the port of Sihanoukville, a vital logistical link that the North Vietnamese had been using since 1966 to supply their forces in South Vietnam. By 1970, virtually all of Hanoi's southbound reinforcements and supplies had to go through Laos. The crowded routes provided easy bombing targets for the American air crews. The North Vietnamese then began a series of operations that pushed west throughout southern Laos in an attempt to widen the corridor, provide more parallel roads, and diminish the effectiveness of the American air interdiction campaign.

As the North Vietnamese moved toward Thailand in the Lao panhandle, they brought a large contingent of antiaircraft units with them. Life for Air America pilots in the south became hazardous. A recent history of Air America offers an example of just how difficult flight operations had become:

Early one morning, an Air America helicopter was badly damaged by enemy fire while attempting to resupply one of the hilltop positions of Thai and Lao guerrilla forces near the Ho Chi Minh Trail. The returning and somewhat unnerved pilot was shocked to find that another flight, this time a C–123 parachute resupply mission, was being sent out to the same spot despite his warning about heavy North Vietnamese antiaircraft fire. Quickly finding the senior Air America captain assigned to the new flight, the chopper pilot warned the veteran of the enemy's capability. He could have saved his breath; he was talking to "Weird Neil" Hansen.

"Weird Neil" had been a Canadian bush pilot and, prior to his recruitment by Air America, the personal pilot for Teamster boss Jimmy Hoffa. He had gained his nickname with the airline because of a consistent pattern of abnormal behavior. As an old-timer, he often instructed new copilots during their training period. His favorite trick was to hand over the controls to the new men on their first flight in Laos. Reaching into his flight bag, he would pull out a child's coloring book and a fistful of crayons. Making a few corrective comments such as, "For Christ's sake don't go over there, it's full of antiaircraft guns!" Hansen concentrated on his coloring chore. His favorite was red barns. If the thoroughly rattled newcomer managed to keep the craft in the air, Hansen figured he might have potential. Needless to say, Hansen accepted the dangerous resupply mission.

Insisting that his crew wear parachutes, an odd demand from an Air America pilot, Hansen departed for the

Pathet Lao soldiers train their antiaircraft guns skyward in 1967. They usually targeted the slower planes and helicopters of Air America.

119

drop. On the first pass over the beleaguered outpost, the C–123 was riddled with machine-gun bullets. "Weird Neil" fought the controls and managed to point the crippled aircraft toward the safety of Pakse. It soon became apparent that the plane would not make it. Hansen headed for a nearby government-held position in order to bail out. Holding the aircraft steady over the chosen spot, the pilot got the crew out of the door. Returning once more, Hansen abandoned the plane himself.

An Air America rescue helicopter arrived and the three-man crew of the crashed C–123 was plucked out of the jungle. Damaging a rotor blade on liftoff, the helicopter had to be nursed along. Bad luck continued as vibrations became more severe over enemy-held territory. The chopper pilot informed the hapless fixed-wing survivors to strap themselves in tight because the helicopter was going down. A rough crash landing was made in the forested area and another rescue helicopter arrived just before the enemy.

Scrambling aboard the second helicopter, Hansen and his crew believed they were living charmed lives. Those thoughts were dismissed in a flash when they heard the new chopper pilot yell out:

"Hell almighty!"

"What's wrong?" the crew chief yelled back.

"You're not going to believe this—we're out of gas!"

A second crash landing was skillfully executed and another rescue helicopter dispatched. Hansen, his crew, and two helicopter crews made it out safely but Air America lost three aircraft that day.

The end of the secret army

The commander of all Thai and Lao units in the panhandle area, Brigadier General Soutchay Vongsavanh, was a big, energetic Lao soldier with a reputation for honesty and courage. Knowing the war was going badly in northern Laos, Soutchay decided he had to abandon guerrilla tactics and fight toe-to-toe battles with the North Vietnamese regulars. Uniting several Thai and Lao guerrilla formations, he created regimental-size forces with their own artillery. He also strengthened a number of Royal Lao Army units.

One of the first battles between Soutchay's new units and Hanoi's regulars was a protracted contest for Muong Phalane, a small district capital midway between Savannakhet and Tchepone along Route 9. The Vietnamese had taken the town in January 1971, pushing the Lao garrison thirty kilometers to the west. Soutchay ordered a newly formed force, Mobile Group 30 (GM 30), composed of former guerrilla and irregular elements, to retake the town. Led by a major named Piewkhao, GM 30 launched its 540-man force toward the objective on March 24, 1970. By evening, Piewkhao's men had moved quietly to the outskirts of Muong Phalane. Using a light aircraft to drop strings of

firecrackers north and south of the town, the crafty major waited until the Vietnamese dispatched patrols from their garrison before he assaulted. By early morning, GM 30 was dug in throughout the district capital.

The counterattack came on the morning of March 26 with the arrival of three Vietnamese battalions. Attacking across open fields, the Communist soldiers were cut down by the heavily outnumbered defenders. Attempting to regroup, the attackers were blitzed once again by a devastating air attack by Lao air force T–28s. That night, a Vietnamese-speaking Lao reported to Piewkhao that he had intercepted a radio transmission from the North Vietnamese commander. The Vietnamese had 365 dead and "many" wounded. It took some time for Hanoi's leadership to cobble together a second try.

In mid-April, GM 30 reconnaissance patrols and reports from the friendly population along Route 9 informed Major Piewkhao that a North Vietnamese officer, General Tuan, was assembling a force of six infantry battalions supported by a unit of antiaircraft artillery for an attack on Muong Phalane. Trying to surround the Lao garrison, Tuan's lead battalion stumbled into one of Soutchay's patrols just west of Muong Phalane. On April 30 the Communists suffered a sharp setback preventing them from cutting a potential withdrawal route for GM 30. The Lao general then decided that the Vietnamese had too many soldiers. He planned to have GM 30 absorb a first assault, to make the northerners pay a heavy price, before he withdrew his men.

The attack came on May 2 and the defenders were ready. Tuan's force lost an entire battalion on the first wave against the well-dug-in positions of GM 30 on the edge of Muong Phalane. A second wave was also demolished by the Lao, but when ammunition began to run low, GM 30 had to retreat. The third North Vietnamese assault found the defenders long gone from the town.

A number of similar battles raged in southern Laos while the siege of Muong Phalane was in progress. Another of Soutchay's units surprised Hanoi's soldiers in the town of Saravane during March and drove them from the city. As at Muong Phalane, the Vietnamese retook Saravane, but in July, the Lao general overwhelmed the invaders at Pak Sane. He then went back to Saravane with two of his regiments, defeated the North Vietnamese regiment there, and again occupied the town. In early 1972, Soutchay struck again. Defeating a Vietnamese regiment, he gained control of Khong Sedone. Mounting a counterattack by two regiments, the North Vietnamese threw the Lao-Thai forces out of their new positions in July. Soutchay came back. This time, in a remarkable performance, two of his regular Lao formations destroyed about one-third of one of the North Vietnamese regiments, put the other to flight, captured large quantities of weapons, and once again reclaimed Khong Sedone. However, the long war and the clandestine army were both coming to an end.

The war ended in a Communist victory because the American people no longer supported it. The entire U.S. support effort had to be phased out and handed over to local forces. The American withdrawal caused the Thais to reconsider their role and begin their own withdrawal. Air America, the CIA, and the U.S. Air Force were ordered out. The clandestine army came to an end. Once again, in the Paris Peace Agreements of 1973, the North Vietnamese solemnly agreed to depart Laos and once again they broke their promise. The Communists won simply by remaining in Laos.

The clandestine army was needed because of the North Vietnamese troops in Laos. Without Hanoi's presence, there would have been no need for the clandestine army. The senior U.S. military officer in Laos during 1961, General Andrew Boyle, told President Kennedy that the Royal Lao Army could handle the Pathet Lao by itself but could not defend itself against the North Vietnamese. Hanoi's activities in the small kingdom led the CIA, Air America, and the Thais to support the Hmoung in Laos. Thirteen years after Boyle spoke, the last U.S. general in Laos, Richard Trefry, said the same thing: Left to themselves, the Lao could take care of their own affairs, but against the North Vietnamese they needed help. In 1973, that help was no longer offered. More than a generation after Boyle's prediction, the North Vietnamese still maintain a force of 50,000 troops in Laos. The clandestine army had been raised to counter an invading army. The clandestine army disappeared when the United States would no longer "bear any burden" or "pay any price."

Of the creators of the clandestine army, many of the Air America pilots traded in their grease-stained gray cotton uniforms for the snappier dress of such companies as Eastern, Pan Am, and United. Most of the CIA men retired in the mid-1970s when the paramilitary arm of the agency was greatly reduced. The Special Forces White Star teams went to Vietnam and another war, so too the Air Force crews. Bull Simons led a raid into North Vietnam, retired from the Army, but surfaced again to lead a dramatic and successful rescue of an American billionaire's employees from prison in Iran. But some of the Americans, particularly the pilots, went into the jungles of Laos and were never seen again. There are continuing reports that some may still be there.

The American who started the first clandestine army in Laos during World War II became famous in the shadowy world of Southeast Asia. Major Jim Thompson, the OSS officer who began arming the Lao against the Japanese, told his friends that he had severed all connections with the U.S. Army after the war. It is certain that he lived in Bangkok and became a millionaire in the Thai silk trade. It is also known that he was often seen in the company of Lao military and political figures. In 1967, Thompson went to Malaysia and registered at a resort hotel high in the mountains. The land there is much like the lofty jungles of northern Laos—cool, jade green, and beautiful. Two days later, a hotel maid saw Thompson walking in the garden. Thompson paused to look at some roses and then stepped into the jungle. Like the clandestine army he inspired, Jim Thompson simply vanished.

Air America

In 1959, the CIA became the owner of an airline—in secret, of course. Given a cover as a commerical air-charter firm, this innocuously named airline, Air America, soon comprised a fleet of more than 100 aircraft that supported CIA covert activities throughout Asia, including those in Burma, Indonesia, Tibet, and South Vietnam. It was in Laos in particular, however, with the CIA's creation of the clandestine army of Hmoung tribesmen, that Air America flourished, growing to rival the largest airlines in the world.

But Air America was not exactly a new airline. Its roots led back to the civil war in China and before. There, in the late 1940s, famed World War II General Claire Lee Chennault enlisted a colorful band of aviators in a commercial airline called Civil Air Transport (CAT), heir to his pre–World War II Flying Tigers. CAT airlifted supplies and troops for the Nationalist Chinese army, but after the Communist victory, Chennault's company began flying for the CIA in that agency's fledgling operations in Asia, serving in both the Korean conflict and French-Indochina War.

Air America quickly outstripped its predecessor in size and influence as a result of its activities in Laos, primarily those in support of the Hmoung army. Air America helicopters flew CIA operatives and Hmoung officers to outlying villages during their periodic recruitment drives and helped maintain communications between scattered bases. In the seesaw battle for the Plain of Jars, Air America helicopters and planes provided the tribesmen with the necessary air trans-

An Air America cargo plane drops supplies to a Meo village in Laos, 1968.

Above. *Maintenance men work on one of the Flying Tigers' P–40s at Mingladon Field, Rangoon, Burma, in 1942. Left. Flying Tigers Commander Claire Chennault stands before his shark-nosed P–40.*

port. They shuttled troops across eastern Laos during their rainy-season attacks and evacuated whole villages during Communist dry-season offensives.

Air America also served as the life line for Hmoung soldiers and their families, airdropping everything the tribespeople needed from weapons and ammunition to rice and live pigs. On one occasion, Air America hauled cases of baby food to remote villages after a CIA study had found that the people lacked certain vitamins in their diet. By 1966 the company was moving an average of 6,000 tons of cargo per month in Laos, predominantly in support of the Hmoung. Eventually, the tribespeople grew dependent on the airline: a popular joke among Air America pilots had Hmoung children pointing to the sky when asked where rice came from.

Air America also conducted numerous CIA pet projects in Laos. These varied from psychological operations (releasing counterfeit Pathet Lao currency over eastern Laos) to deadly combat (secretly trans-

porting small indigenous teams to and from the Ho Chi Minh Trail). Flying in unmarked planes and carrying soldiers wearing enemy uniforms, Air America pilots knew that if they were shot down during one of these missions, their status was SOL—Shit Out of Luck.

For such demanding and hazardous missions, Air America recruited an experienced crew of former Air Force pilots, many of whom had seen combat in World War II and Korea, and Vietnam-hardened helicopter pilots, usually former U.S. Marines. These men joined the airline for a variety of reasons. Some were hooked on Southeast Asia and could not bring themselves to return to America; others simply enjoyed the excitement of war; still others enlisted for the money—Air America pilots could earn annually more than $40,000.

By 1969, Air America controlled a fleet of some 200 planes and 30 helicopters. The fixed-wing aircraft included the remarkable Helio Couriers, which could stay airborne at only 35mph and land on virtually any terrain; World War II–vintage C–46s and C–47s, which made most of the airline's airdrops; and larger C–130s on loan from the Air Force. For helicopters, Air America relied primarily on H–34s, stationed at Udorn, Thailand.

Air America personnel and their Laotian allies attempt to relax inside the cramped interior of a Douglas C–47, a World War II–vintage aircraft used by the CIA airline, during an early morning run to Thakhek, Laos, in 1965.

These began each morning by transporting CIA operatives into Laos, before heading out for their daily runs between the Hmoung camps.

Air America's vast resources, however, could not protect the Hmoung against increasingly fierce Communist offensives, beginning with their sweep across the Plain of Jars in 1968. By the early 1970s, the Hmoung army was in disarray,

and as its depleted ranks retreated west, Air America struggled to evacuate the growing flood of refugees. Following the Paris peace agreements, Air America reduced its operations in Laos. Then, in June 1974, it closed its facilities and followed the rest of the American covert effort out of Laos.

Left. *Hmoung villagers in northern Laos retrieve bags of rice airdropped from an Air America Helio Courier in late 1968.* Right. *An Air America CV–2B Caribou approaches the landing strip at Sam Thong Village, not far from the Hmoung army's Long Cheng headquarters on the Plain of Jars, in September 1966.* Below. *As the battle between government troops and the Pathet Lao nears their village in 1968, Hmoung tribespeople board an Air America CH–34 helicopter for evacuation west.*

A last mission in Indochina. An Air America helicopter evacuates Americans from Saigon on April 29, 1975.

Operation Menu

Far above the rice fields and triple-canopy jungle of Southeast Asia, U.S. aircraft waged a silent, deadly battle against North Vietnamese forces. It was a war fought from the sterility of pressurized cockpits in multimillion-dollar aircraft armed with the latest that modern technology had to offer, against an unseen enemy thousands of feet below. It was an impersonal war filled with the beeps of sophisticated electronic gadgetry and blips on radar screens.

The very solitary nature of the air campaign in Vietnam made it the perfect tool for secret operations. Air warfare was conducted high in the sky, away from the prying eyes of reporters and Congressional investigators. Although many pilots were based in South Vietnam, a large number flew their missions from air bases in Thailand and even from as far away as Guam, where journalists, for the most part, were prohibited. In some air operations even pilots were not required, removing any possible human security problems.

There is no better example of the stealth of aerial operations than the U.S. National Security Agency's spy satellites that circled the globe, scanning the earth below with highly sophisticated surveillance cameras and eavesdropping equipment. The satellites provided detailed intelligence photos of North Vietnam for Air Force and Navy bombing raids.

Below these spy satellites, in the upper reaches of the earth's atmosphere, flew the high-altitude reconnaissance aircraft of the Strategic Air Command—Lockheed U–2s and SR–71s. Operating out of a specially secured portion of the airfield at Takhli, Thailand, both were used extensively during the war to monitor enemy activities in North Vietnam. From the early 1960s on, U–2 aircraft flew routine reconnaissance missions over Southeast Asia. Their cameras could pick out a golf ball on a putting green from an altitude of 55,000 feet and detected the first evidence of the deployment of deadly Soviet-made SA–2 surface-to-air missiles in North Vietnam. The SR–71, constructed with large amounts of titanium to prevent overheating during supersonic flights in the thin air of the stratosphere, could operate from even higher altitudes. The sleek, black aircraft could fly at three times the speed of sound and an altitude of 80,000 feet.

Due to the limited number of U–2s and SR–71s available, however, and the demand for their use in other parts of the world, tactical reconnaissance aircraft performed the bulk of the surveillance missions flown during the war. But Vietnam offered the U.S. an opportunity to test a number of new capabilities and technologies being developed by private contractors. Among the highly classified equipment that received its baptism of fire in Vietnam were unmanned drones and remotely piloted vehicles (RPVs).

The U.S. began flying Teledyne-Ryan Firebee reconnaissance RPVs over North Vietnam, Laos, and China as early as 1964. The RPVs were launched from unmarked C–130 transports, which acted as the controller aircraft, and were recovered either by parachute or by helicopters using nets. The Chinese claimed to have shot down one of these special C–130 transports on November 15, 1964.

Although the U.S. Air Force was initially skeptical of the new RPVs, improvements in North Vietnamese air defenses made manned reconnaissance flights increasingly dangerous. As more and more aircraft and pilots were lost over heavily defended areas, the Air Force became more willing to use the unmanned drones fitted with aerial cameras for reconnaissance missions.

More than 3,400 missions were flown by RPVs during the war, the majority under a classified program given the code name Buffalo Hunter. The project employed twenty different versions of the Teledyne-Ryan Firebee using the basic target drone airframe. In addition to photo reconnaissance missions, RPVs were used for electronic eavesdropping, radar jamming, and propaganda leaflet drops.

Igloo White and SOG

Another unmanned aircraft was the QU–22, a drone version of the Beech Debonaire light aircraft specifically developed to receive signals from sensors strewn along the Ho Chi Minh Trail in Laos to monitor enemy traffic. Code named Pave Eagle, the drone acted as a communications relay platform, transmitting the signals back to the Infiltration Surveillance Center across the border in Thailand at Nakhon Phanom, where they were analyzed and interpreted in order to plan bombing strikes.

The QU–22 flew as part of a classified surveillance effort called Igloo White, which drew on the latest that technology had to offer in an effort to stem the flow of men and materiel from North to South Vietnam. The project was the brain child of a group of scientists pulled together by Defense Secretary Robert McNamara in the summer of 1966. The bombing campaign against the trail had failed to disrupt North Vietnamese supply lines and McNamara was looking for an alternative solution.

The Jason Summer Study Group, as the group was named, developed the idea of an electronic barrier supported by specialized aircraft to detect and deter enemy movements. The main ingredients of the barrier were to include acoustic and seismic sensors, small land mines that could be dispersed over a wide area, and more conventional bombs carried by tactical aircraft.

McNamara approved the concept and created a special group to develop the barrier as a high-priority, top-secret project. The collection of experts was given the cover name Defense Communications Planning Group and worked out of an inconspicuous building in Washington, D.C., rather than the Pentagon. Word of the project eventually leaked out, however, and in September 1967 McNamara acknowledged the existence of a plan to create a barrier of barbed wire and electronic detectors across South Vietnam just south of the demilitarized zone.

Although by 1968 the concept was abandoned as impractical, the electronic surveillance program along the Ho Chi Minh Trail in Laos had by then developed into a full-scale affair. Tens of thousands of acoustic and seismic sensors were airdropped along the trail by tactical aircraft and specially modified Navy OP–2E antisubmarine warfare aircraft. Three kinds of sensors were employed to monitor North Vietnamese movements: acoustic sensors similar to those developed by the Navy for submarine detection, seismic sensors with specially designed transmitters activated by the vibrations from trucks and other heavy equipment, and sensors that combined both acoustic and seismic capabilities.

These sensors were monitored twenty-four hours a day

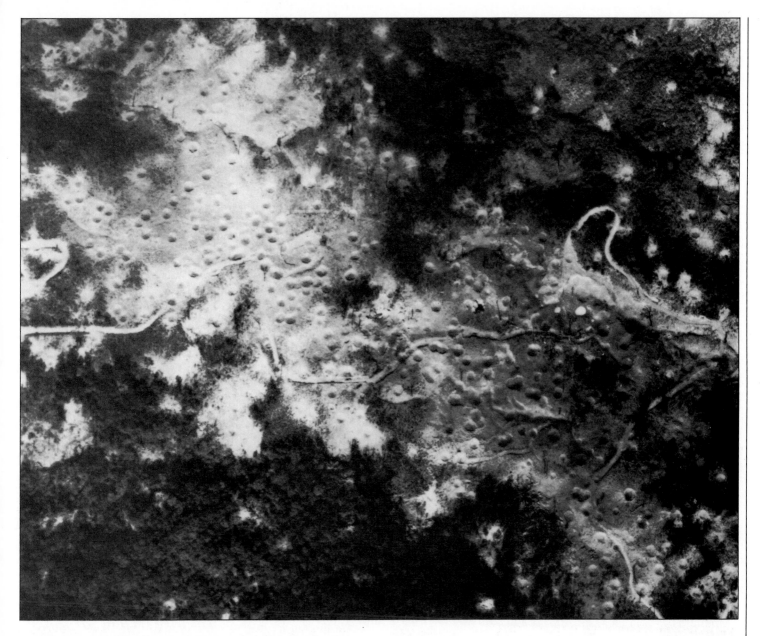

Craters from American B–52 air strikes dot the path of North Vietnam's Route 15, a transport artery leading from Vinh to the start of the Ho Chi Minh Trail in Laos, April 1966.

by air crews flying overhead who relayed the information gathered to the Infiltration Surveillance Center in Nakhon Phanom. Located in the middle of the jungle, the huge data collection and analysis complex was the nerve center of Igloo White operations. Two IBM 360–65 computers, the most sophisticated of that era, processed and stored the mountains of data that were collected by the sensors. The information was analyzed by intelligence experts who looked for patterns in traffic movements and matched them with maps of the network of roads and trails that had been developed from reconnaissance photos. Once a truck convoy's speed and direction were determined, the information could be relayed immediately to forward air controllers airborne over Laos, who could call in fighter-bombers for a rapid strike.

This style of electronic warfare by remote control lent itself perfectly to secrecy. There were few personnel involved to leak the story to inquiring reporters, and all communications were closely guarded. Even Congress was kept in the dark about Igloo White. Senator Stuart Symington, a member of the Senate Armed Services Committee, tried to obtain more information on the project as early as 1967, but the details of the operation and the technologies involved were determined to be too sensitive to reveal even in a closed executive session of the committee. Not until a special hearing was finally convened in November 1970 did Congress realize the full extent and cost of the operation.

Intelligence gathered under Igloo White on North Vietnamese activities along the Ho Chi Minh Trail in Laos was supplemented by the Special Forces ground reconnaissance units of MACV-SOG. A special SOG unit created at Nha Trang in South Vietnam and called the Air Studies Group specialized in airborne intelligence gathering in

off-limit areas such as North Vietnam and Laos. The group had its own clandestine air force composed of unmarked helicopters and transport aircraft to help infiltrate, support, and extricate reconnaissance units on these cross-border operations.

Secret air operations were conducted in Laos as early as September 1965 in support of SOG units operating under the Shining Brass and Prairie Fire programs. While SOG personnel conducted more than 1,798 missions between 1965 and 1972 to monitor enemy movements along the trail, carry out sabotage operations, and occasionally capture prisoners for interrogation, a total of 3,544 helicopter gunship sorties (a single mission by a single aircraft) and 5,410 sorties by tactical aircraft supported these clandestine missions.

When the operating scope of SOG units was expanded to include the lower reaches of the Ho Chi Minh Trail in Cambodia, the Air Force moved south with them. Between 1967 and April 1972, 1,885 SOG missions were carried out under Daniel Boone and Salem House. They were supported by a total of 1,980 tactical air sorties and 2,910 helicopter gunship sorties, according to official Defense Department records.

By 1968, MACV had become more and more concerned over North Vietnamese activities in Cambodia. American military officials were convinced that the bulk of Communist supplies being funneled through Cambodia to support the Vietcong in South Vietnam came through the port of Sihanoukville rather than from the North via the Ho Chi Minh Trail. MACV officials claimed that between October 1967 and November 1968, 10,000 tons of arms passed through Sihanoukville en route to North Vietnamese base camps and supply depots that dotted the border area with South Vietnam. With the exception of some 122MM rockets, all of the weapons and equipment that supported the Communists in military regions IV and III as well as a major part of military region II were coming through Sihanoukville.

As evidence of a mounting buildup of North Vietnamese forces in Cambodia came to light in late 1968, the U.S. stepped up its Daniel Boone forays to verify and amplify photo reconnaissance intelligence reports. One Special Forces officer who began leading Daniel Boone missions into Cambodia in late November 1968 recalled the extent of North Vietnamese and Vietcong activity across the border:

"There were hard-surfaced roads and concrete reinforced bunkers," he said, as well as bulldozers brought in to reinforce the roadbeds. "I personally found some abandoned base camps that were acres in size." He also saw large caches of fifty-five-gallon fuel drums sitting out in the open. "When you get an opportunity to see that blatant

Henry Kissinger, President Nixon's national security adviser and one of the architects of U.S. involvement in Cambodia, sits inside the White House in 1975.

[an] example of their presence there, you scream and beg and do everything you can to get somebody to come in there and blast them."

MACV commanders had long sought approval to hit these Communist sanctuaries, but the Johnson administration, wary of the political consequences of striking against targets in neutral Cambodia, rejected their pleas. That situation was soon to change, however, with the inauguration of a new president.

Nixon sets his course

Richard Nixon was particularly interested in the situation in Cambodia. Ten days before he took the oath of office Nixon instructed his newly appointed national security adviser, Henry Kissinger, to focus on the issue. "I want a precise report on what the enemy has in Cambodia and what, if anything, we are doing to destroy the buildup there," Nixon wrote Kissinger on January 8, 1969. "I think that a very definite change of policy toward Cambodia probably should be one of the first orders of business once we get in." The president-elect was particularly concerned lest the Communists stage another Tet offensive like the one in 1968 that shook the Johnson administration.

Nixon and Kissinger's Vietnam policy eventually evolved into a two-pronged strategy. On the one hand, it aimed at gradually withdrawing U.S. troops while strengthening the South Vietnamese military so that it could stand on its own. On the other hand, it took a carrot-and-stick approach that alternately bullied and cajoled Hanoi toward a negotiated settlement of the war that would be politically acceptable to the U.S.

But Nixon faced a serious dilemma in carrying out the second portion of this strategy. It called for forceful military action, yet American public opinion made any overt escalation of the war impossible. One option offered by the Joint Chiefs of Staff was the resumption of the bombing of North Vietnam, a proposal that was considered political suicide by Kissinger and Defense Secretary Melvin Laird. Secrecy would become an important ingredient of Nixon's plan to end the war, and Cambodia offered a unique opportunity to apply covert pressure against the North Vietnamese.

On January 30, General Earle Wheeler, chairman of the Joint Chiefs of Staff, suggested air strikes against the North Vietnamese sanctuaries in Cambodia. A cable to Wheeler on February 9 from General Abrams made the proposal seem even more enticing. Abrams noted that photo reconnaissance missions had confirmed reports from an enemy deserter that the Communists' Central Office for South Vietnam (COSVN) was located in the Fishhook area along the Cambodian–South Vietnamese border. With MACV intelligence predicting a large-scale offensive against the Saigon area, Abrams recommended a pre-emptive bombing raid by B–52 bombers against COSVN to disrupt the offensive. The U.S. ambassador in Saigon, Ellsworth Bunker, also sent a cable to the State Department endorsing Abrams's request. The JCS stamped its approval on the idea and passed Abrams's recommendation to Defense Secretary Laird on February 11.

Within days Abrams received a top-secret "Eyes Only" cable from Air Force chief of staff General John P. McConnell, acting as JCS chairman in Wheeler's absence. He told Abrams that the president was considering his request. Nixon asked for an estimate of possible Cambodian civilian casualties and insisted that all further communications about the proposal be kept closely held due to the political sensitivity of bombing operations in neutral Cambodia.

The Johnson administration's decision to step up the bombing campaign against the Ho Chi Minh Trail in Laos following the cessation of all air strikes against North Vietnam in early 1968 had carried little political risk, since U.S. military operations in Laos had slowly become public knowledge by then. Initiating air strikes against targets in ostensibly neutral Cambodia was a different matter, however. Unlike Laos, where Communist Pathet Lao rebels backed by North Vietnam were engaged in open hostilities with Royalist forces backed by the U.S., Cambodia had been spared the brunt of the fighting in Southeast Asia.

Although Daniel Boone reconnaissance teams routinely conducted clandestine forays into Cambodia, large-scale military operations would add fuel to the antiwar movement at home and draw further international criticism. There was also the question of how Cambodia's Prince Norodom Sihanouk would react. Cambodia's ruler had been struggling to maintain his country's neutrality since it won independence from France in 1954.

Sihanouk remained on friendly terms with the U.S. until 1965, when the landing of the first American combat troops in South Vietnam led to a break in diplomatic relations with Washington. As the war progressed Sihanouk turned a blind eye to North Vietnamese operations in his country since their activities were concentrated in the sparsely populated areas along the South Vietnamese border.

By 1968, however, Sihanouk had become increasingly concerned about the growing North Vietnamese presence in his country. He was also alarmed by Hanoi's increasing support for the Khmer Rouge, Cambodia's indigenous Communist movement. Sihanouk began to tilt back toward the U.S. again, hinting that he would allow the "hot pursuit" of North Vietnamese and Vietcong units into Cambodia by American troops.

Sihanouk discussed the idea in January 1968 with Chester Bowles, the U.S. ambassador to India. Bowles was sent to Phnom Penh by Washington to convince Sihanouk that the increased number of North Vietnamese and Vietcong units in the Cambodian border areas threatened to widen the war. Although he said he could not publicly approve the concept of hot pursuit, the prince told Bowles,

"I would shut my eyes" to any such activities. Sihanouk thought limited U.S. actions would help counterbalance the Communist presence in Cambodia, Bowles recounted in his memoirs. "We don't want any Vietnamese in Cambodia," the prince said. "We will be very glad if you solve our problem." But nothing ever came from Bowles's mission, as the Johnson administration's attention was quickly diverted by the 1968 Tet offensive.

A little more than a year later, in February 1969, Bowles's findings were resurrected by Kissinger and Nixon as the new administration began contemplating action against the Cambodian sanctuaries. Sihanouk's statements to Bowles were viewed as proof that the Cambodian ruler would not object to U.S. actions against Communist bases along the border regions. "We knew that because of Cambodia's neutral status, Sihanouk could not afford to endorse our actions officially," Nixon later wrote in his memoirs. "Therefore, as long as we bombed secretly, we knew that Sihanouk would be silent; if the bombing became known publicly, however, he would be forced to protest it publicly."

Nixon met with his principal advisers several times during February to discuss the idea of bombing in Cambodia. Abrams sent two staff aides from Saigon to brief Washington officials and push MACV's recommendation for B–52 strikes against the suspected COSVN site. The officials presented MACV's case at a February 18 breakfast meeting at the Pentagon attended by Gen. Wheeler, Kissinger, Laird, Deputy Defense Secretary David Packard, and Laird's military assistant, Colonel Robert E. Pursley.

Laird, a former member of Congress, was concerned about the possible political repercussions of such a move. Although Kissinger approved the concept in principle, he advised the president to postpone any decision until the end of March to allow time to develop a consensus within the cabinet. But within a few short days, events again brought the plan to the fore.

On February 22, just after the Tet holidays, the Communists launched a series of countrywide attacks against U.S. and South Vietnamese military installations. Although the attacks were not nearly as large as in the 1968 Tet offensive, the Communists focused on U.S. forces rather than ARVN units. Within three weeks 1,140 Americans fell victim to the offensive, almost as many as had died in the same period during the 1968 Tet attacks.

Nixon viewed the attacks as a deliberate attempt to humiliate him and test the mettle of his new administration. Convinced that Lyndon Johnson's failure to respond forcefully to Communist acts of aggression had given Hanoi the initiative, Nixon was determined not to let the offensive go unanswered. After consultations with Kissinger, however, he once again decided to delay a decision on the Cambodian bombing operation. The president was preparing to embark on a nine-day trip to meet with Allied leaders in Europe. Nixon feared that if news of the air strikes in neutral Cambodia leaked to the press it could trigger antiwar demonstrations abroad and mar the first diplomatic journey of his presidency. Nixon and Kissinger also wanted to secure the backing of Laird and Secretary of State William Rogers, who remained skeptical of the proposal.

Nixon ordered that Ambassador Bunker be notified through normal channels that all discussions of the proposed bombing raid be suspended. Simultaneously, he sent a "back channel" message, outside the normal communications chain, to Abrams instructing him to ignore the cable to Bunker and to continue contingency planning for the B–52 strikes.

Next day, while en route to Brussels for the first stop in his tour, Nixon abruptly changed course as he received news that the Communist offensive had intensified. He ordered Kissinger to begin the necessary preparations for the bombing strikes. Kissinger quickly cabled Army Colonel Alexander Haig, then an NSC staff aide, to fly to Brussels along with Air Force Colonel Raymond B. Sitton from the JCS staff to help formulate a plan of action.

Upon arriving in Brussels, Haig and Sitton met with Kissinger at the airport aboard Air Force 1. In the presidential plane's small conference area, the three men worked out the general guidelines for the B–52 strikes. The bombing would be restricted to a five-mile-long strip across the border. Fictitious cover targets in South Vietnam would be used to hide the real ones in Cambodia, a practice that members of the Johnson administration had used in certain bombing missions over Laos. In a memorandum dated February 23, 1967, Assistant Secretary of Defense John McNaughton noted that Secretary of Defense Robert McNamara authorized the JCS to conduct covert B–52 strikes in Laos under the cover of routine Arc Light B–52 strikes in South Vietnam along the Laotian border. The strike requests were reviewed and approved by State Department and White House staff members.

Kissinger stressed that knowledge of the strike was to be closely held to avoid unwanted publicity. He even proposed that the B–52 crews not be informed of their real destinations, but Col. Sitton advised him this would be impossible. He said that the B–52 pilots and navigators would realize they were bombing in Cambodia and would begin to talk. Kissinger eventually agreed that it would be better to have them informed and sworn to secrecy, but he gave Sitton the job of formulating a method to keep reports of the real targets of the raids out of the Strategic Air Command's normal command-and-control system. SAC monitored the administrative details of all B–52 operations, such as fuel and ordnance expenditures, and kept detailed records for budgetary purposes.

Since the North Vietnamese could not protest the raid without revealing their illegal presence in neutral Cambodia, Nixon did not expect a public outcry from Hanoi. If Cambodian officials protested and the raid became a subject of press inquiries, government public relations officers were instructed to note that B-52s on routine missions had struck targets in South Vietnam adjacent to the Cambodian border. Reporters were to be told that an investigation would be conducted to ascertain whether any bombs had inadvertently been dropped on Cambodia, and if so an apology and adequate compensation for any damage would be made.

With the wheels set in motion, all Nixon and Kissinger had to do was obtain the support of Laird and Rogers to ensure a united effort. Both secretaries were concerned about the domestic political consequences of bombing in neutral Cambodia. Laird thought it would be impossible to keep the operation secret and worried that its disclosure would fan the flames of public protest and damage the president's relationship with Congress. Rogers shared Laird's concerns and was fearful of the effect renewed bombing might have on the negotiations in Paris.

During a visit to South Vietnam between March 5 and March 12, Laird, Wheeler, and Abrams discussed extensively the issue of troop withdrawals as well as the question of bombing in Cambodia. On his return, Laird recommended that 50,000 to 60,000 troops be withdrawn in 1969. He also came away from Saigon convinced that the B-52 strikes against Communist sanctuaries in Cambodia should begin as soon as possible.

On March 15, Nixon issued the order to the JCS authorizing the B-52 raid against the suspected COSVN site in Base Area 353 for March 18. The mission was code named Operation Breakfast after the February 18 early morning Pentagon briefing by MACV officials.

On March 16, Nixon met with Kissinger, Laird, Wheeler, and Rogers for two hours in the Oval Office to formalize the decision. Laird was now on board, though he was still uneasy about Nixon and Kissinger's demand for secrecy. Rogers was the lone dissenter.

Nixon outlined his belief that such a military action was necessary to save American lives and prod the North Vietnamese into concessions at the Paris peace talks. "I am convinced that the only way to move the negotiations off dead center is to do something on the military front," he said. "That is something they will understand." Faced with the president's decision to act, Rogers finally agreed to the single strike against the suspected COSVN site. The JCS tried to get approval to extend the operation to include additional attacks against North Vietnamese troop concentrations along the demilitarized zone, but the request was denied to maintain consensus in the cabinet.

The bombing begins

On March 18, sixty B-52s roared off the runway at Andersen Air Force Base in Guam on what appeared to be a routine Arc Light mission against enemy troops near Tay Ninh in South Vietnam. Just before reaching the Vietnam-

ese targets, ground controllers diverted forty-eight of the bombers to targets in Base Area 353 across the Cambodian border. The eight-engine bombers, each carrying 24 tons of bombs, rained a total of 1,152 tons of high explosives over the area where MACV intelligence had placed COSVN headquarters. (The other twelve aircraft dropped their ordnance on the original targets in South Vietnam.)

B-52 crews reported seventy-three secondary explosions within the target area, indicating their bombs had hit large ammunition and fuel storage dumps. The reports were enthusiastically received at the White House and the Pentagon, where civilian and military leaders believed they had finally found the elusive COSVN and dealt the North Vietnamese a major blow.

American air crewmen arm B-52 bombs at Andersen Air Force Base in Guam in 1965. A later model of the Air Force B-52 Stratofortress was adapted to carry more than 100 500-pound bombs.

B–52 Stratofortress

O-60684

Tail Gunner

Operation Menu's Secret Warriors

High above Cambodia the six men comprising the crew of the giant B–52 Stratofortress (shown here is the B–52 model D) made the adjustments necessary to drop the aircraft's thousands of pounds of bombs on Operation Menu targets. The pilot was responsible for planning and executing the mission, doing everything possible to insure the safety of his men and aircraft. In addition to assisting the pilot, the copilot oversaw the aircraft's systems and communications. Behind them sat the electronic warfare officer, who operated the B–52's radar-jamming and other electronic countermeasures equipment. Beneath him, in the lower crew compartment, were the radar navigator, who served as bombardier, and the navigator, who used the aircraft's sophisticated systems to direct the aircraft along its preassigned flight path. More than 100 feet aft sat the tail gunner, the only enlisted man aboard; he manned the B–52's four radar-controlled, .50-caliber machine guns used for defense against enemy fighters.

Electronic Warfare Officer

Pilot

Copilot

Navigator

Radar Navigator

A Daniel Boone reconnaissance team flew to the site by helicopter to assess the effectiveness of the strike within minutes after the B–52s dropped their bomb loads. The team, led by Captain William Orthman, had been ordered to scout the area and pick up any survivors for interrogation. Orthman and his company commander, Captain Randolph Harrison, were specially briefed on the mission by a MACV officer who flew to their camp at Ban Me Thuot.

"We were told that we would go in and pick some of these guys up," said Harrison. "If there was anybody still alive out there they would be so stunned that all you would have to do is walk over and lead him by the arm to the helicopter.

"We had been told, as had everyone been told, that these carpet-bombing attacks by B–52s carrying conventional ordnance in the form of 500-pound or 750-pound bombs were totally devastating, that nothing could survive, Harrison said. "If they had a troop concentration there, it would be annihilated."

But Harrison began to have his doubts about the proclaimed effectiveness of the B–52 strikes when he debriefed the survivors of Orthman's team after the mission. Harrison said the team of two Americans and eleven Vietnamese went in literally before the dust from the bombing had settled. As they began running from the helicopters toward a nearby tree line for cover, they were virtually "annihilated" by North Vietnamese gunfire. "They were cut down before they could even get to the trees," said Harrison.

Orthman was hit immediately with two rounds in the stomach. As he crawled into a crater a gas grenade he was carrying ignited, burning his arm and back. The other American frantically radioed for the helicopters to come back and pick them up. "He was calling for help, begging them to come down and get him out, and that everybody was getting hit," said Harrison, who was monitoring the radio traffic. The transmission ended abruptly in midsentence, and all Harrison could hear was an indecipherable scream. One of the Vietnamese survivors later recounted that the man was shot in the head and died instantly.

When the rescue helicopters arrived at the site only two of the Vietnamese managed to scramble aboard. The wounded Orthman was saved by a crewman who dashed from the helicopter and dragged him back to the chopper. The body of the other American was left on the landing zone, along with the rest of the team.

When the battered survivors arrived back at base, Harrison's superiors immediately wanted to run another team into the area. But Harrison and the other team leaders refused when they were instructed to land in exactly the same spot where Orthman's team had been mauled. Three of the men were arrested for failure to obey orders, but no formal charges were brought against them. Higher authorities realized that the unavoidable publicity from a court-martial would sabotage the clandestine bombing of neutral Cambodia.

In spite of the debacle experienced by the Daniel Boone reconnaissance team, Washington believed the bombing strike had accomplished its goals of disrupting North Vietnamese activities in Cambodia and sending a strong signal of American resolve to Hanoi. The perceived success of the mission and the fact that it was not protested by Sihanouk emboldened the Nixon administration to strike again.

In an April 9 memo to the secretary of defense, the JCS identified fifteen Communist base sanctuaries along the Cambodian border, all ripe for further air attacks. The chiefs asserted that air strikes against these targets would be a "strategic blow of major proportions" which could "change the whole balance of forces in Vietnam" and "shorten the war."

The opportunity came on April 15, when a U.S. Navy EC–121 electronic reconnaissance aircraft was shot down by North Korean jets while on a routine intelligence-gathering mission off the coast of North Korea. Nixon's immediate reaction was to retaliate by bombing a North Korean airfield. But his advisers counseled restraint, suggesting that the aerial reconnaissance missions be resumed with combat escorts. The president agreed but curiously ordered a second round of bombing against North Vietnamese sanctuaries in Cambodia in retaliation. Nixon, who clung to the view that all Communist activities in Asia were centrally coordinated, explained in his memoirs that the second strike was intended as a further signal of American resolve to Communist leaders.

A second B–52 raid, code named Operation Lunch, hit Base Area 609, which straddled the borders of Cambodia, Laos, and South Vietnam. Soon after Operation Lunch additional strikes followed against other Cambodian base areas taken from the JCS list. During the next fourteen months, 3,875 sorties were flown by U.S. Air Force B–52s. They dropped a total of 108,823 tons of bombs on six base areas in Cambodia, each identified by a mealtime code name—Breakfast, Lunch, Dinner, Snack, Supper, and Dessert. The entire operation soon became known by the code name Menu.

As predicted Hanoi did not publicly protest the B–52 raids, nor did Prince Sihanouk. But the administration's fear that news of the Cambodian raids would leak to the press was confirmed when the *New York Times* published an article by military reporter William Beecher outlining the rough details of Operation Breakfast on its front page on May 9. The article, which quoted administration officials as the source of the information, drew little notice from outside the administration and was soon forgotten. But Nixon was furious. A few days before, Beecher had also written an article revealing Nixon and Kissinger's deliberations over a response to the EC–121 incident. The president, fearful of the consequences of further leaks, ordered an investigation by the FBI.

The day Beecher's article on Breakfast appeared, Kissinger instructed FBI director J. Edgar Hoover to find Beecher's source in the administration. Suspicion was cast upon Kissinger's own NSC aide, Morton Halperin, whose support for the war in Vietnam was questioned. Later that day the FBI placed a wiretap on Halperin's phone, a surveillance that lasted for twenty-one months. Within weeks the wiretaps grew to include other White House aides and Washington reporters—all in the name of national security. The wiretaps represented the first in a series of questionable actions that later came back to haunt the president during the Watergate investigations.

Wheeler himself later remarked that Nixon was obsessed with secrecy in the planning and execution of the Menu B–52 raids. "His instructions were of a general nature but very emphatic," Wheeler said. "He wanted the matter held in the greatest secrecy," said the chairman of the JCS. "I recall the president saying this to me not just once, but either to me or in my presence at least a half a dozen times.

"In implementation of the president's instructions with regard to security, it was directed that all communications on the subject be very closely held and transmitted by specially secure channels, with distribution limited to named addressees only on a strict need-to-know basis," said Wheeler.

A web of secrecy

Throughout the raids the Pentagon employed an elaborate dual reporting scheme using cover targets in South Vietnam to hide the fact that the B–52s were actually bombing Cambodia. "Many, if not all, of those base areas straddled the border," said Wheeler. "Part of the base area would be in South Vietnam and part would be in Cambodia." Therefore, the covert strikes were often flown within the immediate proximity of legitimate targets within South Vietnam.

A special security, or "back channel," communications system was established to report the information on strikes inside Cambodia. A B–52 strike on a target in South Vietnam in the general vicinity of the desired Cambodian target would be requested by MACV through normal command and communication channels. Simultaneously, MACV would request a strike against the real target through this back-channel network.

These messages were addressed to only a handful of military leaders, including Abrams; the commander-in-chief, Pacific (CINCPAC) in Honolulu; the commander of the B–52 units stationed at Andersen Air Force Base in Guam whose pilots flew the bulk of the Menu missions; the commander of the Strategic Air Command in Omaha, Nebraska; and the Joint Chiefs of Staff in Washington. All messages were stamped "Eyes Only" for the addressees. Robert Seamans, the secretary of the Air Force, was not informed of the strikes, nor was General John P. Ryan, vice chief of staff of the Air Force, until he replaced Gen. McConnell as chief of staff on August 1, 1969.

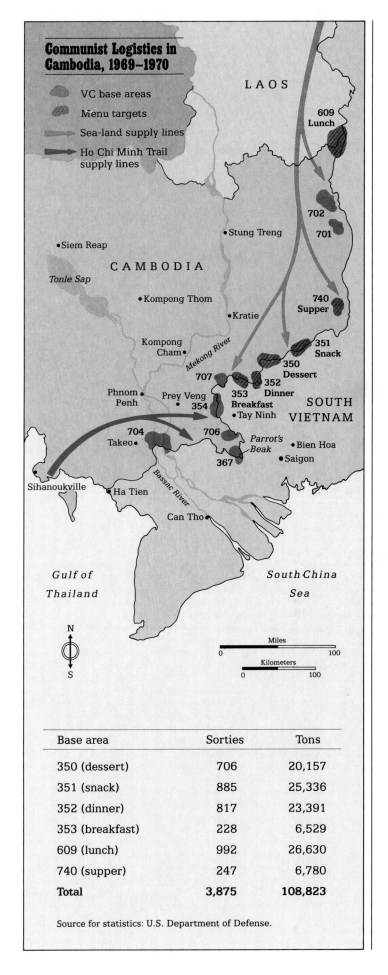

Base area	Sorties	Tons
350 (dessert)	706	20,157
351 (snack)	885	25,336
352 (dinner)	817	23,391
353 (breakfast)	228	6,529
609 (lunch)	992	26,630
740 (supper)	247	6,780
Total	**3,875**	**108,823**

Source for statistics: U.S. Department of Defense.

141

A huge cloud of smoke suggests the power of a B–52 strike. This one hit the Iron Triangle in South Vietnam in 1965, four years before the first raids into Cambodia. Because they released their payloads at 30,000 feet, B–52 bombers could not be seen or heard by the enemy on the ground.

The 11th Armored Cavalry withdraws from Cambodia in June 1970. Like Operation Menu, the May ground incursion into Cambodia was designed to destroy Communist sanctuaries.

Once a Menu request was approved, the mission was flown so that on their way to the actual target in Cambodia the aircraft would pass over the South Vietnamese cover target. During and after the mission, all reports from the aircraft crew and the crews of the ground radar stations that guided the B–52s to their targets were doctored so that they did not reveal the fact that the targets struck were actually in Cambodia.

Normal procedures for Arc Light B–52 strikes in South Vietnam involved a request from MACV that included a list of targets to be struck over a twenty-four-hour period. The request included the map coordinates of each target, the total number of aircraft to be employed, the exact time each aircraft was to reach its target, and a mission code number. This request was forwarded to CINCPAC and the Joint Chiefs for their review. If there were no objections to the strikes, approval was given to Strategic Air Command headquarters in Omaha, Nebraska, to work out the oper-

ational details and assign B–52 units to the targets. SAC's commander then issued an execution order for the strikes through his field commander in Guam. The 3d Air Division, later supplanted by the 8th Air Force, headquartered in Guam, controlled all B–52 operations in Southeast Asia. SAC B–52s operated out of Guam, U Tapao air base in Thailand, and later Okinawa. Acting on SAC's orders, the 8th Air Force issued all its units a fragmentary order, or "frag," which acted as a profile for the mission. The frag included such factors as ground control check-in points, time over target, altitude, and bombing tactics. The strike request and frag were the only two documents that included the target coordinates.

Requests for Menu strikes followed roughly the same procedure except that they were sent through secret back channels. In addition to the regular target coordinates for the next day's mission, MACV transmitted a special top-secret request that included the coordinates for the desired targets in Cambodia. These requests were reviewed by CINCPAC and then the JCS. Once a request was approved by the JCS, a memorandum was sent to the secretary of defense for authority to execute the strikes.

A November 20, 1969, memo from the JCS for a Menu strike that was forwarded to and initialed by Secretary Laird shows how the procedure worked.

The concept of operation is to employ 41 B–52s against Menu targets on each of the two nights during the week of November 23. The remaining available aircraft will be employed to strike cover targets as well as targets elsewhere in-country and in Laos. Strikes on these latter targets will provide a resemblance to normal operations thereby providing a credible story for replies to press inquiries.

Since Menu strikes were always combined with legitimate strikes in South Vietnam, MACV had two sets of strike authorizations for the Arc Light missions—one for a set number of targets in South Vietnam and another secret authorization for those aircraft that would be diverted against targets in Cambodia. B–52s assigned to Menu targets received the same mission-identifier code as the original South Vietnamese targets and retained the same time-over-target schedule so as to maintain a semblance of normality. The only alteration to the standard procedures would be the diversion of the aircraft by radar controllers once they neared their targets.

"The pilots and navigators of the strike aircraft were all briefed," said Wheeler. "They knew where they were supposed to go." Lieutenant General Alvan C. Gillem II, commander of the 3d Air Division on Guam, personally briefed those B–52 pilots and navigators selected for the mission. Very few other SAC personnel at the base knew about the secret bombings.

Once they were over South Vietnam, all B–52 Arc Light missions were directed to their targets by all-weather bombing-control radars code named Combat Skyspot. There were four of these sites, one in each of the four military regions (MR) in South Vietnam. Manned by SAC personnel, the radars were under the operational control of the 7th Air Force, which controlled all aircraft operating in South Vietnam.

Employing sophisticated radar bombing equipment, the Skyspot radar controllers directed B–52 crews along a designated route to a bomb drop point, providing heading and speed corrections as necessary en route. Skyspot ground controllers also computed the ballistics for the bomb loads of the B–52s and provided air crews with the precise moment to drop their ordnance.

For missions in South Vietnam, Skyspot radar operators were provided with Arc Light target coordinates through normal message channels. For Menu bombing operations, however, a representative from the Strategic Air Command Advanced Echelon (SACADVON) at MACV headquarters in Saigon flew directly to the radar site with the revised coordinates.

Major Hal Knight, the supervisor of a Skyspot radar site in MR IV during early 1970, recalled the special procedures for Menu bombing runs. Knight periodically received a phone call from SACADVON in Saigon the morning after he received the normal frag orders for Arc Light strikes for that evening. The caller told him to meet a special courier at the site's airfield later that day. "It was usually around three in the afternoon," said Knight.

The courier handed Knight a plain manila envelope and instructed him to take it back to his office and lock it in his desk. According to his orders, at 6:00 P.M. Knight opened the envelope containing the new target coordinates and passed the information along to the duty controller and crew who plotted the new coordinates on their computers. After the bombing run was completed he was to take all the paperwork from the revised mission and burn it the next morning. At 9:00 A.M. he called a number in Saigon—SACADVON headquarters—and said simply: "The ball game is over."

Knight and his crew then completed the paperwork for the regular mission called for in the original frag orders from MACV. "We worked up the computer tape and everything for the mission that had been fragged," he said. "Then I took the poststrike report which had the coordinates of the mission that had been fragged on them, attached the computer tape to it, and filled out the rest of the form as if the target had actually been run."

This report included information for the actual bombing run, such as air speed and heading at time of bomb release, altitude, weather over the target, and other details that would not give away the actual coordinates of the strike. Knight then sent this doctored poststrike report, which was classified secret, through normal channels to Saigon, where it was reviewed by layer upon layer of officials. The doctored information was then filed in the Defense Department's vast data bank.

The B–52s actually bombed in the general area of the original targets in South Vietnam, normally not farther away than twenty to thirty kilometers, so that there would be little discrepancy in fuel consumption figures and air miles logged. Once they had pulled away from the target, air crews filed a routine radio report back to the unit command post. The report included the aircraft's call sign, a prearranged code word to indicate whether the mission was successful or not, the time over target, and the amount of fuel left for the return trip. There was no mention of the divert order by Skyspot ground controllers.

Intelligence officers at the base used this information to fill out the standard operational report—OPREP–4. This report included all the standard bookkeeping information, which was fed into official SAC and Pentagon records. Since the intelligence officers filling out the OPREP–4 report were unaware of the diversion, the report was filed and forwarded through the normal communications chain as if the mission actually had been flown against the original target in South Vietnam.

Meanwhile, only a small group of approved officials saw the real reports of the missions, which were communicated through the secret back-channel network. The messages, stamped "Eyes Only" for the addressees, went "from MACV to the chairman of the JCS, with information copies to CINCPAC, CINCSAC [commander-in-chief of the Strategic Air Command], and that was it," said Gen. Ryan.

Good Look, Patio, and Freedom Deal

These special reporting procedures were employed for subsequent clandestine bombing operations ordered by the Nixon administration as Washington turned to air power more and more to buy time for the Vietnamese to take over the fighting. Bombing operations were seen as a means of stabilizing the situation on the battlefield while U.S. combat troops withdrew from South Vietnam and as a warning to Hanoi of Washington's determination to obtain an acceptable settlement to the war.

On February 17, 1970, U.S. B–52s were used for the first time against Pathet Lao forces in and around the Plain of Jars in northeastern Laos. Laotian prime minister Souvanna Phouma, seeking U.S. assistance to blunt a Communist offensive to recapture the Plain of Jars, requested the bombing operation, code named Good Look.

Until 1969, U.S. air operations in Laos were mainly centered against the Ho Chi Minh Trail in the country's southern panhandle. American tactical aircraft had also flown a limited number of missions in northeastern Laos against the upper reaches of the infiltration network and occasionally in support of Laotian ground forces in Vang Pao's clandestine army. But with the inception of Operation Good Look the air war in northeastern Laos changed dramatically.

From the first mission on February 17, 1970, until the end of the operation on April 17, 1973, U.S. B–52s flew 2,518 sorties and dropped 58,374 tons of bombs. Initially, the B–52 crews employed their onboard radar bombing systems to locate and strike targets. Later a Skyspot radar system, installed at Udorn, Thailand, directed Good Look missions.

All of the missions flown before April 26, 1972, employed cover targets in southern Laos or South Vietnam for routine reporting. All message traffic to Washington on the actual targets was classified top secret and processed through special security channels. According to Gen. Ryan, the only difference from Operation Menu was that all the members of the B–52 crews knew that they were actually bombing in northern Laos. "There was no attempt to overfly [a cover] target," he said.

Three months after Operation Good Look began, the U.S. secretly expanded its bombing operations in Cambodia. On April 17, 1970, Gen. Abrams requested special authority to employ tactical aircraft against Communist troop and supply movements along an area in northeast Cambodia within thirteen kilometers of the South Viet-

namese border. Since the targets were highly mobile and widely scattered, Abrams and 7th Air Force leaders preferred to employ tactical aircraft rather than B–52s.

The JCS relayed White House approval for the strikes to Abrams on April 20, just ten days before the invasion of Cambodia by U.S. and South Vietnamese forces. The tactical air strikes, code named Patio, began on April 24. The following day, Abrams received approval to extend the boundaries for the strikes to twenty-nine kilometers within Cambodia. U.S. Air Force tactical aircraft flew a total of 156 sorties during Operation Patio, which ended in June.

All requests, instructions, and authorizations pertaining to Patio missions were handled on a closely held basis. After-action and bomb-damage-assessment reports were transmitted through the same back channels that were used for Menu strikes. Unlike Menu operations, however, the majority of Patio strikes were not covered by phony targets.

Patio strikes were curtailed on May 18, 1970, just a few days before Operation Menu also came to a halt after fourteen months of bombing by B–52s. But the halting of these two operations did not spell an end to the secret bombings. After U.S. troops were pulled out of Cambodia on June 30, Washington stepped up its use of American tactical fighters to support South Vietnamese troops that remained in the country and to assist Cambodian forces who had now come under attack by North Vietnamese units. Since the Cooper-Church Amendment prohibited U.S. ground troops from operating in Cambodia or Laos after June 30, U.S. air power was called to help halt the Communist onslaught.

Code named Freedom Deal, these air strikes were restricted to a forty-eight-kilometer–deep area between the South Vietnamese border and the Mekong River. But within two months the strikes were secretly extended to include targets west of the Mekong River. U.S. Air Force tactical fighter-bombers were soon operating in direct support of beleaguered Cambodian forces on the ground, although such strikes were officially denied by the U.S. government. These tactical air strikes outside the normal Freedom Deal operating areas were recorded using false coordinates to hide their existence.

Captain George R. Moses, an intelligence officer with the 31st Tactical Fighter Wing stationed at Tuy Hoa, South Vietnam, during most of 1970, was intimately involved in the falsification of the Freedom Deal reports. Moses was responsible for briefing and debriefing pilots who flew missions in Cambodia and poststrike intelligence reporting. A few weeks after the invasion of Cambodia, Moses and other intelligence officers received a message from 7th Air Force headquarters informing them that any bombing missions west of the Mekong River would not be reported as such.

On these missions the air crews were either assigned to

The Rescue of Black Lion 177

by John F. Guilmartin

At approximately 1:00 P.M. on May 18, 1966, Black Lion 177, a Navy F–4B Phantom II from the U.S.S. *Kittyhawk*, was hit and set ablaze by antiaircraft fire from a small valley in Communist-controlled eastern Laos. Disregarding their wingman's frantic calls to bail out, the jet's two crewmen struggled to maintain control of the damaged aircraft. At the last possible moment, with the Phantom trailing an enormous plume of flame, they ejected about two miles from the North Vietnamese border. The pilot, Lieutenant Commander Carl Sommers, landed safely several miles south of the valley where the aircraft had been hit. His radar observer, Lieutenant Commander Bill Sullivan, was not so fortunate. His parachute malfunctioned, and when he struck the ground at the southern edge of the valley, he injured his lower back.

When hit, Black Lion 177 was making a low pass over the wreckage of an Air Force O–1E Forward Air Control aircraft to mark the site for an oncoming search-and-rescue task force. I was part of this force as pilot of an HH–3E Jolly Green Giant helicopter. My aircraft, designated "low bird," or primary rescue helicopter, along with another HH–3E and four Sandy rescue-escort A–1E fighters, had scrambled from Nakhon Phanom Royal Thai Air Force Base forty-five minutes earlier when the FAC aircraft was reported down. Although we had not heard—and would never hear—from the FAC pilots, their loss put us only minutes away from where Black Lion had crashed, offering us a chance to rescue its crew.

The faster-flying A–1E Sandies, led by Captain Elmer Nelson, arrived at the site ahead of us and quickly located Lieutenant Commander Sommers by homing in on his survival radio transmissions. He was in a relatively secure position on a ridge line just over a crest from Communist antiaircraft emplacements. Elmer told him to sit tight; help was on the way.

Within twenty minutes, we had skirted enemy antiaircraft positions and were headed for Sommers. Elmer detached two Sandies to escort my crew in for the pickup while our back-up helicopter, or "high bird," remained nearby in a safe orbit. As we started in, Nelson called for Sommers to light a flare and my crew immediately spotted it. To save time, Elmer suggested that I dispense with the usual preliminary pass over the survivor to gauge enemy reaction. We had worked together before, and I trusted his judgment. We jettisoned our auxiliary tanks and went in without incident. By 1:40 P.M. Carl Sommers was aboard, hugging flight mechanic Staff Sergeant Mike Holloway.

Meanwhile, the Sandies were having trouble locating Lieutenant Commander Sullivan. They were receiving only sporadic radio transmissions from Sullivan because, unknown to us, he was running for his life. Enemy troops had observed his descent and had set out in pursuit before he hit the ground. Normally, I would have pulled out of the area to minimize exposure while at low air speed and altitude, but under the circumstances my crew—Holloway, copilot Major Don Vavra, and pararescueman Staff Sergeant Dennis Kraft—and I decided to bend the rules. We knew that Sullivan was injured and might need help quickly; departing the pickup area would waste precious minutes. Keeping low to avoid the 57MM and 37MM batteries beyond the ridge lines, we stayed and searched along with the Sandies.

Our determination paid off an hour later. The Sandies made voice contact with an exhausted Sullivan just long enough to fix his position. He was at the head of a box canyon only one ridge line from the valley where Black Lion had been hit; we were less than a minute away.

Elmer directed us in and told Sullivan to set off a flare. Kraft, looking out the helicopter's left window, saw the smoke and called for me to turn left thirty degrees. Elmer called for another flare, and as we headed in on the treetops, Vavra spotted its smoke fifty yards away. For the first time, we picked up Sullivan's radio transmissions; his voice was that of a man at the end of his rope. About 150 yards from his position, we received enemy fire from below. Kraft lurched backward from his window, hit in the right elbow. This was no time to hesitate. Holloway pulled Kraft away from the window and handed his M16 to Sommers, assigning him the duties of left window gunner. Following Holloway's directions, I worked the helicopter in over the dissipating smoke of the flare. Sullivan radioed for us to hold in a hover and Holloway ran the hoist down; a struggling figure burst from the dense underbrush 150 feet below. As Sullivan wrapped his arms around the tree penetrator, Sommers opened fire on Communist soldiers who had appeared less than 50 yards away. Sullivan reached the door of the helicopter with blood on his lips and passed out from shock.

We pulled away amid flak bursts from enemy batteries. Too low on fuel to return to Nakhon Phanom and with wounded aboard, I headed for the Khe Sanh Special Forces camp in South Vietnam, escorted by two Sandies. Though sobered by the loss of the two Air Force FACs and Kraft's injury, we took comfort in knowing that we had beaten the odds: Our tightly knit team of rescue helicopters and air commando A–1s had managed to pluck the crew of Black Lion 177 from deep within Indian Country.

John F. Guilmartin served two tours in Indochina as a Jolly Green Giant rescue helicopter pilot, in 1965–1966 and 1975. He is currently associate professor of history at Ohio State University.

hit a fixed target or ordered to rendezvous with a Forward Air Controller (FAC) or Cambodia Forward Air Guide flying in a small observation plane, who would assign them targets and mark them with small smoke rockets. Normally, the FAC would radio the coordinates of the target to the fighter-bomber air crews after the mission was completed so that they could file them in their poststrike report. But for strikes outside of the Freedom Deal operating zone, the FACs were instructed not to pass coordinates to the air crews over the radio.

When the aircraft landed, Moses would debrief the pilot. "We would get to the point where he mentioned strike coordinates and he would say that the FAC hadn't given any," recounted Moses. They would then ascertain the aircraft's rough position during the bombing strike from the pilot's record of the aircraft's own navigational system. "I would copy these down and go to a map and establish as close as I could exactly where he had been," said Moses. If his calculations confirmed that the strike was indeed outside the normal operating boundaries, Moses was instructed to contact the 7th Air Force's Tactical Air Control Center (TACC) at Tan Son Nhut air base.

"I would go ahead and fill out my complete report leaving blank the area for coordinates," he said. "I would then go to a telephone with a direct line to TACC and say: 'Captain Moses, Tuy Hoa, reporting coordinates position number XXX.' I would hold for a moment and the guy would come back and say: 'Okay, target coordinates X Charlie' and reel off six digits. I would write those coordinates out on my report and send them over to the message center."

Moses said the coordinates that TACC personnel provided for the intelligence officers were those for uninhabited areas in the Freedom Deal zone of operations. Defense Department records indicate that out of more than 8,000 combat sorties flown in Cambodia between July 1970 and February 1971, approximately 44 percent, or 3,634 sorties, were flown outside the Freedom Deal boundaries. On February 17, 1971, the special reporting procedures for these missions were discontinued.

Although the air strikes continued at an even greater level, by late 1972 Congressional criticism of the bombing was coming to a head, fueled by revelations to Congress by former servicemen of the earlier secret Menu operations. In March 1973, acting on information supplied by the veterans, members of the Senate Armed Services Committee asked the Defense Department to provide them with the records of U.S. air operations in Cambodia. The official records provided to the committee by the Pentagon, from which any mention of Menu strikes was withheld, showed no U.S. air operations in Cambodia before May 1970. Congressional critics were not convinced and continued their investigations.

Meanwhile, in June, both houses of Congress adopted amendments to cut off all funds for further bombing in Cambodia. The measure was transmitted to the White House on June 26. Facing continued opposition to the war and the daily revelations of the Watergate hearings, then in full swing, Nixon agreed to halt the bombing within forty-five days, on August 15, 1973.

Less than two weeks after Nixon's grudging acquiescence to Congressional demands, the full story of the secret bombing in Cambodia was finally revealed. On July 12, the Senate Armed Services Committee opened hearings on the nomination of General George Brown to become chief of staff of the Air Force. Gen. Brown was commander of the 7th Air Force and MACV's deputy for air operations, a dual position he had held since August 1968. In a closed session, Brown admitted that air strikes over Cambodia had occurred prior to May 1970. Outraged that the Pentagon had presented them with falsified records, the senators called for a full investigation.

During eight days of testimony in late July and early August, the committee listened to administration officials who recounted the chain of events and attempted to justify the decision to bomb Cambodia. Gen. Wheeler, since retired, testified on the military effectiveness of the bombing missions. "This concentration of firepower—selectively applied—against the enemy's Cambodian sanctuaries, harassed the enemy, destroyed his supplies, kept him off balance, and relieved pressure on allied forces," he said. "The enemy was forced to shift his forces and disperse his supplies over a greater area, imposing increased hardships and frustration on him." Wheeler also pointed out that from the outset, the bombing had resulted in fewer casualties among U.S. troops. "Casualties, which had been running about 250 a week, dropped to about half that number," he said. "And they continued to decline through the rest of the year."

The former chairman of the JCS also testified to the care that was taken to avoid civilian casualties during the missions, noting that only those base areas which were known to be relatively unpopulated by Cambodian civilians were targeted. Wheeler also reminded the committee that Defense Secretary Laird had personally informed a number of senior Congressional leaders of the secret bombings, including Senate Majority Leader Everett Dirksen and Senators Richard Russell and John Stennis, the chairman and ranking member of the Senate Armed Services Committee, respectively, who gave their tacit support.

Senator Stuart Symington, however, challenged Wheeler's assessment of the military effectiveness of the bombing as well as the means that were employed. "From a military point of view it would appear that the raids accomplished very little of a positive nature—since we subsequently had to send ground troops into Cambodia— and on the negative side they apparently caused the North Vietnamese to expand their area of control in Cambodia, thus setting in motion a chain of events which has brought the Cambodian communists to the gates of Phnom Penh.

"In retrospect it is difficult to find any redeeming features of this vast surreptitious bombing campaign," Symington told Wheeler. The Missouri Democrat said the whole operation raised serious questions about "official deception."

"I personally think it is unconstitutional," he said, "because you dropped over a hundred thousand tons [of bombs] on this country and I had no idea you dropped one ton, nor did other members of this committee except those chosen few, all of whom, I might add, supported the war."

The decision to expend funds to bomb targets in a neutral country without Congressional approval and the falsification of government records on the basis of security concerns raised serious questions as to the constitutionality of the actions. The question of the legality of the secret bombings in Cambodia, however, became moot when the House Judiciary Committee voted against a proposal to include the administration's falsification of records in the articles of impeachment against President Nixon by a 26-to-12 vote. The committee's vote also left unanswered the questions concerning the effectiveness and consequences of the operation.

Despite their awesome power, B–52 strikes against Communist base areas exhibited all the effectiveness of trying to swat a fly with a sledgehammer. B–52 pilots dropped their bombs on geographic coordinates based on intelligence reports of suspected enemy camps. While they certainly scored some initial successes against large base areas and storage dumps, the Communists had become adept at defending against such efforts after more than five years of American bombing raids in North Vietnam and Laos.

By 1970, the North Vietnamese had become masters of camouflage and deception, using the dense jungle vegetation to mask their roads and supply caches from aerial observation. By dispersing their camps and supply dumps over large areas they lessened their vulnerability to air attacks. Labor gangs and repair crews were also in high evidence, waiting for the smoke to clear so that they could quickly repair any damage along the roads and trails. At best, the bombings forced the North Vietnamese to divert more time and attention to air defense measures and only hindered, without seriously diminishing, their ability to mount large-scale operations across the border into South Vietnam.

While the air strikes against Communist sanctuaries in Cambodia gave U.S. and South Vietnamese military forces a brief respite to carry out the process of Vietnamization, they irrevocably expanded the scope of the war beyond Vietnam's borders—with disastrous consequences for Cambodia. Coupled with the May 1970 invasion by U.S. and South Vietnamese forces, the Menu bombings ignited full-scale war in Cambodia. The U.S. threw its weight behind Lon Nol, the pro-Western prime minister who overthrew neutralist leader Sihanouk in March 1970. Hanoi

Air Force Major Hal Knight (background) testifies in July 1973 before Senator Stuart Symington (right) and other members of a Senate subcommittee on his role in Operation Menu.

responded by stepping up its backing for the indigenous Khmer Rouge Communist movement.

As the Communists gradually increased their control of the country, the U.S. was forced to devote more of its shrinking resources in Southeast Asia to help stem the tide. U.S. aircraft, including B–52s, were called in to hit enemy targets in heavily populated areas, creating large numbers of refugees. As a former U.S. military attaché in Phnom Penh reported, the areas around the Mekong River were so full of bomb craters from B–52 strikes by 1973 that they "looked like the valleys of the moon." What had begun as a covert show of force intended to prod Hanoi into accepting American terms for a negotiated settlement of the war and buy time for the South Vietnamese ended up costing Cambodia its peace and, ultimately, its independence.

The Secret War of the POWs

There was one common thread to the many wars
America fought in Southeast Asia: Whether it was
the war of attrition in South Vietnam, the secret
bombing of Cambodia, the secret war in Laos,
SOG's cross-border operations, or the Rolling Thunder bombing campaign over North Vietnam, all were
managed in detail and overly supervised from headquarters high above or far removed from the battle.

But there was one war in Southeast Asia that was
planned and managed by the men who did the
fighting and dying: the secret war fought by America's prisoners of war. They fought it to survive
captivity, to unite against their captors, and to return
home with honor. They fought their private, secret
war so fiercely that they became prisoners *at* war
more than prisoners *of* war. Indeed, one of the senior
POWs and heroes of that experience, then Navy
Commander Richard A. Stratton, entitled a book
about his six years in captivity *Prisoner at War*.

As casualties mounted in Southeast Asia and
Americans grew increasingly divided about the Viet-

nam War, one issue united the country: America wanted those prisoners of war home. By the time the Paris peace accords were signed in early 1973, more than 5 million Americans were wearing wristbands inscribed with the name of a serviceman who was either missing in action or known to be a prisoner of war. There were 4,383 of them. For every 12 servicemen killed in Southeast Asia, another was a POW or an MIA. Only 1 in 6 of the POWs and MIAs was ever accounted for.

Only 649 ever came home—28 managed to escape, 30 were released early by their captors, and 566 servicemen and 25 civilians returned after the 1973 peace accords. In addition to those who escaped, 457 came home from North Vietnam, 9 from Laos, 2 from China, and 153 from South Vietnam. Eighty POWs died while in captivity, 1 of every 9 of the men known to have been taken prisoner.

Some men survived almost ten years—some after being kept in solitary confinement for more than three years, a few for more than four years, and one man for fifty-eight months. Seven of every ten men taken prisoner had already been severely wounded or injured by the time they were captured, yet almost all were then tortured in the most inhumane, crude, and senseless way. Some went insane. The rest subsisted on a diet of little more than insipid, vermin-infested, unspiced, boiled pumpkin or cabbage soup—240 consecutive bowls of it for one prisoner who kept count. Most suffered from diarrhea, dysentery, scurvy, beriberi, or hepatitis, confined to bare, unventilated cells that stank of urine, vomit, blood, and feces. Rats, mice, cockroaches, ants, spiders, and mosquitoes were the full-time landlords in the prisoners' cells; the Vietcong, Pathet Lao, or North Vietnamese guards were just the temporary caretakers.

But their rules were strict. The North Vietnamese demanded absolute obedience—and silence. No whistling, singing, or loud talking within a cell; no communication whatsoever between cells. Just silence. When new prisoners tried to communicate—whispering to someone in an adjacent cell or sneaking a message to another prisoner—they learned quickly that their captors spent much of their time looking for excuses to "punish" them, and catching a prisoner communicating was their favorite excuse for more torture.

The punishment hurt beyond comprehension. The most common form in North Vietnamese prisons was putting a man "on the ropes." With hardly an exception, every POW went through it within days of being captured. It was how the North Vietnamese established control, making brutally clear that they held the power of life and death over the POWs and would not hesitate to use it. They put every new POW on the ropes until he "broke"—until he begged for mercy, promised to obey, agreed to "submit"—and surrendered information beyond the "name, rank, serial number, and date of birth" required under the Geneva Convention.

The first interrogation session was usually held in a dark, red-tiled cell known as Room 18 of what came to be called the New Guy Village, or Heartbreak Hotel, part of Hoa Lo Prison, a huge, forty-year-old French jail in downtown Hanoi. Hoa Lo translated roughly to "fiery furnace" or "the place of the cooking fires"—but the first POWs, with gallows humor, quickly dubbed it the Hanoi Hilton.

A POW was invariably introduced to North Vietnamese torture after being bound hand and foot. Seated on a foot-high wooden stool and looking up at an interrogator sitting behind a small, plain table, he was told at some length that he was a war criminal with no rights under the Geneva Convention because there had been no declaration of war. (This was a false assertion, since the Geneva Convention, which North Vietnam signed in 1959, refers not just to declared wars but to any armed conflict.) When he refused to answer questions that went beyond the simple identification required by the Geneva Convention—questions like, "What were you flying?", "Where did you take off from?", "What was your target?", and "How many chickens does your father own?"—the prisoner was told he would have to be "severely punished." (Sometimes the prisoners were not "told" first, and the punishment just began; either way, the message was effective.)

Punishment usually began with a sudden "ka-thwump," an unexpected, sharp blow to the side of the head from a guard standing behind the prisoner, leaving the prisoner lying on the tile floor wondering how he had arrived there so rapidly. The guard working the prisoner over quickly pulled the POW's arms behind his back, turned his palms outward, put manacles on the wrists so tightly that the wrists could not right themselves, and bound the arms tightly together with tourniquet-like loops above the elbows. Then he bound the elbows together, slipped the rope through the wrist manacles, set the prisoner up on his butt, and lifted the POW's arms as high as he could get them to go, thus forcing the head over into a bowed position. The guard then ran a parachute shroud line or rope from the wrist manacles to and around the POW's neck and tied that tightly to his ankles until the prisoner looked like a squashed pretzel. He admonished the prisoner to think more deeply about his crimes, told him to call out "Bao Cao" ("I have something to report") when he was ready to talk, and left the room.

Different interrogators had different versions of putting a prisoner on the ropes. One of the worst was putting him "on the wall"—looping a rope through the wrist bonds, pulling them up behind the prisoner's neck, stringing the

---

Hanoi Hilton

Although there are no actual photographs documenting the abuse of American prisoners of war in North Vietnam, a 1987 film entitled *Hanoi Hilton* attempted to recreate accurately the harrowing experiences —including torture—of American POWs held in North Vietnam's infamous Hoa Lo Prison. To do this, the filmmakers hired thousands of Asian extras and constructed a replica of the Hanoi prison— exact to the last detail—at a former Veterans Administration Hospital in West Los Angeles. The film's director also hired a number of Vietnam War veterans, some of whom had been held captive at Hoa Lo Prison during the war, to serve as technical advisers.

Actors recreate North Vietnamese torture of an American prisoner at Hoa Lo in a still photograph from the movie Hanoi Hilton.

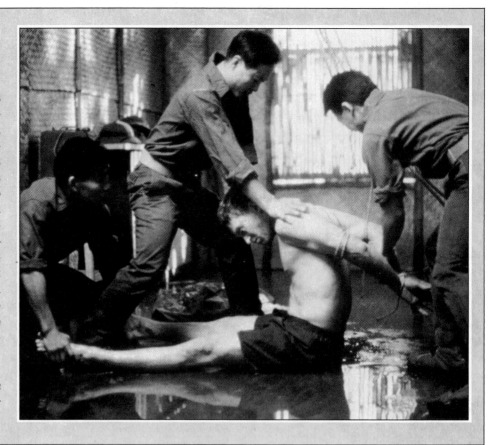

rope over a hook in the ceiling or bolt in the wall, and pulling it taut until the POW's arms were raised behind his back to the point where his shoulders often were pulled out of their sockets.

On the ropes or on the wall, the men were simply left to writhe on the floor or hang in agony—until they screamed out "Bao Cao" and talked.

Recalling his first experience on the ropes a few days after he was shot down on February 20, 1967, Navy Ensign Gary Thornton said, "The North Vietnamese had discovered that 'pain is a wonderful intimidator'; and we discovered that pain reinforces pain. The body is not meant to be in these kinds of positions; your chest starts crackling and feels like it's coming apart at the sternum, and things get increasingly worse. The absence of circulation is a terrifying thing. It starts off as kind of a dull ache, then it grows to a throb, then it's a red hot throb, then just constant, white hot, excruciating pain. And you're claustrophobic by that time and begin to wonder, 'How long can anybody endure this?' " Pain and fear reinforced each other. Thornton recalls at one point using his peripheral vision to glance back up and "seeing some little black clubs sticking up behind my head and literally doing a double-take: 'My God, those are my arms!' " He wondered, "At what point do they have to be amputated?"

Most of the POWs held out for a few hours; a few held out for a week; one or two, it is said, made it for ten days. But they all submitted. "Even an ensign can learn," Thornton jokes today about the first time he broke.

Prisoners in North Vietnam were, for the most part, aviators. During escape-and-evasion training they had learned the POW Code of Conduct, which had evolved from the Korean War. During that conflict, U.S. prisoners of war had no guidelines for the behavior expected of them in captivity, and as many as 70 percent of the roughly 6,000 Americans held prisoner in North Korea were later found to have "collaborated to some degree" with their captors as a result of "brainwashing" or other bestial treatment. The prisoners often had refused to be organized by their superior officers, and the weak were left to fend for themselves while some of the sick, wounded, and dying were preyed upon and often robbed of their rations by some of their healthier comrades. Men held prisoner by the Chinese or North Koreans never organized; morale withered. There were no escapes even though security in most of the POW camps was minimal. Almost 40 percent of the Korean War POWs died in captivity. The conduct of the American POWs in the Korean War, in short, was almost as shocking as their maltreatment, and from that experience grew the Code of Conduct that guided—and yet haunted—Americans held captive in North Vietnam.

The code stated that if captured, a serviceman would "keep faith with my fellow prisoners" and "give no information or take part in any action which might be harmful to my comrades." "If I am senior, I will take command," and "If not [senior], I will obey the lawful orders of those appointed over me and will back them up in every way." And it provided specific guidelines on how to handle interrogation: "When questioned, should I become a prisoner of war, I am bound to give only name, rank, service number, and date of birth. I will evade answering further questions to the utmost of my ability. I will make no oral or written statements disloyal to my country or its allies or harmful to their cause."

What haunted the POWs tortured in North Vietnam was the word *bound*. The men interpreted that to mean "I *swear* to give only name, rank, service number, and date of birth." Thus, when they broke and gave more, they suffered not just from the pain of physical torture, but also from guilt.

(After the Vietnam War, a special review panel convened to study the Code of Conduct and recommended only one change: The word *required* was substituted for *bound*. The change made clear that a prisoner of war under torture was allowed to give more than name, rank, service number, and date of birth without loss of honor or guilt resulting from moral dilemma. President Jimmy Carter signed the revised Code of Conduct on November 5, 1977.)

In Hanoi in the mid-1960s, POWs under torture fell back to a natural first line of defense: When they finally "talked," they waffled, evaded, hedged, and lied. Sometimes it worked; sometimes it did not. But having broken once, the men were tortured again and again—to establish control, to extract information, to punish, and to elicit statements that could be used for propaganda. Almost all of the POWs, for instance, ended up signing some kind of confession or apology for crimes against humanity, although most managed to word it in a way that made clear the statements were products of incredible duress.

Still, the guilt remained because they broke. Their mental despair was as painful as the physical hurt. And their first instinct—once let off the ropes, finished with the first round of interrogation, and left alone to begin healing—was to establish contact with a fellow POW, to share the guilt, to admit having been broken, to ask for forgiveness, and simply to communicate with a rational human being.

The first contact was usually a whispered message from an adjacent or nearby cell, but new POWs quickly learned that the earliest prisoners, the fliers who had arrived at Hoa Lo in 1964 and early 1965, had developed a far more sophisticated and much safer communications system. It was called the tap code, and as soon as contact could be established, new prisoners were told to memorize it, use it, and pass it immediately to any other prisoner they could contact.

Communications: the key to survival

This secret communications system became the blood of POW life, and it proved to be the key to their survival. Its success stemmed from its simplicity. It was based on a twenty-five-letter alphabet arranged box-like into a grid of five rows and five columns:

A	B	C	D	E
F	G	H	I	J
L	M	N	O	P
Q	R	S	T	U
V	W	X	Y	Z

So the code would fit into a simple, five-by-five matrix, the letter *K* was purposely dropped; it is used infrequently and the letter *C* easily substitutes for it. The grid was easy to remember and the code simpler to transmit than Morse code because it used only dots, not dots and dashes. Each letter was represented by two distinct tap patterns, the first to denote its row and the second to denote its position in that row. Thus, a single tap (or dot) followed by another single tap meant letter *A*—first row, first column. Five taps followed by five taps meant *Z*—fifth row, fifth column.

To speed transmission, abbreviations were used extensively. The message prisoners communicated most often was "GBU"—"God Bless You"—and was tapped out as follows:

.. ..

The code could be used on or transmitted through anything that made noise—walls, pipes, buckets, or the swish of brooms. Tapping on the walls between cells was safer than whispering over a transom, for the North Vietnamese guards were always looking for transgressions to punish, and they too had ears.

Various stories about the origins of the tap code exist. One POW recalls having first heard of it during a coffee break in escape-and-evasion training, when a sergeant told how Americans held prisoner in North Korea had tried to use a form of the code in the 1950s, but without much success. The system may be older than can be traced, however; a form of tap code appears in the nineteenth-century novel *The Count of Monte Cristo*. And a former U.S. military attaché to Moscow swears that he saw a Cyrillic version of the five-by-five matrix etched onto a ceramic plaque at the entrance to Number 2, Bolshaia Lubyanka, a building on Dzherzhinsky Square in Moscow that from 1920 until recent years housed the headquarters of the KGB as well as Lubyanka Prison.

The POWs developed endless variations of the code. Prisoners sweeping courtyards used a whisk-whisk, flick-flick pattern that could be "read" by POWs looking out from nearby cells. Even if they could not see the sweeping, they often could hear it. Prisoners exercising in courtyards were not allowed to talk to each other, but they communicated nevertheless by the way they shuffled their feet; the prisoners coughed and cleared their throats a lot, but they were really communicating. When absolute silence was imposed, various forms of hand signals were used, some to transmit the tap code, others using a simplified POW

variation of deaf signing. Even when blindfolded in the back of a truck while being moved from one prison to another, a POW could usually peek out at the floor through the bottom of his blindfold and read the toe-tapping of the prisoner sitting next to a guard opposite him.

POWs used nails twisted out of their cell doors or broken shards of glass to leave behind the tap code's simple matrix on a wall or floor of the cells they first occupied or in the latrines and shower stalls they eventually were allowed to use about once a week.

Over time, the prisoners used this simple, yet versatile tap code to establish an extensive communications system and data bank that became their telephone network—a life line that bound them together, let them console and encourage each other, united them in resisting their captors, and buoyed their spirits because they were able to organize and "beat the system."

Some POWs became more adept at the tap code than others, and the most proficient ones were designated "communicators" while others were used as lookouts to signal an "all clear" or to warn that guards were approaching and that it was time to shut traffic down. A single, loud bang was the standard warning signal, an order to be obeyed instantly—"guards coming" or "stop communicating." The walls would fall silent. To establish or reopen communications, a prisoner would tap out the familiar rhythm of "shave and a haircut"—tap, tap-tap-tap, tap—and the respondent would reply "two bits"—tap-tap.

After they discovered that prisoners were communicating, the North Vietnamese eventually broke the code by torturing it out of the POWs. Occasionally they managed to lure some POWs into a trap by breaking into the prisoners' transmissions with messages or questions of their own and, when they got a reply, using that evidence as an excuse for more torture or solitary confinement. But the North Vietnamese never mastered the signal to initiate communications; "shave and a haircut—two bits" simply made no sense to them. Thus, even after the tap code became compromised and was no longer a secret, only the prisoners knew how to make the walls come alive. Because the POWs outnumbered the guards, they could always "out-communicate" them; and because there was simply no way to obliterate noise in a prison, no matter how strictly silence was imposed, the POWs remained in almost constant communication with one another.

As Stratton later described it, "Talking walls, hand signals, coughs, scrapes, lifelines that allowed a man to survive one hundred days watching his wounds heal and counting his toes, news networks communicating instructions, policies, and the trivia that passed for major events

Apprentice Seaman Douglas Hegdahl (foreground) and Lieutenant Commander Richard Stratton (behind) sweep the prison grounds, an activity that often gave POWs an opportunity to communicate through their code.

in endless, boring, dead days" allowed the POWs to survive. The busy walls revealed to a POW that "he was not the only one who caved in, or who was tortured, or was willing, after the hands turned black from the torture cuffs, to spill his guts. Nor was he the first with thoughts of suicide or mortification over weakness, self-discovered and believed present only in others."

How the POWs organized

The communications network became so organized and efficient that even long, complex messages were sometimes relayed in a single day from one cell block to another, reaching POWs locked up in solitary confinement in remote corners of Hoa Lo. The distance from one end to the other was two full city blocks in the prison.

No matter how often prisoners were shuffled randomly from one cell to another within Hoa Lo's four distinct cell blocks, put into solitary confinement, or moved from one of North Vietnam's eight POW camps to another, they managed to build and pass on an impressive mental data bank about each other. As soon as communication could be established, each new POW was logged into the system along with the fate of any other American about which he was familiar. By the end of 1965, for instance, the North Vietnamese had publicly acknowledged holding only 28 POWs, but the U.S. Air Force alone had lost 264 men shot down over North Vietnam. Within Hoa Lo Prison the POWs had accounted for most of those men. Many had never been seen inside the prison system and, because of the circumstances under which they were shot down, were considered almost certainly dead. Others were categorized as possible survivors but not yet accounted for, and thus were carried as missing in action. The POWs also correctly logged into their data bank exactly 61 Air Force members seen or heard from one way or another within the prison system, even though no more than about 10 of them had ever been in the same cell block at any one time. And by early 1970, the POWs had managed to log in almost every one of their 370 fellow prisoners, even though North Vietnam had admitted by then to holding only 339 POWs.

The prisoners also used the communications system to remain organized, to update each other on the name of the senior ranking officer (SRO) in each cell block and in each prison, and to pass on new policies or forms of resistance. The POWs decided early to use a prisoner's rank as of the date he was shot down or taken captive, except in those rare instances when word of a subsequent promotion was confirmed by external public sources. Thus, the second Navy prisoner, Lieutenant Commander Robert H. Shumaker, became the SRO when he was shot down on February 11, 1965, because he outranked the first, Navy Lieutenant Everett Alvarez, Jr., who had been in prison since August 5, 1964, the day of the Tonkin Gulf retaliatory strikes. Navy Commander Jeremiah A. Denton, Jr., suc-

ceeded Shumaker as SRO when he was shot down on July 18, 1965, and in turn was succeeded by a more senior commander, James B. Stockdale, on September 9. Stockdale remained the senior ranking officer until late 1970, even though several Air Force officers successively more senior to him were taken prisoner between 1965 and 1970. These officers—Air Force Lieutenant Colonel Robinson Risner (shot down September 16, 1965), then Air Force Colonel Norman C. Gaddis (shot down May 12, 1967, the first full colonel or Navy captain–equivalent to become a POW), and finally Air Force Colonel John P. Flynn (October 27, 1967)—were known by their fellow POWs to have been taken prisoner but were kept so isolated that effective communication with them was not established for years. Through it all, in six years of incarceration, Ensign Gary Thornton remained the most junior commissioned officer of all POWs, even though it seemed certain that he would have been promoted while in captivity and thus, by the time of his release in 1973, would have been senior in rank to some of the later, junior-ranking prisoners.

Keeping track of the SROs was a continuous task because the North Vietnamese, whenever they suspected that a cell block or prison was becoming too organized, shuffled the more senior officers about without warning or explanation. One remote camp, for instance, had four senior ranking officers in less than two years.

Remembering the directives or guidelines of the SROs was not difficult because they kept them simple. The most important early guidance was to resist as much as possible, but not to the extent of risking permanently disabling injuries or of making inadvertent, serious revelations during torture. One of Stockdale's first directives was for the POWs to "back the U.S.," in other words, to hold out as long as possible and then evade, waffle, and lie, if need be, but never submit to the point of demeaning their country. Another directive was "no early return": the POWs would remain together and go home together, refusing North Vietnamese promises of an early return home to those prisoners who "cooperated."

What preyed on the minds of the POWs about the torture they endured was that it was all so senseless; it produced so little that was useful to their captors. The propaganda statements were transparently coerced, and most of the information the North Vietnamese finally extracted was useless. It was either too dated to be of value or just random bits and pieces of "intelligence" that the interrogators seldom correlated with what they learned from another prisoner. Air Force Major Elmo C. Baker recalls one session after he was shot down in 1967 in which the North Vietnamese seemed determined to put together an air order of battle and tortured all the POWs in his cell block, one by one, for the names of other pilots in their squadrons. By tap code, the men passed to each other word of what the interrogators wanted. They agreed that each man would try to hold out for ten days. At that rate, it would take the

A POW uses a nail to carve the tap code matrix into the floor of his Hanoi cell in this artist's rendition.

North Vietnamese a year and a half to extract the information. As each POW finished his interrogation, he reported to the others exactly which names he had divulged: Dizzy Dean was Mo Baker's squadron commander, Stan Musial the operations officer, and the rest of the St. Louis Cardinals were his flying mates. Other POWs revealed that they had served with Clark Kent, Captain Marvel, and Bruce Wayne. America's lifestyle was so foreign to the interrogators (some of whom spoke little English in any case) that such stratagems often worked. Some of the sessions, brutal as they were, left the POWs amused. One interrogator pressed hard for a working diagram of an aircraft carrier, including where its chicken and pig pens were located. Word of such encounters passed quickly among the cell blocks and boosted morale. Despite their suffering, the POWs could find occasional bits of humor through their communications system.

Failed rescues

One task that kept the communicators especially busy was the effort to develop precise layouts of each of the prisons and its regimen. That was essential not only for better communications, but also for plotting escapes.

The men dreamed of escape. But most of them, especially pilots shot down over North Vietnam or Laos, had been wounded or injured so severely when they ejected that they were incapable of even trying to evade capture after they hit the ground. One of every five had broken an elbow, an arm, or a knee on the side of his cockpit while ejecting, wrenched a shoulder when his parachute opened, or fractured a bone or dislocated a joint when he hit the ground. Those injuries were one reason that Air Force search-and-rescue teams, flying their Jolly Green Giants, H–3 helicopters, were able to recover only one of every nine aviators shot down over North Vietnam. Still, that was a remarkable number of rescues deep within enemy territory, for by the time of the 1973 Paris peace accords, 938 American planes had been downed over the North.

Even for those with only minor injuries, evading capture was virtually impossible, for these were robust, tall, and very white or very black Americans, and they were conspicuous in a land of thin, short Asians. It took the North Vietnamese only three weeks to pick up the man who

evaded capture the longest: A Navy pilot decided to head inland instead of toward the coast, hoping to reach a friendly CIA outpost on the Laotian border. The North Vietnamese found his flight helmet and tracked him down with dogs. It took the North Vietnamese only twelve days to capture the man at large for the second-longest time, Air Force Colonel George E. "Bud" Day, a half-blind F–100 pilot who managed to escape soon after being captured even though he had lost his eyeglasses when he ejected, broken his right arm in three places, and badly sprained his left knee.

Once captured, the prisoners were too weak from their initial torture, too bent from brutal treatment, and too debilitated from malnutrition and disease to attempt escape. Only four or five men ever managed to escape prison in North Vietnam, and none ever made it to freedom. One, Air Force Captain Edwin L. Atterbury, escaped in May 1969 from a remote prison while he was in what fellow prisoners later described as "fairly robust health," but he was recaptured the next day and was never seen or heard from again. The North Vietnamese would only report that he "died in captivity," on May 18, 1969. Atterbury, it was later determined, was beaten to death. Air Force Lieutenant Colonel John Dramesi escaped twice (once with Atterbury), but each time he was soon recaptured and brutally tortured. The reprisals on other POWs following each escape attempt were so harsh that further efforts were forbidden by the SRO in each POW camp.

This step by the SROs was all the more remarkable because the POW Code of Conduct required prisoners to make every reasonable effort to escape. The requirement had a therapeutic as well as a practical purpose: to force POWs to consider themselves active participants in the war rather than passive victims. That the senior officers forbade such attempts reveals just how hopeless the situation of the POWs in North Vietnam had become.

Elsewhere in Southeast Asia, escape attempts were only marginally more successful. Of the 649 Americans who eventually survived captivity during the Vietnam War, only 28 escaped successfully: 2 from the Pathet Lao and 26 from the Vietcong. Two of those men escaped in 1962, 13 escaped during the confusion of the 1968 Tet offensive fighting, and the last ones escaped from Vietcong prisons in 1969. Thus, during the last three-and-a-half years of American involvement in the Vietnam conflict, when concern for the POWs and MIAs was at its peak, not one American escaped captivity anywhere in Southeast Asia.

But throughout Indochina, throughout the war, American prisoners dreamed constantly of being rescued. Over

Air Force Colonel Robinson Risner, held by the Communists for seven-and-a-half years, leads a group of POWs in the Hanoi Hilton back to their cells in 1973. Risner was the ranking U.S. officer in the prison at the time.

American POW Camps Outside Hanoi

CHINA

NORTH VIETNAM

Dogpatch

Mountain Camp

Son Tay · Camp Faith
Briarpatch · · Hanoi
Skidrow ·
Farnsworth · · Haiphong
Rockpile ·

Red River

Gulf of Tonkin

LAOS

Kilometers
0   100

Miles
0   100

THAILAND

SOUTH VIETNAM

time, 119 rescue missions were mounted in South Vietnam, Cambodia, Laos, and North Vietnam to bring those men home. Ninety-eight of those operations involved pre-planned raids against prisoner-of-war compounds.

Only one American POW, Army Specialist 4th Class Larry D. Aiken, was rescued—from a Vietcong prison on July 10, 1969. He died fifteen days later of wounds inflicted by his captors just before his rescue. The raid to save him apparently had been compromised at the last minute.

All but one of the rescue missions were handled by the Joint Personnel Recovery Center (JPRC), a separate staff detachment within MACV headquarters in Saigon. Its operations did succeed in liberating 318 South Vietnamese soldiers and 60 civilians, all held by the Vietcong. But most of the attempts were heartbreaking. In December 1966, for instance, an informant supplied information on American prisoners being held by the Vietcong. The JPRC found the information credible, launched a raid, and the rescue team ended up in an intense firefight during which thirty-five Vietcong were killed and thirty-four others detained. During interrogation, they confirmed that Americans had been held in the camp but were moved just before the raid. Like that one, some of the raids failed because intelligence was compromised, but others failed because the rescue missions were not launched quickly enough. Such was the case when a South Vietnamese prisoner escaped from a Vietcong POW camp in 1967 and reported the location of two camps containing Americans.

Authorities challenged his reports at first but eventually verified them. More than thirty days after the man's escape, a raid was launched, and twenty-one South Vietnamese prisoners were rescued from one of the camps. The other camp was empty, but evidence showed that Americans had, in fact, been there. The South Vietnamese POWs who had been freed said that the Americans had been moved about a month before—as events unfolded, soon after the escapee had first reported their presence.

Of the ninety-eight raids launched to free American POWs in Southeast Asia, only the seventy-first and most dramatic raid—the only one into North Vietnam—was planned and run from the Pentagon, one of twenty-five rescue missions mounted in 1970. It involved one of the boldest, most secret, complex, bizarre, and controversial operations of the Vietnam War. It too failed—not one POW was rescued; yet the Americans who eventually came home from captivity in North Vietnam would report that it did more for their well-being than any other single event of the war. Some said that it saved their sanity.

It was the Son Tay raid of 1970. The Son Tay story began that spring, when more than 462 Americans were believed to be POWs in Southeast Asia, 80 percent of them in North Vietnam. Only the North Vietnamese knew where the prisoners were. In spite of an extensive intelligence-collection effort, not one prison compound outside of downtown Hanoi had been located, even though the U.S. had known since 1968—from interrogating North Vietnamese soldiers captured in the South and from three POWs whom North Vietnam had released early—that there was at least one camp said to be located about fifty kilometers west of Hanoi.

By late spring of 1970, some of the POWs had been in captivity for more than 2,100 days, longer than any serviceman in America's history. By then, the North had released nine POWs, and some had reported that at least a few of those left behind were near death and that all the POWs were being held in conditions so primitive and brutal that U.S. authorities wondered if any of them would return home alive and sane. The reports merely confirmed the grim news that had become apparent in the spring of 1966, when Navy Commander Jeremiah A. Denton, Jr., shot down in 1965, was paraded before television cameras to tell of his "humane treatment" and blinked out the word *torture* in Morse code.

Accounting for the number of POWs, much less their whereabouts, was a near-hopeless task. In violation of the Geneva Convention, Hanoi announced very few captures, and, even when pressed about specific cases during the Paris peace talks, frequently refused even to acknowledge holding an American prisoner.

(Indeed, when Hanoi finally released a list of POWs on January 27, 1973, four days after the Paris peace accords were signed, the list proved to be cruelly inaccurate. It accounted for 617 POWs, 53 about whom North Vietnam

American prisoner of war Toren Harvey Torkelson is interviewed in North Vietnam by a German film crew for a documentary on the POWs.

had given out no information whatsoever during the entire time they were held prisoner. There had been another 55 POWs who, the North Vietnamese said, had died in captivity; but in the weeks that immediately followed, 566 Americans, not 562, returned home alive. In the ensuing months, another 25 POWs and MIAs were returned to U.S. control, and the U.S. eventually accounted for 80 POWs, not 55, who had died in prison.)

Developing intelligence on the prisoner-of-war situation was also made difficult because many of the men were never allowed to write home. Ninety-five of the 566 who returned to America in 1973 had never received a letter from home; 80 families had never received a letter from the prisoners.

Although sometimes delayed for weeks or months in transit, a letter to his family was the best hard evidence that an American was indeed alive. Some prisoners devised homespun double talk to pass information on their fellow POWs, especially those who were not allowed to write home. In 1966, for instance, an Air Force captain wrote to his father, "Oh, by the way, Dad, hold on to those houses in Indiana and New Jersey"—he even listed their street addresses—"I'm sure the price is going to skyrocket some day." The houses were the home addresses of two other POWs who had not been allowed to write home.

A few prisoners tried to communicate with the outside world on a much more systematic basis. One POW told in a book that he had regularly attempted to use homemade

invisible inks, such as urine diluted with water or lemon juice, to provide his wife more detailed information on his condition as a prisoner of war.

But it was hard to piece together a comprehensive mosaic from such tidbits, in part because the POWs were frequently moved in random shifts from one camp to another. One POW, Navy Lieutenant Charles Plumb, was imprisoned in five camps within three years. Gary Thornton moved nine times among five different camps in six years, and within Hoa Lo Prison itself (which he called "home plate," his other prisons being only "temporary duty" assignments), he moved six times among the four parts of the prison.

But in 1969 a POW released by the North, Seaman Apprentice Douglas Hegdahl, brought home an encyclopedia of information on his fellow prisoners. In 1967, he had fallen off the fantail of the cruiser *Canberra* when it was shelling the North Vietnamese coast. It took him months to persuade the North Vietnamese that he was not a pilot or a commando; they did not believe that anyone could fall off a huge ship. In 1969 the North Vietnamese told Hegdahl he could go home—if he would ask for an early release in writing. At first he refused, since the POWs had agreed that no one would accept preferential treatment, but the senior POWs finally ordered Hegdahl to accept the offer and gave him a cram course to remember the names of more than 200 prisoners whom the POWs had accounted for in one way or another and logged into their mental data banks. Hegdahl also carried firsthand details of the brutal treatment many of the POWs were being subjected to, a message the senior POWs wanted to make sure got home. But such windfalls were rare, and the fate of the POWs became a vexing problem that increasingly preoccupied not just the administration, but the public as well.

By May 1970, America was growing desperate for a resolution to the Vietnam War. President Richard Nixon had just ordered the invasion of Cambodia to destroy the Vietcong headquarters called COSVN and root out the VC sanctuaries there, but it resulted only in the discovery of sixty-five tons of rice and several large arms caches. A riot that ensued at Kent State University and subsequent protests at the White House made clear that the war was tearing America apart. The only issue Americans remained united on was that they wanted their POWs home and the missing in action accounted for. But the prospect of that happening soon was dim: The Nixon withdrawal program was under way, but the North Vietnamese negotiating in Paris had made it clear that the prisoners would be released only when the U.S. pulled *all* of its forces out.

In those bleak hours, the POW situation suddenly took a dramatic turn. On Saturday, May 9, POW experts in a special intelligence unit at Fort Belvoir, Virginia—euphemistically called the 1127th Field Activity Group—discovered in reconnaissance photos unmistakable signs of a prisoner-of-war compound in an area thirty kilometers west of Hanoi. The compound had been photographed before. So thorough had the search for POWs become that the U.S. was systematically photographing every installation in North Vietnam with a wall around it. That made a sizable list in a country where almost every family raised pigs or chickens and did not want them running loose and where almost every school had an enclosed courtyard.

As photo interpreters from the 1127th were routinely comparing new and old photos of the area, they noticed that one compound had been enlarged. Stereoscopic pairs of photos soon revealed a new wall and what might have been a guard tower in the northwest corner. Air Force Colonel George J. Iles, who had been a prisoner in World War II and headed the unit's Evasion and Escape Branch, noticed that someone had recently spelled out the number *55* in hieroglyphics on the ground and added the letter *K*, a search-and-rescue code that meant "Come get us." Iles and his team thought they could also make out the numbers *6* and *8* and an arrow pointing roughly west. That could mean six of the POWs were ready to escape and were calling for a pickup, either eight miles to the west or on the eighth of the following month, June.

The Son Tay compound was on the edge of the Song Cong River, 37 kilometers west of downtown Hanoi and about 101 kilometers from the Laotian border. Further scrutiny of the photos revealed another possible POW camp, Ap Lo, roughly 8 kilometers farther west. Several kilometers to the southwest was a foothill called Mount Ba Vi.

Iles quickly took the photos to the Pentagon, for it was clear they were onto something big. What made the jigsaw puzzle fit together was that Mount Ba Vi was one of several prearranged places in North Vietnam and Laos that American air crews had always been instructed to try to reach if shot down so they could be rescued by friendly agents. Some of them, like Ba Vi, had small caches of food, radios, and medical supplies. To the intelligence and covert-operations experts whom Iles briefed in Air Force headquarters, the Son Tay–Ap Lo–Ba Vi connection looked like the POW breakthrough they had been awaiting for years.

But the prison camps' remote locations raised haunting questions. Why had the North Vietnamese put the POWs in such isolated compounds? Why were they not locked up in Hoa Lo Prison in downtown Hanoi, where most of the prisoners were thought to be held? Were these the "basket cases"—the prisoners who were most seriously injured, the most tortured, or the ones who had gone insane? That would explain why the North Vietnamese wanted them out of Hanoi; that way, there would be no risk of a visiting peace delegation ever seeing them or hearing about them. Although it would turn out that the prisoners in Son Tay had been sent there almost at random, concern about the state of these remote POWs made their plea for a rescue all the more urgent.

Brigadier General James R. Allen, the chief Air Force planner for special operations, immediately put a small team to work devising that rescue. Allen instructed them to "go hide somewhere for a week" and think about all the prisoners at Son Tay and Ap Lo, not just the six in Son Tay who might make it to Ba Vi.

Allen was not the kind of general who needed a big staff study to prod him into gear, but the sketchy plan his team came back with reminded him that a major rescue operation deep into North Vietnam went far beyond his authority. About ten days after discovery of the Son Tay and Ap Lo camps, Allen asked permission of his boss, Lieutenant General Russell E. Dougherty, the USAF's deputy chief of staff for operations and plans, to "go joint." That meant taking the matter up with the office of the Joint Chiefs of Staff, where Allen went on May 25. The Vietnam War had, in fact, become so bureaucratized by 1970 that it took two weeks to get word of a breakthrough on the POW issue and an urgent request for a rescue to the only people who could really do something about it.

An iron door opens onto the compound of Hoa Lo Prison. The building's history dates back to the 1930s, when French colonialists used it as a jail for political prisoners.

The Raid at Son Tay

The one person in the Washington bureaucracy who could begin to make something happen about an urgent prisoner-of-war rescue was a young Army brigadier general who, twenty-nine years earlier, had disobeyed orders to avoid becoming a POW himself. As a newly commissioned lieutenant in World War II, Donald D. Blackburn had refused to surrender after Corregidor fell. Instead, he headed into the jungles and mountains of northern Luzon, where he helped organize 20,000 Filipino guerrillas and eventually commanded one of their five regiments. The unit was made up of his favorite warriors, Igorot head-hunters. In 1970, he was known as SACSA, the Special Assistant for Counterinsurgency and Special Activities to the chairman of the Joint Chiefs of Staff, the same man who controlled SOG activities from the Pentagon.

Early in the Vietnam War, Blackburn had become one of the first commanders of SOG. He was especially proud that not one American life had been lost during SOG's first forty-five "cross-border" opera-

tions. Some of those operations involved "CAS" teams—"Controlled American Sources." These were Vietnamese (many of whom had fled the North when Vietnam was divided) whom SOG had recruited, specially trained, and sent back north on intelligence-gathering and, occasionally, sabotage missions. (Contrary to most perceptions, all such operations in the North were the military's responsibility after 1965, not the CIA's.) SACSA had always controlled the CAS operations, and as he listened on May 25 to General Jim Allen's rough concept of a rescue for the men in the camp called Son Tay, Blackburn realized that any plan involving the "safe site" on Mount Ba Vi was out of the question.

The site, in all likelihood, had been hopelessly compromised, although only a handful of people knew of it. When President Lyndon Johnson ordered the bombing halt over all of North Vietnam in 1968, the military not only lost authority to mount any special operations or agent insertions there, but was even forbidden to resupply its CAS teams. For months, all they were told in guarded radio messages was to "hang in there," there were "problems with resupply," et cetera. Nine teams, forty-five carefully trained Vietnamese, were simply abandoned. It was one of the greatest tragedies and biggest secrets of the Vietnam War. In time, some of the agents were picked up by the North Vietnamese; a few defected; others simply died. Ironically, one of the last CAS teams to remain in contact had operated from the safe site at Mount Ba Vi, but SOG (and thus SACSA) had lost contact with the team just a few months before Allen's visit to Blackburn. And while it was considered "beautiful" at the time, it had become tragic that the site had been guarded for the CAS team by North Vietnamese soldiers who were, in effect "double dipping": They were full-time North Vietnamese soldiers but were poorly motivated because of their dull, seemingly unimportant jobs in a remote area. They had been working for the Americans unwittingly by accepting special favors—money, food, sewing kits, medicines, and sometimes even dope from CAS agents to help protect the safe sites from becoming discovered. But by late May 1970, Mount Ba Vi had become about the last place in Southeast Asia Blackburn wanted escaping POWs to head for.

Blackburn told Allen only that he liked the idea of a larger rescue operation, not just picking up six POWs, but that it was out of his purview as well, something the Joint Chiefs of Staff would have to decide. In World War II, rescuing prisoners of war was something a regimental or division commander could have decided to do on the spot. But this was the Vietnam War, and going into North Vietnam probably meant that the ultimate decision would have to be made in the Oval Office of the White House.

Preceding page. *Secretary of Defense Melvin Laird, testifying before Congress on November 24, 1970, displays a model of the Son Tay Prison compound.*

The bureaucracy gets organized

Brigadier generals did not normally pick up the telephone and ask to see the chairman of the Joint Chiefs, but as SACSA, Blackburn had access when he needed it. Within hours of Allen's visit, Blackburn and the head of his Special Operations Division, Army Colonel Edward E. Mayer, were in JCS chairman Wheeler's office with a five-minute summary of the information the 1127th had uncovered and an outline of possibilities for a rescue operation. Wheeler's response was, "Jesus Christ, how many battalions is this going to take?" His response was understandable: President Richard Nixon's withdrawal program had been underway for over a year; the U.S. had brought home, and in most cases deactivated, more than a third of the 536,000 men and 254 maneuver battalions fighting in South Vietnam at the war's peak in 1968. The country was now short on battalions, down to its lowest number of deployable units since World War II.

Wheeler had been chairman since mid-1964, before the Gulf of Tonkin incident. Worn down by the war and in ill health, he was just weeks away from retiring—and here was SACSA, on the heels of the Cambodian incursion, proposing an "invasion" of North Vietnam. Blackburn quickly assured Wheeler that he was thinking not in terms of battalions but of a small team of Special Forces volunteers. Wheeler told Blackburn to brief his successor, Admiral Thomas H. Moorer.

On Tuesday, May 26, Blackburn and Mayer asked the Defense Intelligence Agency (DIA) to lay on special reconnaissance coverage of the Son Tay and Ap Lo camps; on May 27, Blackburn told the JCS's director of operations, Air Force Lieutenant General John Vogt, that he had a "requirement," an assigned task, to put together a quick prisoner-of-war rescue-feasibility study for the chairman. Vogt arranged for Blackburn to brief Moorer on the twenty-ninth and told him to have a recommendation ready for Wheeler by June 1. That afternoon, Blackburn briefed Vogt and Army Lieutenant General Donald V. Bennett, the director of the Defense Intelligence Agency, with several options for a rescue operation dubbed Polar Circle. One option was to insert an agent near the camps who would call in rescue helicopters and a raiding party positioned to launch on a standby basis from CIA sites on the Laotian border. But Blackburn and Bennett agreed that entailed too much risk of compromise. For one thing, they knew the North Vietnamese and Vietcong had often gained advance warning of B–52 raids launched from Guam, 2,400 miles away; they might sense that something was up as the U.S. helicopters waited for the summer's monsoon weather to break, alert their air-defense warning system, and tighten defenses accordingly.

The second option involved a much more complex operation that would take off from Thailand, with a Navy diversion over Haiphong launched from the Gulf of Tonkin

Pilotless Buffalo Hunter drone reconnaissance aircraft, like the one pictured here, made seven unsuccessful attempts to photograph at treetop level the inside of Son Tay Prison.

to draw attention away from Son Tay. But that meant the rescue helicopters would have to refuel in-flight, and weather would be a key factor. Precise forecasts would have to be available, and the first good weather window was not predicted until October.

(Concern about weather would prove a determining factor in delaying the rescue attempt, but somehow its planners ignored the fact that from July through September of the preceding year, the weather had been good enough for the U.S. to fly 9,214 sorties over North Vietnam, the second most active quarter of the year for air operations there. Those operations had included 1,144 reconnaissance sorties, when presumably the weather had been good enough to see something, and that was almost twice as many reconnaissance flights as were flown during October, November, and December, the period when forecasters predicted the best 1970 weather windows.)

By June 2, when Blackburn, Vogt, and Bennett briefed Wheeler, Bennett had new, high-altitude SR–71 photos of Son Tay and Ap Lo; they confirmed that "someone" was in Son Tay and at Ap Lo. Wheeler said he wanted the other four members of the Joint Chiefs of Staff briefed. The earliest that briefing could be scheduled was on Friday, June 5. Blackburn recommended and the Chiefs approved

a two-phase approach: a more detailed "feasibility study" of rescue alternatives to be completed by June 30, followed by the detailed planning, training, and, finally, execution of the raid. On Monday, June 8, Blackburn briefed the Army, Air Force, Navy, and Marine Corps "OPS DEPS," as the three-star service deputies were called. They controlled whatever forces and equipment a major rescue operation might entail. Next day, he and Mayer advised the CIA of its plans. Exactly one month had passed since the plea for an "urgent" rescue had been spotted. The following day, Blackburn convened a fifteen-man feasibility study group at the DIA's Arlington Hall annex near the Pentagon.

The June 30 deadline the JCS had set came and went. It was that time of the year for a Pentagon ballet known as "musical chairs": On July 1, Admiral Moorer was relieved as chief of naval operations by Admiral Elmo R. Zumwalt; the next day Wheeler retired, and Moorer succeeded him as JCS chairman.

The new Joint Chiefs of Staff did not convene until July

10 to reconsider the rescue—more than two months after the 1127th's "POW breakthrough." By then, reconnaissance photos showed the camp at Ap Lo was empty, but intelligence suggested there were now sixty-one, not fifty-five, prisoners in Son Tay. Moorer was concerned that a rescue might backfire. What would success or failure mean for the other prisoners left behind? Would they suffer even more from North Vietnamese reprisals?

The DIA and the CIA had consulted a Vietnam specialist on the National Security Council staff, Dolf Droge, on that very issue. Droge had served three tours in Vietnam and Laos with the Agency for International Development, spoke Vietnamese fluently, and understood the culture and people well. Droge was not told that a rescue was being planned; he was just asked hypothetically, "What do you think would happen if one of the camps was raided and some POWs rescued?" Without hesitation, Droge said that would be the greatest thing America could do for all the prisoners. Their treatment, he predicted, would improve dramatically, almost instantly. There would be a general tightening of security, but no reprisals on the prisoners left behind, he reasoned.

Blackburn's briefing to the Joint Chiefs noted that while Son Tay Prison was isolated, there were several North Vietnamese installations within a few kilometers. In all, the CIA and the DIA had estimated there might be as many as 12,000 North Vietnamese troops nearby, mostly from the 12th Infantry Regiment, an artillery school, a supply depot, and an air-defense installation, all about ten kilometers away. The only facility in the prison's immediate vicinity was a compound about 400 meters to the south. On their maps of the area, intelligence specialists had labeled it "Secondary School." Blackburn's feasibility study team had reasoned that a night raid would achieve the most surprise, that it would take the closest North Vietnamese troops about thirty minutes to get to the prison, twelve minutes to be alerted, grab their weapons, and board trucks, and eighteen minutes to race to the compound. On that basis, the plan called for the whole raid to be over in twenty-six minutes.

Low-altitude photos taken by a Buffalo Hunter reconnaissance drone and high-altitude SR–71s showed that the prison consisted of two compounds, one with four large buildings housing the POWs and an open courtyard about the size of a volleyball court, all surrounded by seven-foot walls with three guard towers. The other was an administrative support area outside the east wall housing about forty-five guards.

The plan called for launching the mission from Thailand, flying north over Laos, and then east to Son Tay. A small team would land by helicopter inside the compound and race into the cell blocks before the guards could react. The rest of the raiding force would land in a large clearing south of the prison, blow a hole in the wall, and guide the prisoners out. A separate team would take care of the guards in the prison support area and block off the north-south road just east of the prison to prevent reaction forces from reaching the area. Blackburn estimated that about fifty men could handle the mission. Weather experts argued that October and November offered the best launch windows, when the moon would also be just high enough above the eastern horizon to give the helicopter pilots good visibility on their 160-plus-kilometer flight from the Laotian border, yet low enough to reduce the possibility of their being detected.

Blackburn convinced the Chiefs he could pull it off. They renamed the operation Ivory Coast and authorized Blackburn to organize a joint contingency task group to complete the planning and begin training for the mission. The following Monday, July 13, he and Mayer flew to Fort Bragg, North Carolina. Over lunch, without providing any details of the mission ahead, they asked Army Colonel Arthur D. "Bull" Simons, an old friend who had fought with the 6th Rangers in the Philippines, if he would be interested in a "very sensitive mission" that might be "kind of rough." Simons, who headed the first White Star team Blackburn had recruited in 1960 to train a Laotian army and who had served under Blackburn in SOG, reasoned that if Blackburn was involved, it would at least be more interesting than his current assignment as the G–4, or supply officer, for the XVIII Airborne Corps. Simons answered, "Hell, yes." There was no discussion of a raid, no mention of North Vietnam.

Before leaving Fort Bragg, Blackburn called on the commander of the Special Warfare Center to ask if they could use a secure area at Smoke Bomb Hill to train a special force for an unspecified operation they explained was of the highest national priority. The major general objected; his personnel records section and judge advocate general's office had just moved into the compound they wanted. He suggested some empty World War II barracks elsewhere on the post. Although Fort Bragg's 130,698-acre reservation would have been an ideal training site, Blackburn left the post in disgust; he and Mayer decided to use the 464,980-acre complex at Eglin Air Force Base, Florida. That also meant that, simply to ease coordination, an Air Force officer would command the task group. The man picked was Brigadier General Leroy J. Manor, a tall, quiet veteran with 345 combat missions, 275 of them in Southeast Asia, who was serving as commander of the Air Force's Special Operations Force at Eglin. He had once trained the unconventional warfare teams that supported SOG, later became the Air Force's top briefing officer on Southeast Asia, and understood, like Bull Simons, that the war in Vietnam involved a lot more than body counts, search-and-destroy operations, and the fighter-bomber missions that made up most newspaper accounts of the war. Simons, it was agreed, would be the task force deputy commander and the operation's ground commander.

All this was progress, but the Son Tay raid soon turned

into an administrative, intelligence, and logistics nightmare.

Training the force

Americans had been held prisoner in Southeast Asia since 1964. Getting the POWs home had become the highest priority in the land, and it had long been evident that any effort to rescue POWs from North Vietnam, where about three-fourths of the prisoners were held, would have to involve a well-trained, specially equipped Army–Air Force team. Yet by the summer of 1970 no one had been trained or equipped to rescue anybody, other than the Air Force H–3 Jolly Green Giant crews whose helicopters swooped in to pluck a downed aviator to safety before he could be taken prisoner.

Thus, Simons and Manor spent the last weeks of July and the first week of August recruiting volunteers—for a mission they could not even describe—and getting them assigned to temporary duty at a remote corner of Eglin Air Force Base called Auxiliary Field Number Three. Doolittle's Raiders had trained there twenty-eight years earlier for the first B–25 raid over Tokyo.

Manor picked three rescue veterans for his deputies and lead helicopter pilots. Lieutenant Colonel Warner A. Britton had been the operations and training officer for the Aerospace Rescue and Recovery Service; moreover, he had served in Blackburn's feasibility study group. Lieutenant Colonel John Allison was another experienced Jolly Green pilot and commanded a flight of the huge HH–53s at Eglin. Lieutenant Colonel Herbert E. Zehnder had set a long-distance world record flying the smaller HH–3 nonstop from New York to Paris in 1967. Flying rescue missions in that plane in Vietnam, he was credited with 84 saves. Major Frederic M. Donohue had been project officer for capsule recovery on the Apollo space launches, had flown 131 missions in Southeast Asia, had made 4 rescues over North Vietnam, and had logged almost 6,000 hours as a test pilot, the last ones on the world's first trans-Pacific helicopter flight. It had involved thirteen HH–53 refuelings by HC–130 tankers.

Simons picked Lieutenant Colonel Elliott P. "Bud" Sydnor, a tall, quiet, lean, and mean Southeast Asia Special Forces veteran, to be his ground force deputy and to lead a twenty-man command-and-security group that would land outside the compound, secure the guard quarters, and seal off the roads. Major Richard J. Meadows would head a fourteen-man assault team that would crash-land inside the compound. Meadows was a Special Forces sergeant who had captured the first North Vietnamese artillery pieces in Laos, earned a battlefield commission, and served with Simons in Panama and in SOG. Meadows already had one mission into North Vietnam under his belt, involving an attempted rescue from an aircraft carrier of some Controlled American Sources agents who were in

Army Brigadier General Donald D. Blackburn. As the JCS's Special Assistant for Counterinsurgency and Special Activities (SACSA), Blackburn was responsible for planning the Son Tay raid.

"a real pickle." He arrived too late to rescue them but got his team out safely. Simons would also land just south of the prison compound with a twenty-two-man support group.

Simons needed one other key volunteer, a doctor, but there were few volunteers. Lieutenant Colonel Joseph R. Cataldo, who had once been chief surgeon for the Green Berets at Fort Bragg and was parachute qualified, walked into his office one day, having been told only that Simons needed a doctor with Special Forces experience for some kind of "special assignment." Simons told him flat out that a prisoner-of-war rescue was being planned involving a raid deep into North Vietnam and that he needed a doctor to help plan the mission and go along. Cataldo told him, "I'm your surgeon." Simons and Cataldo finally selected fifteen officers and eighty-two enlisted men to train for the mission. Except for Sydnor and Meadows, the other volunteers had been told only that it might be "moderately hazardous." Only about a third had served under Simons

Lockheed's SR–71 reconnaissance aircraft, streaking across the sky at 80,000 feet, provided most of the photographic intelligence on the Son Tay Prison.

before; six had never seen combat, but Simons liked their mettle.

On August 8, the Joint Chiefs of Staff sent a message to unified and specified commanders worldwide announcing formation of a Joint Contingency Task Group under Manor and Simons, ordering full support of their work; but there was no hint what their work was about. On August 10, Blackburn, Manor, and Simons met in the Pentagon basement with a thirty-eight-man Ivory Coast Planning Group. Four of its members would end up flying into Son Tay, but the mission they would execute still existed only as a concept whose intricate details had yet to be worked out.

Three months had passed since receipt of the Son Tay rescue message.

The planners agreed to have a training plan ready by August 20, an operations plan by August 28. Training would begin September 9 (by which time four months would have passed); night training on September 17; joint training on September 28; and finish by October 6. The task force should be ready to deploy by October 10. Five months would have passed, but that would be in time to launch the raid during the first good weather window, predicted between October 20 and 25.

By mid-August, the DIA's target folder on Son Tay filled several file drawers, and the planning group knew the location of every building, every wall, every ditch, and every tree in or near the compound. Equal attention had been paid to and detailed photo mosaics prepared of the 1,106-kilometer route from Thailand over Laos to the objective and back. The CIA prepared a $60,000, table-size replica of the compound. It was rigged with special viewing devices so Simons's men could see the camp from every conceivable angle exactly as it would look to them on the ground the night of the raid. By varying the optical viewers, the camp could appear to be lit by quarter- or half-moon, by flares, or in near-total darkness. Simons wanted every member of the force to be able to fight into the POW cells even if he was blind, deaf, or wounded.

But Simons did not train men on sand tables or map exercises. He decided to replicate Son Tay Prison on the ground—buildings as well as walls—using 4x4 posts, 2x4 lumber, and canvas target cloth with gates, windows, and doors painted on or cut out. Trees were planted to conform with those at the real target. Because a Soviet reconnaissance satellite, Cosmos 355, flew over Eglin Air Force Base twice every twenty-four hours, after each four-hour training period (conducted only when the satellite was not in position to photograph the area) the mockup was dismantled. The post holes were even covered by lids so that the outline of the camp could not be spotted.

Over the ensuing weeks, Simons and his men collected an arsenal of weapons and special equipment. Only fifty-six men would land at Son Tay, but they would carry 111 weapons, 213 grenades, 15 claymore mines, 11 special demolition charges, 6 night-vision devices, 11 axes, 12 pairs of wire cutters, 11 bolt cutters, 5 crowbars, 7 coils of rope, 2 oxyacetylene torches, 2 chain saws, 17 machetes, a fourteen-foot ladder, 4 fire extinguishers, 5 bullhorns, 34 miner's lamps, 2 cameras, and 92 radios.

Even though the task group had the highest possible special-supply priority, getting some of the equipment without arousing suspicion proved an administrative and logistical nightmare for Simons's six-man supply team. Almost none of the equipment they needed existed in the Pentagon's mammoth supply system. To pry open doors or barricades, for instance, each man needed a knife smaller than a machete but with a heavier blade and sharper point. The Army was testing one, but even with an expedited requisition through special channels, Simons's men were told, it would take four months to get them, so they made the knives on local grinding wheels. Ever since the Korean War, the Army had placed a premium on night combat and had spent $18.4 billion on research and development to better equip its soldiers to fight—half of the time, obviously, at night. But Simons found in 1970 that neither the Army nor the CIA yet owned a decent night sight, and even his best shooters were getting only 25 percent of the rounds fired at fifty meters into the torso-size targets that simulated enemy guards standing up in a foxhole. Unless night-firing accuracy could be improved, the raiders would jeopardize the POWs they were trying to save. Simons's men finally found a night sight they could use; it was advertised for $49.50 in a sporting magazine. Every gun buff in America probably knew about it, but not the Army. With it, almost every round went through the torso-size targets at fifty meters. Simons also needed some larger night-vision devices. He had to get the permission of a brigadier general in the Pentagon to release the only six the Army had that proved suitable for the raid.

Doc Cataldo compounded the supply headache. Given the likely condition of the POWs, he wanted 2,690 pounds of special medical suppplies loaded aboard the helicopters that would bring the men back from Son Tay. They included 150 cans of water; 100 cans of survival food; earplugs, thermal ponchos, and a blanket for every prisoner; 100 sets of pajamas and bathrobes; specially made sneakers with reinforced sponge soles; medical kits with a very fast-acting, "knockout" anesthetic plus hemostats and inflatable splints; and, finally, cartons of boxes of Heinz baby food (mashed rice). It was repackaged in plain sealed foil because, realizing that baby food is generally given to newly released prisoners or hostages, some might have guessed its purpose.

But even though America was still in the middle of a big war, with the Army spending a fourth of its budget on ammunition, $10 million a day, getting ammunition that worked proved to be a problem. Twenty-two percent of the 1,000 blasting caps Simons ordered to set off his special demolition charges misfired in training. At one time during the training, Simons was told he had exhausted the Army's entire supply of the M79 grenade-launched, 40MM white star clusters his men would need to mark targets. Distribution of the entire stateside supply of 66MM rounds for the Army's standard hand-held, antivehicle rockets had been suspended because of reliability problems, and 250 rounds had to be diverted from a shipment bound for Vietnam. The Army's standard automatic shotgun fired too small a pattern at twenty meters for area fire while clearing buildings. Simons's men found the perfect 12-gauge model in a sporting- goods catalogue. Similar problems abounded. At times it must have seemed to Simons and his men that the Pentagon's logistics system was more of a threat than the guards at Son Tay would be.

By early October, nevertheless, Simons's men were equipped and ready, although all but four of them did not know what they were training for. Simons explained only that they might have to rescue diplomatic hostages from an embassy. By that time, his men had "assaulted" the Son Tay mockup 170 times. Every man had been cross-trained so he could take over several other jobs. Doc Cataldo, for instance, had become especially proficient with an ax. Each of the three assault teams had practiced filling in for the others in case one of the helicopters might have to abort or was shot down.

In mid-September, the tempo increased—several rehearsals during the day and several more at night, some with live ammunition. On September 28, the Air Force and Army teams began jointly practicing the assault in earnest—three helicopter landings or "insertions" were rehearsed each day, three more each night, some with empty weapons, the others with tracer ammunition and satchel charges, grenades, the works. By the time Manor and Simons took their men through a full-scale, live-fire, night dress rehearsal on October 6, Simons's men had walked, run, and crawled through the mockup so many times that they knew where every round was going—every friendly round, that is.

Manor's air crews had become just as proficient. In all,

they flew 1,017 hours and 368 sorties training for the 1,106-kilometer mission into Son Tay and back to Thailand: 697 of those hours and 268 sorties were spent rehearsing the assault itself and getting the POWs and Simons's men out of Son Tay. Herb Zehnder, for instance, had practiced landing his HH–3 inside the cramped compound 31 times: It was a tight fit to squeeze sixty-two–foot rotor blades between trees sixty-five feet apart and to maneuver a seventy-three-foot–long fuselage into an eighty-five–foot clearing. Marty Donohue, who would fly the lead helicopter into Son Tay, flew 15 live-fire missions, practicing shooting out the camp's guard towers with the side-firing Gatling guns on his HH–53.

None of this was normal flying, not even normal combat flying. The pilots were inventing new tactics and maneuvering their aircraft on the very edge of their performance capabilities. Two four-engine, MC–130 Combat Talon "mother ships," escorted by five A–1 propeller-driven attack planes, would guide five HH–53 and one HH–3 helicopters, like Seeing Eye dogs, on the 3.4-hour, 543.7-kilometer flight across Laos and into Son Tay. An HC–130 would refuel them en route. All of this had to be done in radio silence with the crews wearing night-vision goggles and the planes in tight formation, often twisting and weaving at treetop level over rugged terrain without any beacon lights.

The normal cruise speed of a C–130 at low altitude is about 250 knots, but for the Son Tay raid they had to fly at 105 knots, only about 10 knots above the plane's stall speed, because the HH–53 could not fly any faster. Both it and the HH–53s were so overloaded and so underpowered for the mission that they had to fly tucked in close behind the Combat Talons, literally sucked along in the plane's vacuum. At 105 knots, the HH–3 was pushing the upper boundary of its performance envelope; at 105 knots, the C–130 was at the rock bottom of its performance curve. That meant the C–130 crews had to fly using full power and 70-percent flaps, a configuration normally used for landing and one at which the plane is inherently unstable. Thus, the pilots would have to fly manually, unable to rely on their autopilots. The slowest an A–1 could fly with bombs, rockets, and fuel was about 145 knots, so its pilots had to devise tight circling and S-turn maneuvers to keep formation with the C–130s that they too depended on to guide them into the target.

By early October, the intricate aerial ballet was ready; so were Bull Simons's men. But no one else was.

Throughout September, Blackburn and Manor had been busy coordinating the mission with the Pentagon bureaucracy. On September 16, they appeared before the Joint Chiefs of Staff for a progress report. Manor said the task force would be ready to deploy by October 8, and he recommended that the rescue be scheduled for October 21. Then he had to fly to Military Airlift Command (MAC) headquarters in Illinois to arrange medical evacuation of

the POWs once they were safe in Thailand, to assure on-the-spot support in Southeast Asia for the mission from MAC's Air Weather Service, and to borrow HH–53s and an HH–3 in Thailand from MAC's Aerospace Rescue and Recovery Service. He carried with him a letter from Air Force Chief of Staff General John D. Ryan directing commanders worldwide to give Manor their full support on a "no questions asked" basis. Manor could not even tell four-star generals what he was up to; just what help he needed, but not when. At Tactical Air Command headquarters in southern Virginia he had to arrange use of the C–130s and A–1s he would need in Thailand.

On September 24 Manor was called to Washington to brief Defense Secretary Melvin R. Laird and CIA Director Richard Helms. Again he said that October 20–25 would present the best launch window, but Laird told him he would have to defer approval pending "coordination with higher authority." He did not tell Manor that the president's national security adviser, Henry Kissinger, had met secretly in Paris twice that month with Xuan Thuy, North Vietnam's chief negotiator, hoping to get a diplomatic solution to the POW issue.

The next day, Blackburn and Manor met in the Pentagon with Admiral John S. McCain, Jr., the commander-in-chief, Pacific. They were finally cleared to tell him of the rescue they would be conducting in McCain's back yard, but they had to tell him also that McCain's son, a Navy pilot taken prisoner three years earlier and known to be in bad shape, was not one of the prisoners believed to be in Son Tay. McCain said simply that he understood the implications. He promised everything in his power to help the operation succeed and agreed that only his chief of staff in Hawaii needed to know of the mission. Not even the commander-in-chief of the Pacific Fleet would be told, even though Task Force 77 under his command in the Gulf of Tonkin would be used to launch a diversion over Haiphong.

Two days later President Nixon left for a five-day trip to Europe. He tried to enlist Yugoslavia's help as well as the Pope's on the POW issue and then met with Laird and JCS chairman Moorer aboard the flagship *Springfield* on maneuvers in the Mediterranean. They told him of the rescue attempt that was ready to be launched.

Nixon approved the operation "in principle," but deferred a decision on when it would be made, saying only that first he wanted Kissinger briefed thoroughly. Soon after the president returned to the U.S. on October 5, Laird, Moorer, and Blackburn got word that the raid on Son Tay "might" have to be postponed. No one said so, but there were too many diplomatic initiatives under way on other fronts, particularly Nixon's hoped-for reconciliation with Communist China, and, as events would unfold, the timing for a major military operation in Vietnam late in October was hardly propitious. American writer Edgar Snow, for instance, had been invited to stand next to Chairman Mao Tse-tung at China's National Day ceremonies on October 1, a clear signal that Mao had given his blessing to a dialogue with President Nixon, his bitter enemy of twenty-five years, rekindling an initiative that had come to a screeching halt after the invasion of Cambodia in April and May. October 24, moreover, would be the twenty-fifth anniversary of the United Nations, and the next day Nixon would meet with the president of Pakistan to discuss a mid-November trip by the Pakistani to China in which he would quietly convey Nixon's hopes for "talks in Peking at a 'high level.' " And at a state dinner for the president of Rumania on the twenty-sixth, Nixon would toast that country's unique "good relations with the United States . . . the Soviet Union . . . and the People's Republic of China," the first reference ever by an American president to Communist China as "the People's Republic of China."

On Thursday, October 8, Blackburn, Manor, and Simons met with Henry Kissinger for thirty minutes in the West Wing of the White House and briefed him on Operation Ivory Coast. Blackburn emphasized that the mission had a "ninety-five to ninety-seven percent assurance of success." Kissinger was very complimentary of the plan and told Simons to "use whatever restraint is appropriate, but whatever force is essential." But when told the task force would have to begin deploying in two days for an October 20–25 launch window or else delay the raid until late November, the next suitable weather window, Kissinger said only vaguely that the president would have to decide.

Soon after the meeting, Blackburn and Manor were told the raid would be postponed and to reschedule everything for late November. Both of them remembered one odd thing about the briefing to Kissinger: He had not even asked how many prisoners were in Son Tay.

That was now a burning question, for the intelligence was becoming very garbled. Cloud cover had obscured the compound on some of the high-altitude reconnaissance flights flown in August and September, but some of the photos suggested there was "a decline in activity" at the camp, a euphemism meaning there was no sign of anyone there. For one thing, weeds were growing where the POWs would normally have trampled them. The low-altitude Buffalo Hunter drones, whose photos would show the height, color, eyes, and facial expressions of every man in the compound, but which the DIA used only sparingly lest too many flights tip off interest in the area, had run into a streak of bad luck. Seven drone "shots" were flown in September and October; at least two were downed by North Vietnamese gunners, and four had mechanical failures. The last one, on October 28, was a perfect launch, but it banked an instant too soon as it flew past the prison at treetop level. The drone was recovered with perfect pictures, but only of the horizon beyond Son Tay. The DIA decided it could not risk any more Buffalo Hunter flights as the date for the raid approached, yet the need for updated information on the camp was becoming critical. On Octo-

ber 3, for instance, an SR–71 flying at over three times the speed of sound had taken excellent photos of the camp from fifteen miles above the earth. The plane's technical objective camera produced stereoscopic photos sharp enough to count the number of people inside the camp, but the photo interpreters could not find any signs of POWs. Some analysts reasoned that the prisoners were being punished for something and confined to their cell blocks.

The DIA and the CIA considered inserting an agent near the camp, an option that had been ruled out earlier for fear of compromising the mission. But the CIA, the Pentagon learned, had just lost the one site in Laos from which an agent insertion might have been feasible. (Later, the raid's planners would admit that they never thought of seeding the area with the airdropped, remotely controlled sensors that had been implanted to monitor North Vietnamese traffic all along the Ho Chi Minh Trail under Igloo White. The listening devices could have been strewn randomly all

Colonel Arthur D. "Bull" Simons briefs his team in November 1970, just prior to their departure from Thailand en route to Son Tay.

over North Vietnam to avoid focusing undue attention on any discovered near Son Tay. Nor is it clear why low-altitude, manned reconnaissance flights were not flown over the compound. Notwithstanding the 1968 bombing stand down, an incredible 9,168 aircraft sorties were flown over North Vietnam between July and September of 1970, and 1,091 of those were reconnaissance sorties. Another 963 reconnaissance missions were flown there in October, November, and December.)

Amid this muddled intelligence picture, Blackburn, Manor, and Simons left on November 1 to fly across the Pacific to coordinate final details of the raid. A small staff flew separately to visit every base and unit that would have to support the operation. Admiral McCain was brought up to date, as was General Creighton Abrams, the commander of U.S. Military Assistance Command, Vietnam. Everything about the rescue had been so "compartmentalized," so tightly held, that it was the first time Abrams learned of an operation in his front yard that the Pentagon had been working on for five-and-a-half months. Abrams's chief of staff and his air deputy, the commander of the 7th Air Force, were the only other people in Saigon told of the mission. Manor and Simons then flew to an aircraft carrier in the Tonkin Gulf and briefed the commander of Task Force 77 on the diversionary raid over Haiphong that his aircraft would have to fly the night of the raid. The admiral clued in only two members of his staff, his operations officer and his intelligence officer, on what was about to take place.

By the time Blackburn arrived back at the Pentagon on November 10, SR–71 missions flown on November 2 and 6 had revealed "a definite increase in activity" at Son Tay; the "secondary school" south of the compound, which once also looked dormant, apparently had been "reactivated." Thus, the first contingent of the rescue task force left Eglin for Thailand on November 12, and three final SR–71 missions were added for November 13, 18, and 20 to provide the last-minute intelligence Manor and Simons would need. But that afternoon, November 12, Admiral Moorer asked Blackburn what the impact would be if the raid had to be delayed until December. Blackburn said it would be "devastating." The assault force was already en route; everyone was "up," psychologically "peaked"; there would not be another weather window for months; a recall now would mean serious risk of compromise. Minutes later, Blackburn's office received word that Moorer had just seen Laird, who was on his way to the White House. Not long after, Blackburn got good news: "It's a 'go.' "

The next day brought grim news: Six more POWs were dead. Peace activist Cora Weiss had been given their names by a North Vietnamese front organization. All six names had been counted as POWs held in the North. That made eleven POWs whose deaths had become known in 1970. The news renewed concern about the treatment of the Americans held prisoner and gave an even greater sense of urgency to the rescue that, by then, had been incubating for over six months. Manor and Simons left for Thailand the next afternoon.

While they were still en route, on November 16, the CIA tried to borrow the HH–53 helicopters they would need for the raid. Abrams had opposed it, but could not tell the station chief in Saigon why, and CIA action officers were screaming for the aircraft to support an urgent operation in southern Laos. Blackburn's deputy, Ed Mayer, defused the imbroglio by quickly arranging for the Air Force to temporarily ground all HH–53s worldwide because of a "potentially catastrophic technical problem": Only "safety-related test flights" were authorized until further notice. No sooner was that problem resolved than a message arrived that the president wanted a complete briefing on the raid the next afternoon, and that Moorer would need a whole new set of briefing charts, all done to a special White House format. But Blackburn and Mayer were in a quandary on what to say about the status of the task force because the prearranged, coded message that was supposed to notify them of Manor and Simons's arrival in Thailand was either lost or waylaid, or else their plane had gone down and no one had notified the National Military Command Center.

Just as the briefing charts were completed, instructions arrived for a completely new set in a different format and with more detail; the presidents's briefing had been postponed until next day. By that time, the only draftsman cleared for the operation was home baby-sitting, and Ed Mayer had to finish the charts and maps himself. By then, late on November 17, word should have arrived that the final contingent of Simons's assault force had arrived in Thailand, but that message too got waylaid, tied up in an automatic switching station in Japan that could not handle the special codes being used.

Execute

At 11:00 A.M. on Wednesday, November 18, Moorer's eighteen-minute briefing for the president went smoothly. His twenty-by-thirty-inch briefing charts were now labeled Operation Kingpin, the raid's third code name in six months; Moorer flipped the charts himself. Secretary of State William Rogers was present and learned for the first time that an "invasion" of North Vietnam would soon be under way. Nixon mused that the POWs at Son Tay—which, Moorer said, was still "the only confirmed active POW camp outside Hanoi"—might even be home in time for Thanksgiving dinner "right here at the White House." Moorer told him, "The ground commander is positive that the operation will succeed, Mr. President." Nixon asked what cover stories had been devised in case the raid failed. There were five of them. Late that afternoon Nixon gave Laird the go-ahead, and at 5:30 P.M. the National Military Command Center sent Manor the coded "Red Rocket" message to "execute."

The raid had been scheduled for the fall because of weather windows. Now that the president had given the final okay, Blackburn learned that the meteorologists could not have been more wrong in their prediction of good weather. Typhoon Patsy hit the Philippines with 105-mile-per-hour winds and gusts to 140, and it was headed for North Vietnam at 80 miles an hour. He was awakened about 4:00 A.M. the next morning with a message from Manor that "a delay due to weather was possible."

Twelve hours later, a typhoon of a different nature hit Washington: At 4:30 P.M. on November 19, the DIA's General Bennett caught up with Blackburn on his way to Moorer's office with "bad news." He told Moorer and Blackburn, "It looks like Son Tay is empty. I'm afraid we're too late." The prisoners had been moved. His information was straight from Hanoi.

The word had come from Nguyen Van Hoang, a middle-level but well-informed bureaucrat in the "Enemy Proselytizing Office," North Vietnam's euphemism for the group supervising POWs and their detention areas. Hoang was a senior research official there. "Research" meant that he dealt in particular with POW interrogations. Through a contact code named Alfred in the three-nation International Control Commission set up as a result of the 1954 Geneva accords dividing North and South Vietnam, the

U.S. had been cultivating Hoang for years. Alfred would feed him nuggets of information that Hoang's interrogators had been trying to extract from the POWs but which American officials were reasonably sure, from their debriefings of POWs released by the North, had not been compromised. Hoang, of course, could report that he had pieced the data together from POW interrogations, and the DIA and SACSA had worked hard to make sure the information was eventually corroborated for North Vietnam's defense ministry through other sources.

By late September of 1970, Alfred was reasonably sure that Hoang was ready for the "hook"—an outright trade of information. That opportunity arose in early November when Alfred was to fly home for "consultations" and, he confided to Hoang, possibly a big promotion. The only thing conceivably blocking it was his foreign ministry's inability to evoke any response from Hanoi on the POW issue. Like the other two neutral nations on the I.C.C., Alfred's foreign office was playing both sides against the middle, trying to please Washington as well as Hanoi.

Members of the assault force load into a C–130 bound for Udorn AFB, Thailand, where they will transfer to helicopters. Stored among the fire extinguishers (center) is one of the 30-pound wall-breaching charges.

Alfred complained that he had almost been "challenged" in a recent cable for information on how many POWs were really held in the North, because America was not "buying" the list of only the 339 men whom Hanoi had accounted for early in the year. Alfred remarked that the bureaucrats back home "must really be uptight" and speculated derisively, "I bet they would give anything for an answer."

A day or two before Alfred left Hanoi, Hoang wished Alfred success on his pending promotion and gave him a package of Thuoc La Bien cigarettes to enjoy on the flight home. Alfred noticed that the pack was partially open; Hoang said he wanted to make sure they were fresh. "They're pretty strong, so don't smoke them too fast," he joked. But Alfred did not smoke, and he was pretty sure Hoang knew that. In Hong Kong, he turned the pack over to a friend for further examination. The cigarettes were decoded in Washington by the following Thursday, just before Bennett met with Moorer and Blackburn. The DIA's analysts were intrigued with how Hoang had used a version of the POW's own tap code to spell out the number of men held in each prison camp. Son Tay was not on the list. Most of them were in a new camp DIA had never heard of, called Dan Hoi.

The SR-71's latest infrared imagery of Son Tay, however, showed that the camp was active. Someone was there. The photos taken on November 6 had produced only a picture of a cloud, the only one within a mile or so of the camp, but it was directly over the compound. On the November 13 mission there had been wisps of clouds over the camp and so many shadows that the photos were inconclusive. The last chance for photographic verification of prisoners had been the mission flown on November 18, the day before, but that SR-71 developed an airborne emergency and had to land in Thailand where there was none of the special equipment needed to process its film. The film had to be flown to Japan, but by the time it could be processed there, the raid would be under way.

Bennett's comment about being "too late" carried another grim connotation, for he had also learned through a special intelligence intercept called Gamma that North Vietnam would make known on November 23 that eleven more POWs were dead. One had died only fifteen days earlier. That made seventeen in 1970. Thus, with cruel irony, the Pentagon learned that day from one source that the raid on Son Tay might be too late, but from another source that rescuing the POWs was all the more urgent.

Bennett added a last-minute SR-71 mission that would make two passes over the prison early the next morning. A quick read-out of its "dump" could be relayed to Manor three-and-a-half hours before Simons's men would have to take off for Son Tay. If the photos confirmed the camp was empty, the raid could be recalled by a Red Rocket emergency message. But at 3:56 A.M. Washington time, 3:56 P.M.

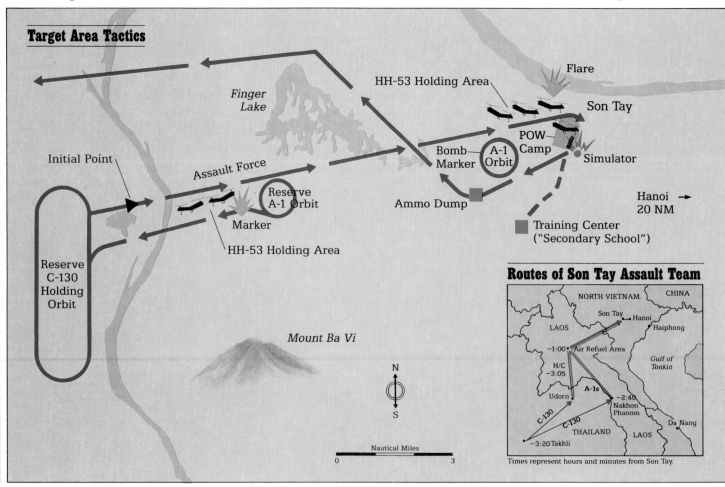

Target Area Tactics

Finger Lake

HH-53 Holding Area

Flare

Son Tay

Initial Point

Assault Force

Reserve A-1 Orbit

Marker

HH-53 Holding Area

Bomb Marker

A-1 Orbit

POW Camp

Simulator

Ammo Dump

Hanoi → 20 NM

Training Center ("Secondary School")

Reserve C-130 Holding Orbit

Mount Ba Vi

N

S

Nautical Miles

0   3

Routes of Son Tay Assault Team

NORTH VIETNAM   CHINA

Son Tay Hanoi

LAOS   Haiphong

−1:00 Air Refuel Area

H/C −3:05   Gulf of Tonkin

A-1s

Udorn   −2:40 Nakhon Phanom   Da Nang

C-130 C-130   LAOS

THAILAND

−3:20 Takhli

Times represent hours and minutes from Son Tay.

in Thailand, Manor sent a message to the Pentagon that he had decided to advance the raid by twenty-four hours: They would launch at 10:32 A.M. Washington time. A high-pressure ridge had formed over Hanoi and the weather was clearing there, but then Typhoon Patsy would move in with full force. It was the only launch window he would have for at least a week.

Moorer and Bennett conferred with Laird over breakfast. A decision needed to be made by 9:18 A.M.; the last chance to abort prior to launch would be at 10:08 A.M. Bennett was candid: He held a stack of photos, cables, and messages in one hand. "I've got this much that says 'They've been moved.'" In his other hand was a thick folder: "And I've got this much that says, 'They're still there.'" Like Blackburn, Bennett felt that it was worth the try. If it turned out the POWs had been moved back to Son Tay but the raid was canceled, it would be unforgivable. Moreover, they might never be given another chance. He told Moorer, "I recommend we go." Moorer agreed; he told Laird there was still a 50-50 chance and he wanted to go even if there was only a "10 percent chance." Laird talked with Richard Helms; he too thought the raid should go as planned. Laird picked up the secure phone to the White House, told Nixon of the conflicting reports about Son Tay, the weather crunch, and the Gamma intercepts that eleven more POWs were dead. Laird said he had decided to let the raid go. Nixon agreed.

At 6:00 P.M. in Thailand, Simons's men got their final briefing. Simons spoke for less than three minutes. "We are going to rescue seventy American prisoners of war, maybe more, from a camp called Son Tay. This is something American prisoners have a right to expect from their fellow soldiers. The target is twenty-three miles west of Hanoi." For a second or two, there was absolute silence. A few men let out low whistles. Then, spontaneously, they stood up and began applauding.

Five hours and eighteen minutes later, the last HH–53 took off from Udorn. Simons slept for most of the three-hour flight to Son Tay. He told his men to wake him twenty minutes away from the objective. As the last helicopter began refueling over Laos, fifty-five minutes from Son Tay, three aircraft carriers from Task Force 77 began launching the biggest air strike flown over North Vietnam since October 1968. Their target was Haiphong Harbor, so that the North Vietnamese air-defense system would focus its attention to the east, away from the route into Son Tay. But all the Navy planes were dropping over the densest air defenses in the world were flares, and none of the pilots knew why. To them the war had turned truly bizarre.

Minutes before Marty Donohue's HH–53 began its firing run on the guard towers at Son Tay, he saw the sky beyond Hanoi, over Haiphong, "lit up like the Fourth of July." Just as the prison came in sight, the sky above Son Tay exploded in brilliant light from flares dropped by one of the C–130s. It was 2:18 A.M., Hanoi time. Donohue could see firefight simulators exploding three kilometers east of Son Tay City, as if ground battles were raging all over the place. Suddenly, a yellow warning light in his cockpit began flashing, "transmission, transmission," as a buzzer signaled its impending disintegration and what was tantamount to an order for an emergency landing. Donohue told his copilot, "Ignore the sonovabitch." Seconds after he ordered his gunners to fire, the guard towers crashed into the ground, their 4x4-inch support posts chewed into sawdust by an almost solid hail of bullets.

Herb Zehnder's crash-landing inside the compound was much harder than Meadows and his thirteen men had expected. The trees in Son Tay's courtyard had grown much bigger than anyone had calculated and the helicopter twisted violently thirty or forty degrees to the right as its rotors tore through the limbs. The impact was so hard that a fire extinguisher tore loose from its bracket and broke the flight engineer's ankle. One of Meadows's men was thrown off the open, rear ramp. Meadows ran about fifteen meters from the helicopter and, as the whine of its engines died, pressed the trigger on his bullhorn and announced as calmly as he could, "We're Americans. Keep your heads down. This is a rescue. We're here to get you out. Keep your heads down." But as his men raced for the cell blocks and east gate, there were no answering cries.

Three minutes into the raid, Meadows was relieved to hear a blast behind him, leaving a gaping hole in the south wall that Bull Simons's team presumably had blown open with satchel charges so they could get the POWs out quickly and into the HH–53s waiting there. But the men who rushed through the breach into covering positions inside the compound were Sydnor's men, not Simons's.

Bull Simons had landed at the wrong camp. His twenty-two–man contingent, the largest part of the raiding force, was now 400 meters south of the target, plunked down outside the compound that the "spooks" had labeled "secondary school." It was a horrendous blunder, but one easily made. The two compounds were about the same size, and a canal north of the school was easily mistaken in the moonlight for the Song Cong River as it turned east just north of the prison. The helicopter carrying Sydnor, ahead of Simons, had drifted a few hundred meters south as it approached the prison and corrected course only at the last minute, but Simons's HH–53 was too far atrail, and Warner Britton was too busy concentrating on his landing zone to see the ship ahead of him change course in the last few seconds. Sydnor saw the mistake as soon as he hit the ground two minutes and forty-five seconds into the raid, and he calmly ordered one of the alternate plans they had rehearsed so often put into effect.

Britton's blunder proved one of the most fortuitous mistakes of the Vietnam War. The school's walls were ringed with barbed wire with guards all around the outside. Seconds after landing, Simons and his men were engaged in an intense firefight. But they had the advantage of surprise: Simons launched what he called a "pre-emptive

The raid. Just seconds after their helicopter has landed in the Son Tay Prison compound, the rescue team fans out according to its meticulously rehearsed plan.

strike," and in five minutes the school was a blazing ruin. By the time Britton wracked his HH–53 back into a tight turn to land amid what looked like an exploding ammunition dump, eight minutes into the raid, Simons and his men had killed somewhere between 100 and 200 very well-armed North Vietnamese and Chinese or Russian soldiers. As he was racing back aboard the helicopter, Captain Udo Walther's belt broke and he stripped a belt off a nearby body to hold his pants up.

Nine minutes into the raid, Simons called for insurance, an air strike between the prison and the school. Thirty seconds later, as Britton was landing outside the walls of Son Tay, Simons radioed Sydnor and Meadows to revert back to the basic plan.

Britton had set a new record—three combat assault sorties in nine-and-a-half minutes. By the time his helicopter set down at the right camp, Meadows's men had finished searching the cell blocks and he was radioing, "Search complete. Negative items." Most of the North Vietnamese at Son Tay were dead or wounded, shot before their eyes could focus on the crazy Americans who were shooting up a prison that was empty.

Simons sent one of his men to photograph the empty cells and, fourteen minutes into the raid, signaled Meadows to blow up what was left of the HH–3 in the compound and for the HH–53s to begin extracting his men. Twenty-eight minutes after it began, the raid on Son Tay was over.

Save for the landing at the "secondary school," Simons's men and Britton's pilots had performed flawlessly. The Navy diversion had worked. Surprise was total. There were only two minor casualties, one man with a broken ankle, another with a flesh wound in the thigh. The assault had been fast and violent; the search had been swift, the fire precise, the reactions unflappable, the withdrawal smooth. There was only one thing missing—there were no prisoners with them as Simons's men headed west to marry up with the tankers that would refuel them over Laos. The men flew back to Thailand in disappointed silence.

Aftermath

There was nothing quiet about world reaction to the raid. Within hours of landing at Udorn at 4:28 A.M., Simons and Manor were directed to fly back to Washington. They landed at Andrews Air Force Base about 3:00 A.M. Monday morning, November 25, got a few hours sleep, and were driven to the Pentagon for breakfast with Laird. Simons would recall later that most of the discussion centered on what to say at a press conference Laird would hold that afternoon. He was taken aback by Laird's questions about whether the raid could be kept secret, how long the "lid" could be kept on it, and what was the "least" that could be said. Exasperated, Simons urged Laird to go public with everything he could; there was nothing to be ashamed of.

Laird's press conference lasted forty-two minutes; reporters asked thirty-five questions; Laird fielded ten of them and let Manor and Simons handle the rest.

It was not the most informative or candid report America received on the Vietnam War. Asked how many men were on the mission, if it had a code name, if the rescue force had flown from an aircraft carrier, what kind of "helicopter" was involved, how many men they hoped to free, if they had taken any prisoners, and if they had an alternate target, the three "briefers" answered only, "I can't answer that." Forty percent of the questions received such nonanswers. Asked if he had killed anybody, Simons said only, "Yes, I would imagine so."

Almost six years would pass before America learned that the Pentagon had been forewarned Son Tay was probably empty; that, ironically, the prisoners there had been moved on July 14, just one day after Bull Simons was picked to command the rescue team; and that part of his raiding force had landed at the wrong compound and killed hundreds of enemy soldiers at a "secondary school." Even then it still was not clear whether they were North Koreans, Russians, or Chinese. That they were Chinese was not confirmed until ten years after the raid when the belt buckle Captain Walther had taken was identified as that of a Chinese officer.

Given what little the Pentagon made known about the Son Tay raid immediately after it, it is little wonder that press, public, and Congressional reactions were mixed at best. Some newspapers damned it with faint praise, others were outright hostile. Headlines like these were typical:

"U.S. Raid to Rescue POWs Fails"
"Senators Appalled at Forays"
"Incursions by U.S. Raise New Peril for Nixon Policy"
"Paris Session Canceled As Reds Protest Raids"

Editorials expressed pride that America had tried to free its POWs, but ridiculed the intelligence failure that led the Pentagon to raid an empty prison. The harshest criticism came from Capitol Hill and the evening television newscasts. Eric Sevareid of CBS noted caustically that although "everyone admires the brave men who tried it, a great many cannot help feeling there was something hare-brained about the concept." ABC's John Scali charged that "outdated, inadequate intelligence is being blamed for the failure. And the finger," he added, "is being pointed at the Pentagon's Defense Intelligence Agency, not the government's Central Intelligence Agency, which was not involved." That, obviously, was the product of a "cover-your-ass" leak from the CIA. Other news reports would insist that the raid had been "planned and executed without consulting the CIA." Even Vice President Spiro Agnew decried the "faulty intelligence" behind the raid—although he was never briefed on it, before or after.

At one of many hearings about the raid on Capitol Hill,

Operation Popeye

The perfectly executed attempt to rescue American POWs at Son Tay Prison in North Vietnam ended in disappointment when American raiders landed inside the compound only to find the prison's cell blocks empty. Later, they would learn that the North Vietnamese had moved the POWs months earlier when a flood, caused by the summer monsoon's torrential rains, had threatened the prison camp. Nature seemed to have played a cruel trick on the rescue party.

But the flood that undermined the mission may not have been simply a whim of nature. Even as the Son Tay raiders trained for the rescue during the summer of 1970, another group of Americans was engaged in a top-secret operation whose goal was to increase the seasonal rainfall in northeastern Laos, west of Son Tay. This operation, code named Popeye, may

have inadvertently triggered the flood near the POW camp.

Popeye was one of several designations for a weather-modification program initiated by the Department of Defense and the CIA in March 1967. Its aim was to intensify the monsoon rains in Laos and North Vietnam in order to inhibit North Vietnamese traffic along the Ho Chi Minh Trail. To do this, U.S. pilots airdropped cloud-seeding pellets of lead and silver iodide, which, if successful, would provoke rains that would wash away river crossings, create landslides, and render roads impassable. CIA teams in northern Laos also released tons of emulsifiers to make trails and riverbanks even more slippery.

Between 1967 and 1972, American pilots flew 2,602 sorties in Operation Popeye, and many of these drops targeted the region west of Son Tay Prison. In the program's first two years pilots seeded primarily over North Vietnam, but with the bombing halt in that country in November 1968, they shifted their operations to Laos, concentrating on an area contiguous with the North Vietnamese border west and southwest of Son Tay. In 1970

Operation Popeye expanded to include the southern section of Laos, but the target area west of the prison camp also doubled. And most missions in 1970 occurred between March and November, during the organizing and planning of the rescue.

The Son Tay planners and raiders were never informed of the odd air strikes in eastern Laos even though weather conditions were an important factor in the success of the rescue mission. This is not surprising, however, for Operation Popeye was one of the most closely held secrets of the Vietnam War. Information about the program was so highly classified that some of President Nixon's closest advisers knew nothing of it.

Whether or not Operation Popeye played a role in the flooding of Son Tay can never be absolutely determined. Important statistics for the operation are no longer available, and they probably would prove inconclusive given the ambiguous nature of any weather-modification program. Operation Popeye remains an intriguing footnote to the raid on Son Tay, one that raises more questions than it answers.

Senator J. William Fulbright, chairman of the Foreign Relations Committee, upbraided Laird: "I personally asked the Director of Central Intelligence Board [sic] if he was consulted and he said 'No.' " Laird replied simply, "I don't think that can quite be the case." Fulbright called the raid a "major escalation of the war," and said, "It was a very provocative act to mount a physical invasion." Senator Birch Bayh told newsmen he feared the operation might "result in POWs being executed." Laird predicted that, on the contrary, POW treatment would improve. But Congressman Charles Vanik said, "This vain action jeopardizes the life of the prisoners of war who still survive in North Vietnam," and Representative Robert Leggett insisted that the raid had "radically decreased our chances of negotiating better treatment" for the POWs.

But 9,500 miles away from Washington, a totally different picture emerged. At "very early daylight" on the morning after the Son Tay raid, the POWs in Dan Hoi Prison, where most of the Son Tay prisoners had been moved in July, found out what a panic move was like. Guards told them to "roll up"—dishes, drinking cups, everything. Blindfolded, slapped into manacles, they were jammed into trucks and driven late that evening to downtown Hanoi and thrown into Hoa Lo Prison, the Hanoi Hilton. Close to fifty POWs from one entire compound at Dan Hoi were jammed into a single, huge room at Hoa Lo in an old part

of the prison in which Americans had never before been held. Similar POW roundups continued for weeks from the eight other prison camps outside of Hanoi that were scattered over North Vietnam.

One POW, who had been moved five times in three years with only one, two, three, two, and then (in September of 1970) seven cell-mates, suddenly found himself back in Hoa Lo Prison with fifty-seven cell-mates. Another man, Ernie Brace, a CIA Air America pilot who had been shot down over Laos in May 1965 but managed to pass himself as an Air Force major, had spent two-and-a-half years chained up in a damp, dark, vermin-infested cave near Dien Bien Phu, eight kilometers from the Laotian border. Kept in irons for over 900 days, he was later moved, again in solitary, to a closet-like room at a prison in North Vietnam called the Plantation. Inexplicably, he found himself in the Hanoi Hilton late in November 1970, still in solitary, but surrounded by scores of Americans with whom he could communicate. Air Force Col. Theodore W. Guy, shot down over Laos in 1968, had been in solitary for almost 1,000 days; moved to Hoa Lo in November 1970, he saw his first American in almost three years of captivity. Air Force Col. Norman C. Gaddis, shot down in May 1967, had spent over 1,000 days in solitary; none of the other POWs had seen him. After Son Tay, he got his first roommate in four-and-a-half years.

Crowded into Hoa Lo, the POWs became "incredibly well organized." They defied their captors, giving each other medical care; holding church services; teaching each other college-level algebra, differential calculus, French, German, and Spanish; and reenacting movies. In fact, many of the POWs would joke later that they became *too* organized. They formed themselves into the Fourth Allied POW Wing—"fourth" because they were POWs in the fourth war America had fought in the twentieth century, "allied" because locked up among them were two Thais and one Vietnamese, a pilot nicknamed Max. Born in Hanoi, he had fled to South Vietnam in 1954 and was shot down over North Vietnam on a 1966 air strike led by Marshal Nguyen Cao Ky. The wing was organized along standard Air Force lines: Different cell blocks were designated squadrons, and each squadron was broken down into flights, each led by its senior ranking officer with responsibility for preparing periodic Officer Efficiency Reports, determining awards and decorations, and administering the Uniform Code of Military Justice, to include nonjudicial punishment as well as summary and special court-martials. (Some prisoners were, in fact, court-martialed by their superiors and fellow inmates, although details on who and why remain classified.) Each squadron organization, by formal directive of the wing commander (now Colonel John P. Flynn, who was at last in communication with the other POWs), included a full staff—including men designated as athletic, medical, or sanitation officers. But one POW later quipped that "it all went too far" when his flight leader "insisted on holding formal staff meetings every morning."

What it meant to the POWs was that the slow passage of time ceased to be so oppressive—although the men still suffered from horrible prison conditions. As the POWs in Hoa Lo Prison compared notes, sometimes through the tap code with prisoners still held in isolation, they learned that at least three fellow POWs had gone insane. The men came from a group known as "the Lonely Hearts," eleven POWs identified by a fellow captive as being held by the North Vietnamese but who were kept isolated even after the Son Tay roundup—men who never came home.

But as one Son Tay POW summed it up after he came home in 1973, "The Son Tay raid may have saved the sanity of some others." When he stepped off an airplane at Clark Air Force Base in the Philippines on March 14, 1973, in the second contingent of prisoners of war returned from North Vietnam, a television audience even bigger than had seen Neil Armstrong and Buzz Aldrin land on the moon in 1969 was watching—choked with emotion, grateful the ordeal was over.

America's longest-held POW, Lieutenant Commander Everett Alvarez, Jr., departs Clark Air Force Base in the Philippines to begin the final leg of his long journey home in 1973.

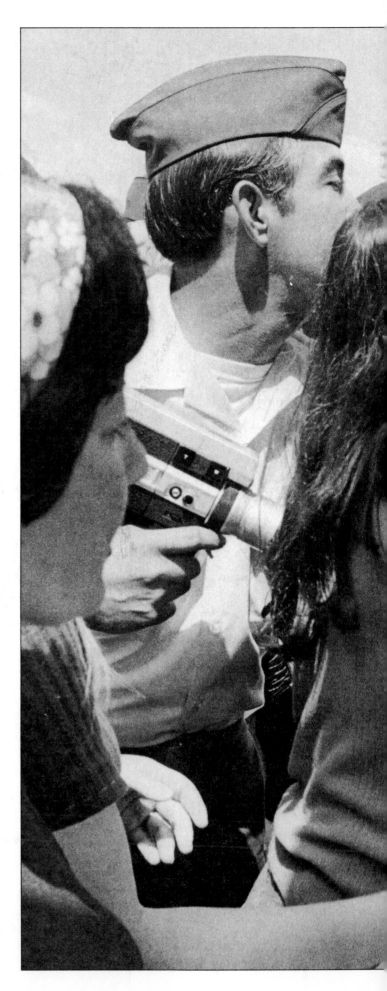

Bibliography

I. Books and Articles

American Enterprise Institute for Public Policy Research. *Vietnam Settlement: Why 1973, Not 1969?*, 1973.

Asprey, Robert B. *War in the Shadows: The Guerrilla in History.* Vols. 1 and 2. Doubleday, 1975.

Austin, Anthony. *The President's War.* J.B. Lippincott, 1971.

Bamford, James. *The Puzzle Palace.* Penguin Bks., 1983.

"Better Deal for Service Spooks?" *Armed Forces Journal*, December 1971.

Blaufarb, Douglas S. *The Counterinsurgency Era: U.S. Doctrine and Performance.* Free Pr., 1977.

Burchett, Wilfred G. *Inside Story of the Guerrilla War.* International Publishers, 1965.

Buttinger, Joseph. *Vietnam: A Dragon Embattled.* Vol. 2. Praeger, 1967.

Colby, William E., and Peter Forbath. *Honorable Men: My Life in the CIA.* Simon & Schuster, 1978.

Cook, Capt. John L. *The Advisor.* Dorrance & Co., 1973.

Cooper, Chester L. *The Lost Crusade: America in Vietnam.* Dodd, Mead, 1970.

Corson, William R. *The Betrayal.* Norton, 1968.

Daniels, Ian. "The Five-Week Siege of Phalane." *Eagle*, September 1985.

Daugherty, William E., and Morris Janowitz. *A Psychological Warfare Casebook.* Johns Hopkins Univ. Pr., 1958.

David, Heather. *Operation Rescue.* Pinnacle Bks., 1971.

De Silva, Peer. *Sub Rosa: The CIA and the Uses of Intelligence.* Times Bks., 1978.

Dessaint, Alain Y. "The Poppies Are Beautiful This Year." *Natural History*, February 1972.

Dickinson, Paul. *The Electronic Battlefield.* Indiana Univ. Pr., 1976.

"Dissent." *Armed Forces Journal*, July 1974.

Donlon, Roger H.C., and Warren Rogers. *Outpost of Freedom.* McGraw-Hill, 1965.

Dramesi, John A. *Code of Honor.* Norton, 1975.

Duiker, William J. *The Road to Communist Power in Vietnam.* Westview Pr., 1982.

Effros, William G., ed. *Quotations, Vietnam: 1945-1970.* Random House, 1970.

Eisenhower, Dwight D. *Waging Peace: The White House Years.* Doubleday, 1965.

Frisbee, John L. "Igloo White." *Air Force*, June 1981.

Gaither, Ralph, as told to Steve Henry. *With God in a POW Camp.* Broadman Pr., 1973.

Gallucci, Robert L. *Neither Peace nor Honor: The Politics of American Policy in Vietnam.* Johns Hopkins Univ. Pr., 1975.

Gibbons, William C. *The U.S. Government and the Vietnam War.* Part 2: *1961-1964.* Princeton Univ. Pr., 1986.

Gibson, James William. *The Perfect War: Technowar in Vietnam.* Atlantic Monthly Pr., 1986.

Goodman, Allen E. "Political Implications of Rural Development Problems in South Vietnam: Creating Public Interest." *Asian Survey*, August 1970.

Goulden, Joseph C. *Truth Is the First Casualty.* Rand-McNally, 1968.

Halberstam, David. *The Best and the Brightest.* Random House, 1972.

Harkins, Philip. *Blackburn's Headhunters.* Norton, 1956.

Hersh, Seymour M. *The Price of Power: Kissinger in the Nixon White House.* Summit Bks., 1983.

Hilsman, Roger A. *To Move a Nation: The Politics of Foreign Policy in the Administration of John Fitzgerald Kennedy.* Doubleday, 1967.

How We Won the War. Recon Publications, 1976.

Hubbell, John G. *P.O.W.* Reader's Digest Pr., 1976.

Johnson, Lyndon Baines. *The Vantage Point: Perspectives of the Presidency.* Holt, Rinehart & Winston, 1971.

Johnson, U. Alexis, with Jef Olivarius McAllister. *The Right Hand of Power: The Memoirs of an American Diplomat.* Prentice-Hall, 1984.

Kahin, George McT. *Intervention: How America Became Involved in Vietnam.* Knopf, 1986.

Kalb, Bernard, and Marvin Kalb. *Kissinger.* Little, Brown, 1974.

Karnow, Stanley. *Vietnam: A History.* Viking Pr., 1983.

Kerby, Robert L. "American Military Airlift During the Laotian Civil War." *Aerospace Historian*, Spring 1977.

Kissinger, Henry. *The White House Years.* Little, Brown, 1979.

Krepinevich, Andrew F., Jr. *The Army and Vietnam.* Johns Hopkins Univ. Pr., 1986.

Lansdale, Edward Geary. *In the Midst of Wars: An American's Mission to Southeast Asia.* Harper & Row, 1972.

Lasky, Victor. *JFK: The Man and the Myth.* Macmillan, 1963.

"Last Medals of Honor of the Vietnam War." *Armed Forces Journal*, March 1976.

Leary, William M. *Perilous Missions.* Univ. of Alabama Pr., 1984.

Lewis, Flora. "Heroin and the CIA." *Atlantic Monthly*, November 1972.

Littauer, Ralph, and Norman Uphoff, eds. *The Air War in Indochina.* Revised ed. Beacon Pr., 1972.

Lodge, Henry Cabot. *The Storm Has Many Eyes: A Personal Narrative.* Norton, 1973.

MacCloskey, Gen. Monro. *Alert the Fifth Force.* Richards Rosen Pr., 1969.

McCoy, Alfred W. "Flowers of Evil." *Harper's*, July 1972.

_____ . *The Politics of Heroin in Southeast Asia.* Harper & Row, 1972.

McCullouch, Frank. "Laos: The Awakening." *Time*, June 26, 1964.

McGleish, Wayland. "Opium and the Hill Tribes." *America*, June 10, 1972.

McGrath, John M. *Prisoner of War: Six Years in Hanoi.* Naval Institute Pr., 1975.

Mecklin, John. *Mission in Torment: An Intimate Account of the U.S. Role in Vietnam.* Doubleday, 1965.

Mersky, Peter B., and Norman Polmar. *The Naval Air War in Vietnam.* Nautical & Aviation Publishing, 1981.

Meyerson, Harvey. *Vinh Long.* Houghton Mifflin, 1970.

Molnar, Andrew R., et al. *Undergrounds in Insurgent, Revolutionary, and Resistance Warfare.* Special Operations Research Office, American Univ., 1963.

My Visit to the Liberated Zones of South Vietnam. Foreign Languages Publishing House, 1964.

Nalty, Bernard C., et al. *An Illustrated Guide to the Air War over North Vietnam.* Arco, 1981.

Nguyen Cao Ky. *Twenty Years and Twenty Days.* Stein & Day, 1976.

Nixon, Richard M. *RN: The Memoirs of Richard Nixon.* Grosset & Dunlap, 1978.

Noble, Dennis L. "Cutters and Sampans." In *U.S. Naval Institute Proceedings*, June 1984.

Norodom Sihanouk, as related to Wilfred Burchett. *My War with the CIA: The Memoirs of Prince Norodom Sihanouk.* Penguin Bks., 1973.

"Our Outgunned Spies." *Armed Forces Journal*, December 1971.

Phan Thi Quyen and Tran Dinh Van. *Nguyen Van Troi as He Was.* Foreign Languages Publishing House, 1965.

Phillips, Brig. Gen. T.R., ed. *Roots of Strategy.* Military Service Publishing Co., 1955.

Pike, Douglas. *Viet Cong: The Organization and Techniques of the National Liberation Front of South Vietnam.* MIT Pr., 1966.

Plumb, Charles. *I'm No Hero: A P.O.W. Story as Told to Gwen de Werff.* Independence Pr., 1973.

"POW Profile: The Upward Trend in Letter-Writing." *Armed Forces Journal*, October 5, 1970.

Prados, John. *Presidents' Secret Wars: CIA and Pentagon Covert Operations Since World War II.* Morrow, 1986.

Race, Jeffrey. *War Comes to Long An: Revolutionary Conflict in a Vietnamese Province.* Univ. of California Pr., 1972.

Risner, Robinson. *The Passing of the Night: My Seven Years as a Prisoner of the North Vietnamese.* Ballantine Bks., 1973.

Robbins, Christopher. *Air America.* G.P. Putnam's Sons, 1979.

Rodman, Peter W. "Sideswipe: Kissinger, Shawcross, and the Responsibility for Cambodia." *American Spectator*, March 1981.

Rowan, Roy. *The Four Days of the Mayaguez.* Norton, 1975.

Rowe, James N. *Five Years to Freedom.* Little, Brown, 1971.

Ruhl, Robert K. "Raid at Son Tay." *Airman*, August 1975.

Rust, William J., and the editors of U.S. News Bks. *Kennedy in Vietnam: American Vietnam Policy, 1961-1963.* Scribner's, 1985.

Schanche, Don A. *Mister Pop.* David McKay Co., 1967.

Schemmer, Benjamin F. *The Raid.* Harper & Row, 1976.

Schemmer, Benjamin F., and the editors of *Armed Forces Journal.* *Almanac of Liberty.* Macmillan, 1974.

Schlesinger, Arthur M. *A Thousand Days.* Houghton Mifflin, 1963.

Schwanhausser, Robert R. "RPV's: Angel in the Battle, Victim in the Budget." *Armed Forces Journal*, November 1974.

Sharp, Adm. U.S.G. *Strategy for Defeat: Vietnam in Retrospect.* Presidio Pr., 1978.

Shawcross, William. *Sideshow: Kissinger, Nixon, and the Destruction of Cambodia.* Simon & Schuster, 1979.

Sheehan, Neil. "C.I.A. Says VC Hold Vital Posts in Saigon." *New York Times*, October 19, 1970.

Simpson, Col. Charles M., III. *Inside the Green Berets.* Berkley Bks., 1984.

Sisouk Na Champassak. *Storm Over Laos: A Contemporary History.* Praeger, 1961.

Smith, Joseph Burkholder. *Portrait of a Cold War Warrior.* G.P. Putnam's Sons, 1976.

Smith, Nicol, and Blake Clark. *Into Siam: Underground Kingdom.* Bobbs-Merrill, 1945.

Sochurek, Howard. "American Special Forces in Action in Vietnam." *National Geographic*, January 1965.

Stanton, Shelby L. *Green Berets at War: U.S. Army Special Forces in Southeast Asia, 1965-1975*. Presidio Pr., 1986.

_____ . *Vietnam Order of Battle*. U.S. News Bks., 1981.

Steinhauser, Thomas C. "How to Make Flag Rank." *Armed Forces Journal*, July 1972.

Stockdale, Jim, and Sybil Stockdale. *In Love and War*. Harper & Row, 1984.

Taylor, Gen. Maxwell. *Swords and Plowshares*. Norton, 1972.

Thayer, Thomas C. "Territorial Forces." In *The Lessons of Vietnam*, edited by W. Scott Thompson and Donaldson D. Frizzell. Crane, Russak, 1977.

"There's Always a Chance." *Armed Forces Journal*, March 1973.

To Arm the Revolutionary Masses, To Build the People's Army. Foreign Languages Publishing House, 1975.

Truong Nhu Tang, with David Chanoff and Doan Van Toai. *A Vietcong Memoir*. Harcourt Brace Jovanovich, 1985.

"U.S. Raiders Killed 100-200 Chinese Troops in 1970 North Vietnam Foray." *Armed Forces Journal*, January 1980.

Van Dyke, Jon M. *North Vietnam's Strategy for Survival*. Pacific Bks., 1972.

Van Tien Dung, Gen. *Our Great Spring Victory: An Account of the Liberation of South Vietnam*. Monthly Review Pr., 1977.

Vo Nguyen Giap, Gen. *Big Victory, Great Task*. Praeger, 1968.

Weaver, Robert A. "A New Expanded 1975 Version of the Army Writer's Dictionary (6th Edition)." *Armed Force Journal*, May 1975.

Weiss, George. "Battle for Control of the Ho Chi Minh Trail." *Armed Forces Journal*, February 15, 1971.

Westmoreland, Gen. William C. *A Soldier Reports*. Doubleday, 1976.

Zapinski, Leonard E. *Ten Days in November 1970: An Incredible Story*. Unpublished ms., 1984.

II. Government and Government-Sponsored Published Reports

Berger, Carl, ed. *The United States Air Force in Southeast Asia, 1961-1973*. Office of Air Force History, 1977.

Bowers, Raymond L. *The United States Air Force in Southeast Asia: Tactical Airlift*. Office of Air Force History, 1983.

Cabinet Committee on International Narcotics Control. "World Opium Survey 1972." In *Drug Use in America*, Appendix 3. GPO, 1973.

Conley, Michael Charles. *The Communist Insurgent Infrastructure in South Vietnam*. Vols. 1 and 2. Prepared by the Center for Research in Social Systems, American Univ., for the U.S. Army, 1967.

Futrell, Robert F. *The United States Air Force in Southeast Asia: The Advisory Years to 1965*. Office of Air Force History, 1981.

Hanoi's Strategy of Terror. Southeast Asia Treaty Organization, 1970.

Hoang Ngoc Lung, Col. *Indochina Monographs: Intelligence*. U.S. Army, Office of the Chief of Military History, 1981.

_____ . *Indochina Refugee Authored Monograph Program: Intelligence*. Study OAD-CR-155, General Research Corp., 1976.

Hosmer, Stephen T. *Viet Cong Repression and Its Implications for the Future*. Study R-475-ARPA, Rand Corp., 1970.

Kelly, Col. Francis J. *Vietnam Studies: U.S. Army Special Forces, 1961-1971*. Department of the Army, 1973.

Komer, Robert W. *Bureaucracy Does Its Thing: Institutional Constraints on U.S.-GVN Performance in Vietnam*. Rand Corp., 1972.

Leites, Nathan. *The Viet Cong Style of Politics*. Memorandum RM-5487-ISA/ARPA, Rand Corp., 1969.

Marolda, Edward J., and Oscar P. Fitzgerald. *The United States Navy and the Vietnam Conflict. Vol. 2: From Military Assistance to Combat, 1959-1965*. Naval Historical Center, 1986.

Oudone Sananikone, Maj. Gen. *The Royal Lao Army and U.S. Army Advice and Support*. U.S. Army, Office of the Chief of Military History, 1978.

The Pentagon Papers: The Defense Department History of the United States Decisionmaking on Vietnam. 4 vols. Beacon Pr., 1972.

Republic of Vietnam. Ministry of Information. *Vietnam, 1967-1971: Toward Peace and Prosperity*. GPO, 1971.

Scoville, Thomas W. *Vietnam Studies: Reorganization for Pacification Support*. U.S. Army Center of Military History. GPO, 1982.

Sharp, Adm. U.S.G., and Gen. W.C. Westmoreland. *Report on the War in Vietnam*. GPO, 1968.

Soutchay Vongsavanh, Maj. Gen. *RLG Operations and Activities in the Laotian Panhandle*. U.S. Army, Office of the Chief of Military History, 1978.

Spector, Ronald H. *The U.S. Army in Vietnam: The Early Years*. U.S. Army Center of Military History, 1983.

Thayer, Thomas C. "How to Analyze a War without Fronts: Vietnam, 1965-1972." *Journal of Defense Research, Section B: Tactical Warfare*, Fall 1975.

U.S. Congress. House. Committee on Armed Services. *United States-Vietnam Relations: 1945-1967* [Pentagon Papers]. GPO, 1971.

_____ . Subcommittee on Procurement and Military Nuclear Systems. Testimony of Donald N. Fredericksen. "Unmanned Aerial Vehicle System Applications in the Department of Defense," February 25, 1986.

_____ . Committee on Foreign Affairs. *The U.S. Heroin Problem and Southeast Asia*. 93d Congress, 1st sess., 1973.

_____ . Subcommittee on Oceans and International Environment. *Weather Modifications*. 93d Congress, 2d sess., 1974.

_____ . Select Committee on Missing Persons in Southeast Asia. *Americans Missing in Southeast Asia*. Parts 1 and 2. 94th Congress, 1st sess., 1975 and 1976.

_____ . *Written Report of Lieutenant General Vernon A. Walters, USA, Deputy Director, Central Intelligence Agency*. Submitted March 17, 1976.

_____ . Subcommittee of the Committee on Government Operations. *Hearings on U.S. Assistance Programs in Vietnam*. 92d Congress, 1st sess., 1971.

_____ . Senate. Committee on Armed Services. *Bombing in Cambodia*. 93d Congress, 1st sess., 1973.

_____ . Committee on Foreign Relations. *Bombing Operations and the Prisoner-of-War Rescue Mission in North Vietnam*. 91st Congress, 2d sess., 1971.

_____ . *U.S. Air Operations in Cambodia, April 1973*. Staff report. 93d Congress, 1st sess., 1973.

_____ . Subcommittee on National Security Policy and Scientific Developments. *American Prisoners of War in Southeast Asia, 1971*. Parts 1 and 2. 92d Congress, 1st sess., 1971 and 1972.

_____ . Select Committee to Study Governmental Operations with Respect to Intelligence Activities. Book 1: *Foreign and Military Intelligence*. Book 2: *Intelligence Activities and the Rights of Americans*. 94th Congress, 2d sess., 1976.

U.S. Department of Defense. Office Assistant Secretary of Defense (Comptroller). *Southeast Asia Statistical Digest*, Table 6. 1966-1973.

_____ . Office Assistant Secretary of Defense (Public Affairs). Transcript of secretary of defense's press conference on the Son Tay prisoner-of-war raid. November 23, 1970.

U.S. Joint Chiefs of Staff. Historical Office. *Chronology of the Vietnam War. 1955-1972*.

The Viet-Cong Strategy of Terror. U.S. Mission in Vietnam, 1970.

III. Unpublished Government and Military Sources

Eisenhower Papers. "Laos Visit." September 24, 1956, memorandum.

Indochina Archive, Univ. of California (Berkeley), various documents.
    Donn F. Downing. "A Political Homiletic," n.d.

Lyndon Baines Johnson Library. National Security File: NSC Aides File (Bundy); Country File: Vietnam; Agency File.

John Fitzgerald Kennedy Library. National Security File: Meetings and Memos File; Country File: Vietnam.

MACV-SOG AVGB-CCS Letter, Subject: MIA Board Proceedings and Recommendations, May 2, 1968.

MACV-SOG Commander Letter from Colonel Blackburn to Colonel Marttinen, Office of the Deputy Chief of Staff for Military Operations, November 3, 1965.

National Archives. Records Group 273: Records of the National Security Council.

National Security Archive. George McTurnan Kahin Collection (consisting of Vietnam documents released under the Freedom of Information Act or drawn from the Kennedy and Johnson archives).

National Security Council. National Security Study Memorandum 1. In *Congressional Record*, May 10, 1972.

Special Operations Association, Fact Sheet, Subject: Major Thorne, June 30, 1983.

U.S. Air Force. Briefing on the Son Tay Raid. Brig. Gen. Leroy J. Manor. 1971. Untitled.

U.S. Army Military History Institute. Document Collection.
    United States Army. Field Training Team 39. "Mission After Action Report."
    United States Operations Mission to Laos. January 10, 1957, report. "Country Statement on Military Assistance Program."
    _____ . Program Evaluation Office. September 1959. "Narrative Statement."
    _____ . Oral History Collection.
    Blackburn, Brig. Gen. Donald D. 1978.
    Boyle, Maj. Gen. Andrew L. 1980.
    Heintges, Lieut. Gen. John A. 1978.
    Trefry, Lieut. Gen. Richard G. 1986.

U.S. Department of the Army. General orders no. 32. Headquarters. July 13, 1971.

U.S. Joint Chiefs of Staff.
    "Report on the Son Tay Prisoner of War Rescue Operation." Parts 1 and 2. Brig. Gen. Leroy J. Manor, USAF, Commander, JCS Joint Contingency Task Group, Office. 1971.
    Operation Kingpin. Briefing Book for the Joint Chiefs of Staff and National Command Authorities. Office. November 1970.

Wheeler, Gen. Earle G. "Authority for B-52 Strikes Against Targets in Cambodia." CM-4003-69, memo to the secretary of defense, March 13, 1969, Carrollton Pr.

_____ . "Cambodia." JSCM-207-69, memo to the secretary of defense, April 9, 1969. Carrollton Pr.

IV. Interviews

Col. Alan Armstrong, former USA military adviser in Cambodia, 1970-1971, 1974-1975.

Robert Bechtoldt, former sergeant and SOG team commander in CCS.

Lt. Col. Kenneth R. Bowra, USA, former SOG team commander in CCN.

Col. William R. Corson, USMC (Ret.), former Vietnam battalion commander.

Col. James Dingeman, USA (Ret.), former aide to General Maxwell Taylor.

Robert J. Graham, former staff sergeant and SOG team commander in CCS.

Samuel Halpern, CIA (Ret.), former Vietnam desk officer.

Col. Roger M. Pezzelle, USA (Ret.), former commander of SOG ground operations in Laos.

Col. L. Fletcher Prouty, USAF (Ret.), former action officer for Department of Defense Special Assistant for Counterinsurgency and Special Activities.

Maj. Clyde J. Sincere, Jr., USA (Ret.), former executive officer of SOG Forward Operating Base 1.

Col. Rolf W. Utegaard, USA (Ret.), former commander of Project Sigma.

Picture Credits

Map Credits

Index

Names, Acronyms, Terms

ARVN–Army of the Republic of (South) Vietnam.

CAS team–Controlled American Sources Team. Squad of Vietnamese agents trained by Americans and sent into North Vietnam to gather intelligence and conduct sabotage missions.

CCS, CCC, CCN–Command & Control South, Central, and North. MACV-SOG field commands established in 1968 to control unconventional warfare operations in different regions of Indochina.

CD–civilian defendant.

Chieu Hoi–the "open arms" program promising clemency and financial aid to guerrillas who stopped fighting and returned to live under South Vietnamese government authority.

CIA–U.S. Central Intelligence Agency.

CI–counterinsurgency.

CIDG–Civilian Irregular Defense Group. Project devised by the CIA that combined self-defense with economic and social programs designed to raise the standard of living and win the loyalty of the mountain people. Chief work of the U.S. Special Forces.

CINCPAC–commander-in-chief, Pacific. Commander of American forces in the Pacific, including Southeast Asia.

CIO–Central Intelligence Organization. South Vietnamese agency established by Ngo Dinh Diem in May 1961 to collect intelligence and conduct paramilitary operations.

Code of Conduct–Set of rules of behavior for American servicemen held in captivity.

CORDS–Civilian Operations and Revolutionary Development Support. Pacification high command established under MACV in 1967. Organized all U.S. civilian agencies in Vietnam within the military chain of command.

COSVN–Central Office for South Vietnam. Communist military and political headquarters for southern South Vietnam.

CSG–Combined Studies Group. CIA detachment in Saigon that managed covert operations in North Vietnam in the early 1960s.

dau tranh–Communist grand strategy of the "struggle movement" that combines Marxist-Leninist, Maoist, and indigenous Vietnamese military doctrines. Assumes two forms: political struggle and armed struggle.

DCI–Director of Central Intelligence. Head of U.S. CIA.

DIA–Defense Intelligence Agency.

FAC–forward air controller. Low-flying pilot who directs high-altitude strike aircraft engaged in close air support of ground troops.

GVN–Government of (South) Vietnam.

Igloo White–Classified surveillance program that used seismic and acoustic sensors to monitor enemy movement along the Ho Chi Minh Trail.

Infiltration Surveillance Center–Complex in Nakhon Phanom, Thailand, that collected and analyzed data from Igloo White operations.

JCS–U.S. Joint Chiefs of Staff. Consists of chairman, Army chief of staff, chief of naval operations, Air Force chief of staff, and Marine commandant. Advises the president, the National Security Council, and the secretary of defense.

JPRC–Joint Personnel Recovery Center. Staff detachment within MACV headquarters responsible for maintaining records on and rescuing all POWs during the Vietnam War.

Khmer Rouge–Literally, Red Khmers. Cambodia's indigenous Communist movement and its members.

MAAG–Military Assistance Advisory Group. First U.S. military advisory program to South Vietnam, established in 1955.

MAC–Military Airlift Command. Responsible for maintaining a continuous strategic and tactical airlift of personnel and materiel from the U.S. to Southeast Asia and within the combat theater.

MACV–Military Assistance Command, (South) Vietnam.

MACV-SOG–MACV Studies and Observation Group. Conducted unconventional warfare, including cross-border missions in Laos, Cambodia, and North Vietnam throughout the Vietnam War.

Main-Force unit–regular forces of NVA/VC military.

MAROP–maritime operation.

Mike Force–Mobile Strike Force. Reaction unit of montagnard troops trained and led by Army Special Forces.

montagnards–the mountain tribes of Indochina, wooed by both sides in the war because of their knowledge of the rugged highland terrain and for their fighting ability.

MR–Military Region. One of four geographic zones into which South Vietnam was divided for purposes of military and civil administration.

Navy SEAL–SEa, Air, and Land. Elite U.S. Navy commando skilled in underwater, airborne, and ground combat.

NLF–National Liberation Front. Officially the National Front for the Liberation of the South, it aimed to overthrow the GVN and reunite North and South Vietnam.

NSC–National Security Council.

NVA–U.S. designation for the North Vietnamese Army. Officially PAVN (People's Army of Vietnam).

OSS–Office of Strategic Services. Predecessor of CIA.

pacification–unofficial term given to various programs of the South Vietnamese and U.S. governments to destroy enemy influence in the villages and gain support for the government of South Vietnam.

Pathet Lao–Laotian Communist insurgents supported by North Vietnam.

PAVN–People's Army of (North) Vietnam.

POW–prisoner of war.

PRU–Provincial Reconnaissance Unit. Elite Vietnamese commando squad used to capture suspected members of the VCI in the Phoenix Program.

PSC–Provincial Security Committee. Governing body that judged and sentenced VCI suspects apprehended in the Phoenix Program.

RD cadre–Revolutionary Development cadre. South Vietnamese trained to use Vietcong political tactics to carry out GVN pacification.

RF/PF–South Vietnamese Regional and Popular Forces. Paramilitary units organized to provide provincial and rural defense. The U.S. nickname Ruff-Puffs is derived from the abbreviation.

RPV–remotely piloted vehicle.

SAC–Strategic Air Command.

SACADVON–SAC Advanced Echelon. SAC's Forward Command post at MACV headquarters.

SACSA–Special Assistant for Counterinsurgency and Special Activities. Head of a top-secret section of the Joint Chiefs of Staff that oversaw MACV-SOG operations and organized the raid on Son Tay.

SRO–senior ranking officer. Among POWs, the officer with the highest rank.

Special Group (CI)–NSC unit formed by President Kennedy in 1962 to supervise the implementation of counterinsurgency programs.

TACC–Tactical Air Control Center.

USAID–U.S. Agency for International Development.

USIA–United States Information Agency.

"van" program–tactical program employed by the Vietcong in the struggle in South Vietnam. Included *dich van* (action among the enemy), *binh van* (action among the military), and *dan van* (action among the people).

VC–Vietcong. Originally derogatory slang for Vietnamese Communist; a contraction of Vietnam Cong San (Vietnamese Communist).

VCI–Vietcong infrastructure.